'Andrew Griffiths is real, raw and relevant'—*The Sunday Mail*

'Andrew Griffiths has a unique gift. He is one of the greatest communicators of our time. Part philosopher, part futurist and part advocate for entrepreneurs everywhere'—**Shelley Evans-Wild, Managing Director, NeuroPower**

'Andrew Griffiths is one of the best authorities I know on how to do business better. He is a never ending source of smart information and powerful inspiration'—**Brian Haverty, CBS Interactive**

'Big on knowledge. Big on passion. Another cracker, Andrew!'—**Robert Gerrish, Flying Solo**

'There is no one else like Andrew Griffiths. He's larger than life, totally driven to help others and he makes doing business a blast'—**Anh Do, author of** *The Happiest Refugee*

'Andrew Griffiths—we salute you'—*Weekend Sunrise*

'Andrew Griffiths is an incredibly gifted author and international speaker who is able to take complex business issues and make them easy to understand and even easier to implement. It is no wonder that top business people in 50 countries read and apply his material. Quite simply, the value he provides is immense.'—**Blake Beattie, author of** *Bullseye* **and founder of Pay it Forward Day**

'As a weekly regular on our morning show, Andrew is a wealth of amazing practical strategies to get ahead in life. Totally inspirational'—**Liam Renton, Program Director, 96.5 FM Brisbane**

'Andrew is an inspirational and charismatic entrepreneur who can communicate the strategies and tactics that will help you get from where you are today to where you want to go'—**Sam Harrop, Action Coach—Top 100 Platinum Coach**

ALSO BY ANDREW GRIFFITHS

101 Ways to Market Your Business
101 Ways to Advertise Your Business
101 Ways to Really Satisfy Your Customers
101 Ways to Boost Your Business
101 Ways to Have a Business and a Life
101 Ways to Build a Successful Network Marketing Business
101 Secrets to Building a Winning Business
101 Ways to Sell More of Anything to Anyone
Bulletproof Your Business Now
The Me Myth

THE BIG BOOK of SMALL BUSINESS

Andrew Griffiths

THE BIG BOOK of SMALL BUSINESS

The #1 guide to growing, prospering and succeeding today

ALLEN&UNWIN

First published in 2011
Copyright © Andrew Griffiths 2011

Allen & Unwin
Sydney, Melbourne, Auckland, London

83 Alexander Street
Crows Nest NSW 2065
Australia
Phone: (61 2) 8425 0100
Fax: (61 2) 9906 2218
Email: info@allenandunwin.com
Web: www.allenandunwin.com

Cataloguing-in-Publication details are available
from the National Library of Australia
www.trove.nla.gov.au

ISBN 978 1 74237 428 4

Text design by Squirt Creative
Set in 12/15 pt Sabon by Midland Typesetters, Australia
Printed in Australia by Ligare Pty Ltd, Sydney

10 9 8 7 6 5 4 3 2 1

CONTENTS

Acknowledgements

The *Big Book of Small Business* is the culmination of my business experiences, observations, successes and failures so far. The more I learn about small business the more I love it. It is dynamic, vibrant, challenging, rewarding and so much more.

We are so lucky to live in the age of the entrepreneur, a time when more people are starting businesses than ever before. I have so much admiration for anyone who is brave enough to throw away the security of a paying job to pursue their entrepreneurial dream and all the risks associated with it. Rest assured, there are many rewards that come with these risks, and the biggest is being in control of your own destiny. Once you experience this sense of independence it is hard to ever go back to your old way of life.

So this book is a tribute to each small business owner on the face of the planet. You are my inspiration. Keep doing what you do, remember the extraordinary riches that your business gives you and never lose the passion for the life you are creating; and, along the way, make the world a better place.

Introduction: The age of the entrepreneur

I t's been ten years since I wrote my first book, *101 Ways to Market Your Business*. A lot has certainly happened in my world and the business world in this time. How we do business has changed, technology has become firmly entrenched in our daily lives and we have had one of the most financially challenging periods in the best part of a century.

For the modern business owner it has been a roller-coaster ride, to say the least. Many older businesses have faded away and new shining stars appeared out of nowhere, taking a good idea and becoming commercially successful in a ridiculously short time. We are finding ourselves in need of new skills, relevant advice, revised perceptions and a greater range of communication tools.

I believe that the greatest risk to any business today is a failure to evolve. Sadly, there are a lot of businesses with this malady, not to mention entire industries that somehow can't seem to let go of the past and morph into something that is more relevant for today's consumers. I get to see them firsthand and listen to their arguments as they put their heads in the sand, and I see the writing on the wall. They don't go out with a big bang, they tend to slowly fade to black. The past two years have seen a major shift in the business world for both large corporations and small businesses alike. But interestingly enough, the challenges of evolution apply equally to the big and the small of the business world.

However, the other side of the coin is that we live at a time when unbelievable opportunities exist for smart entrepreneurs. In fact, I call it the 'age of the entrepreneur', a time when just about anybody can start a business, with not a lot of money, or even time, and end up creating a successful enterprise. Sure, most of these revolve around the online world, but that is the point: if you are in business and you are not embracing the online world and the limitless potential that it provides, you are heading the same way as the tyrannosaurus.

In saying that, this is certainly not a book about building an online business. It is a book about having an open mind, about doing what you do better, about gaining and keeping a competitive edge and learning from those who are out there and succeeding. Too many of us make the same mistakes in business, over and over. My book aims to give you a clear-cut pathway to avoid these pitfalls and mirror the actions that make others successful.

What makes a successful entrepreneur?

I am a strong believer in finding successful people and mirroring their attitude and behaviour as a strategy for increasing your own chances of success, at whatever level you want. Having worked with, interviewed, presented to and read about many of the world's most successful entrepreneurs, I've been able to compile the following profile of the sort of people succeeding today.

These people are quick to see an opportunity, particularly in the niches that already exist. They are positive, energetic and not afraid to ask for help if they don't understand something. They embrace technology but avoid being enslaved by it. They know their customers and they put them above all else. They have a hunger for doing what they do better than their competitors, and this attitude of constant and never-ending improvement is ingrained in their business culture. This is reinforced by their open mind and willingness to try new ideas and concepts. They consider investment in self-development and business development as essential and they combine this with an ability to network, both face to face and online, to help them build strategic relationships. They are detective-like in their ability to research and make smart decisions based on the findings of that research. And most importantly, they back themselves and believe in themselves, completely.

Much more than a 'greatest tips' book

My publishers asked me to put together a compendium book of my 'greatest tips', based on my ten other bestselling business books, which cover every topic from marketing to selling, advertising and business–life balance. But as I started pulling this book together I realised that it needed to be much more. It needed to provide a broad overview of the state of business today, it needed to explore the entrepreneurs' world and their way of thinking, it needed to show how to evolve and succeed in this new landscape, and it also had to provide a clear understanding of where the dinosaurs go wrong.

A word of warning

This book contains a lot of information. In fact, I have tried very hard to cover every aspect of running a business, and for some people this could prove a little overwhelming. Please don't let it be. There will be parts of this book that are really relevant to you now, but in a year's time there will be other parts that strike a chord. We tend to find the right information at the right times and I hope this book works for you in this way.

So, the point I am trying to make is that it is easy to get overwhelmed with all of the things we should be doing to make our businesses successful. Many of you will have heard the old joke, 'How do you eat an elephant?'—'One mouthful at a time': this also applies to building a business. Do what you can, when you can. The more time and energy you can put into this process, though, the faster you will get results.

How to get the most out of this book

Like every book I write for business owners, I aim to get to the point quickly. We are all battling against time, so if we have to hunt too hard for the information that we need we tend to move on. In many ways we are drowning in information but thirsty for knowledge.

In this book I have addressed the most common topics that I get asked about or that I see business owners struggling with. I have provided some background as well as information about the challenges and opportunities, and some practical tips that you can implement right now. This means that you can read this book cover to cover, or open it at any page and find information and practical advice that can be used immediately.

There are a number of key themes and specific strategies that are reiterated throughout this book, and these may cross over several chapters. If I am repeating information it is because I think it is important.

You will notice that some sections are longer than others. Some of my advice might take a sentence, some a page or two. It doesn't mean that any of the information I am sharing is any less or more important, just that some key points can be said in a few lines while others need more explanation.

I suggest that, as you are reading, you take note of particular points that resonate with you and write down the action you intend to take. Great information is pointless if we don't act upon it.

From here, it's up to you.

1

What is the difference between success and failure?

get asked this question a lot and it is not an easy one to answer. Sure we could look at a bank-account balance, but if that was the only indicator we had to measure an entrepreneur's success it would be a sad world indeed.

Personally, I believe anyone who is brave enough to step out of their comfort zone and enter the challenging realm of self-employment should already be classified as a significant success, because there is no doubt that running your own business is tough. However, I have noticed that most financially successful entrepreneurs share common personality characteristics, including an overriding desire to be good at what they do. I discuss these characteristics throughout this book and you may be surprised to notice how many you already have. Often what drives people to be entrepreneurs in the first place is the fact that they *are* good at what they do and they know it, and they would rather make money for themselves than someone else.

If I had to pick one defining characteristic that separates success and failure, it would have to be passion. Those entrepreneurs who are passionate about their businesses will not accept half measures—they sincerely want to be the best at what they do. They are passionate about their products and services, their customers and their staff. This passion enables them to embrace change and meet head-on the everyday challenges that all business owners face. Sure, they encounter setbacks, but they don't get caught up in the negatives, preferring instead to move forward, learning from their mistakes and refining the way they do things. They are passionate enough to share their triumphs and tragedies in a philosophical way, and they will help other people to succeed wherever they can.

In this opening chapter I want to explore the concept of attitude and how it is, without doubt, the single most important aspect of success. Most of the time, success is about changing the way we think, learning from others or even gaining a greater understanding about ourselves.

In this chapter we are going to explore the following topics and discover why having the right attitude is so important for the successful small business entrepreneur.

- Some things can never be measured in dollars and cents
- How proud of your business are you?
- Size doesn't matter
- Do you have the commitment to build a successful business?
- What every business owner and entrepreneur needs
- Always think big (how big is up to you)
- Have a strong moral code—with no shades of grey
- Develop a reputation for being fair
- Be more than your business
- Make decisions—procrastination is a killer
- Successful people don't play the victim
- Back yourself completely
- Remember to celebrate your victories
- It's not that serious—have some fun

Some things can never be measured in dollars and cents

All too often business success or failure is measured purely in terms of profit. I find this approach really wrong; a change in attitude is needed. From working with literally thousands of business owners around the world, either through my books or through seminars, I've found that most of them seem caught up on the same issue: they overlook their other successes and evaluate what they do based on what kind of car they drive or the size of their house.

I love small business and everything it stands for. It represents people willing to give life a go, to go out on a limb and be brave enough to take a risk and put everything on the line. But most of all I love the fact that most small businesses are actually very good at what they do—and this is because of that vested interest and risk. They know that losing a customer will have an immediate effect on their personal income. By contrast, if a person working for a large organisation loses a customer it is unlikely to cost them anything personally (unless it is a very big customer); their income is reasonably secure regardless of the loss.

But to me the real success of small businesses is what their owners build and achieve. I encounter truly amazing people doing amazing things, often for marginal profit or sometimes none at all. But they are proud of what they do, the service they provide, the jobs they create and the reputation they are building.

Many of us need to stop and take stock more often. Rather than just looking at how much money is in the bank at the end of the week, we should post a victory board highlighting the successes we have had that week as well. What great things did we achieve?

Changing the way we think about success makes us more forgiving and understanding of ourselves. We start to say things like, 'I haven't got a lot of money in the bank, but I do have a lot of very happy customers. The money will come.' And believe me, it does.

How proud of your business are you?

After being on the road for a few weeks I decided I had better get my car cleaned, so I drove it to an automated car wash I use now and then. As I waited patiently in line, the owner of the business came over to say hello. He is a very positive fella and I always like his energy.

Today he was carrying a squirt bottle with some special cleaning liquid in it that was supposed to make my wheels look brand new. He walked around the car, squirted it on each wheel, gave me a big smile, two thumbs up and then headed to the car behind me. He didn't try to sell me anything, there was no ulterior motive—he was simply being professional. When he got to the next car he pulled out a tin of spray and started to attack some stubborn stains on the bonnet as the people in that car waited for their turn in the wash. Once again, he did this for no reason other than because he is a motivated and professional business owner who is clearly proud of his business.

This man could have just as easily sat in his office reading the paper, emptying the coin machines a few times throughout the day. Instead he was all over the car wash, helping people, chatting, laughing and, most importantly, making sure his customers were leaving happy and contented.

To me this is the sign of a man who is not only smart but also very proud of his business, and boy does it show. I happen to know that since he has taken over the company, revenue has increased by 70 per cent. Interesting what happens when you add some passion and energy to a business.

If you own your own business, be proud. It represents a lot of blood, sweat and tears. All too often we forget the hard work we have put in to get here and simply look at where we are today, not where we have come from. So rather than finding fault in your business and looking for the things you haven't had a chance to do yet, give yourself a big pat on the back for what you have achieved and walk a little taller today.

When a business owner is proud of their business it shows, and remember: passion plus energy equals profit—ALWAYS.

Size doesn't matter

One of my greatest frustrations, and one I refer to often in my books, is what I call the 'Small Business Syndrome'. Have you ever held back on taking your business to its full potential because it's 'only a small business'? That's the Small Business Syndrome.

Experience has shown me that the best-run businesses are small ones, and size is certainly no excuse for not providing great service, doing smart marketing, making great products or being innovative and dynamic. Often small business owners are almost apologetic for being a small business. I think it is well and truly time to move on from this mindset and embrace the fact that small businesses are the engine of the business world—there are millions of them and they generally lead the way in all industries.

Being small is in fact a wonderful opportunity. Imagine being the CEO of a huge multinational corporation—how do you make a change to the way the business operates? Countless meetings and arguments may eventually lead to board approval, then the sanctioned changes would need to be handed down to the next level to start the long and winding road to implementation. Once this road is navigated, the changes eventually reach the frontline staff who actually sell the product or service. But in a small business, if you want to make a change, you just do it. How empowering is that?

My main message here is to be proud of your business, regardless of the size. Building a winning business has nothing to do with size—it is all about attitude.

Do you have the commitment to build a successful business?

As an author, I meet a lot of people who want to write a book. In fact I am amazed at how many people have this dream. But of all those people who want to write a book, very few actually do it. The real question here is:

why don't they? Coming up with an idea for a book is pretty easy. I'm sure most of us could sit down with a pen and paper and rustle up a few good ideas in a couple of minutes. But what happens once these great ideas are staring back at us from a sheet of paper?

Writing a book takes time, commitment and discipline—just like running a successful business. When I got the phone call from my publishers saying they liked the manuscript for my first book enough to publish it, I assumed I could sit back, put my feet up, hit eBay and buy my first Porsche. The reality was a little different. My publishers did like the idea, but I had to rewrite the entire manuscript from start to finish. They edited it three times and it took almost twelve months before it was ready to go to the printers. Finally the book was ready for the shelves, and this was when the real business of selling my idea stepped up.

Running a successful business is a lot like writing and publishing a book. It's very easy to fall in love with the idea, but the reality is that it will take a lot of time, dedication, discipline and hard work just to get it up and running, and then there is no guarantee it will work. Successful business entrepreneurs have this commitment and dedication and, from my observations, this is a characteristic of their personality type. It is not something they have to decide to do—it just happens.

My advice here is simple: if you're not 100 per cent committed to building a very successful business . . . get a job. Enjoy a weekly pay cheque (there is nothing wrong with that) and forget the romantic concept of owning your own business. If you are not completely dedicated it will only end in tears and heartache.

What every business owner and entrepreneur needs

One of the best skills I have learned, that has not only helped me to build better relationships but also to reduce stress in my life, is how to have more empathy. To me this means the ability to put myself in the shoes of another person and look at a situation from their point of view.

It is an interesting exercise, and one that we all need to do a little more often, especially when we are feeling overwhelmed by events going on around us. When you make the conscious decision to think about a situation from another person's perspective, it takes you out of your own stressed-out head and lets you see the situation in a way that may not have occurred to you before.

Being empathic generally makes us more compassionate, more under-standing and more tolerant—not feelings we necessarily experience enough in an increasingly chaotic world.

So, how do you become more empathic? Like most things in life worth learning, it takes some time and energy. If a difficult situation arises, instead of simply reacting with anger or frustration, stop and take a moment to start thinking empathically. Ask for time to think the matter over. Try to ignore your own feelings for now and look at the situation from the other person's perspective. How would you feel if you were in their shoes? Are their problems, complaints or actions reasonable? You might come full circle and end up back where you started, but at least you will have thought the situation through fully.

With empathy comes understanding, and I have learned this from some quite exceptional businesspeople. It is the basic principle of great salesmanship; it is the force behind humanitarian movements the world over. Empathy is powerful stuff, but how does it help us to reduce stress and improve relationships? It shifts the centre of our universe (being us) to another point, and this gives us a fresh view of the situation at hand.

Just as it is hard to feel pain when you laugh, it is hard to be stressed out and angry when you look at any situation with empathy. Try it—I guarantee that you will be surprised by how calming it is.

Always think big (how big is up to you)

What is the difference between the person who opens and runs a success-ful pizza restaurant and the person who opens and runs a chain of pizza restaurants around the world? I believe it is all in the thinking process. If you think big you can be big, but most of us get too busy doing what we do to let thoughts about where we are going manifest and form. There is nothing wrong with being a small successful business, but likewise there is nothing wrong with building that small successful business into a hugely successful big business.

I know there will be some people reading this who will feel there are a multitude of limitations that prevent them from achieving world domination (in the nicest possible way) but, from my own experiences and observations of entrepreneurs, there is little doubt that those who aim high and think big tend to achieve more.

I personally have a series of big plans, which I have broken into timeframes. For example, in the short term, I would be happy to pay off my credit cards (like most of us); longer term, I want to sell a million books. Both plans are significant to me and I believe I will do them, even if I am not sure when. I have a list of about ten major goals, and when I read the longer-term ones my analytical brain goes into seizures—but I honestly and sincerely believe I will achieve them all.

Think big and go for it.

Have a strong moral code—with no shades of grey

How many examples do you know of high-profile people who were shining stars but became corporate disgraces? It really is quite disheartening when business leaders once featured on the front of dozens of major magazines are just a few years later being dragged into court and often prison. Why does this happen? How can they have fallen so far? What corrupted them?

In reality, the answer is most likely that they were always corruptible. It's often the case that no one was looking closely enough to catch them out earlier.

We all need to live by a strong moral code. Be very clear about what is right and what is wrong. There should be no shades of grey, because often these are places where you falter. What is your moral code? Do you have situations that you have to deal with which could be considered grey areas?

Of course there are differences between moral, ethical and legal codes, but in reality they are closely linked. Once you cross a line, it is a lot easier to keep crossing it and most offenders do.

My philosophy is simple—I will not do anything, ever, that can come back to haunt me. I don't want to ever leave my office with a towel over my head, scurrying away from a host of reporters. Apart from the devastating impact it has on your fashion sense, it ruins lives, often those of innocent parties.

Develop a reputation for being fair

There is a saying that for a negotiation to work, all parties need to win. The level of the win varies, but that is the ideal outcome. Some people adopt an egotistical stance of having to win everything at any cost whenever they enter a negotiation. We all know these kinds of people. They negotiate on the purchase of a bus ticket. They are obsessed with winning, to the point where they spend their life burning other people and, eventually, people don't want to deal with them.

Negotiating is a part of life. In business we need to be good negotiators to make sure we can run our businesses as profitably as possible. But the key word here is fair. I have to negotiate with suppliers, such as graphic designers, media outlets, printers and subcontractors. I want to have a good relationship with these companies and I want them to do the best job possible for my clients. If I negotiate them down on price to the point where the project is only marginally profitable, they will lose interest, I will get a marginal quality job from them and the loser is my client.

I make it clear to my clients from the start: we want to do the best job at the fairest price. If they want a cheaper job done, they have to go somewhere else. This philosophy has enabled me to build an excellent network of suppliers who do a great job every time. They make good money out of each project, my company makes good money and the client gets the best end result possible.

Be more than your business

Businesses come and go—what you are doing today is unlikely to be what you will be doing in ten years' time. You are the most significant asset in your life and it is important to realise this.

I encounter a lot of people who become their business—it is everything to them, from their first waking moment to their last thought at night (and often it fills their dreams too). When they no longer have this business, their life falls apart. They don't know what to do, their life feels empty, and dissatisfaction and depression can set in.

Look at the lives of a few high-profile entrepreneurs. Rarely do they have only one business interest. They may start new businesses, sell old ones, go broke in some, do a joint venture in others—they are not attached to one business. They are passionate about what they do but they realise they are the resource and the skill centre used to make the other businesses work. They are more than any of the businesses that they own.

Whatever you are doing, there is life after your current business. For this reason you too need to be more than your business. You need to have more substance, more interests, more beliefs and more of a long-term view about how you fit into your business life. Don't let your business consume or control you—you are in the driving seat, not the other way around.

Ponder this thought: what would you do if you got a letter in the mail that said you had to close down your business in 24 hours? How would you cope? What would you do next? This is an interesting situation to spend a few minutes considering.

Make decisions—procrastination is a killer

Personally I find that the busier I become, the harder it is to make a decision. I get bombarded with literally hundreds of messages every day, from the fax, the phone, email, letters and internally from my team. There is so much to do that finding the time to make a decision on any one thing can be really difficult. But if I don't make decisions, my workload backs up, my clients get frustrated and so do my staff.

A friend of mine who has run some very large corporations pulled me aside a little while ago and gave me some important advice. She said I had to learn to start making decisions right now, not to keep putting them on the backburner for when I would have more time to think about them. If I didn't, all I would end up with was an ever-expanding list of 'decisions to be made' that I would never get to the end of. I took her advice and discovered she was spot on.

I now make immediate decisions as often as possible. Some things need a little more time to ponder, but in reality the vast majority of my decisions are simple 'yes' or 'no' ones that someone else needs to action. This has had quite an amazing flow on to my daily workload: it seems I have a lot less to do, I don't go home with a never-ending list of things to think about and everyone I deal with is happier because they are getting their decisions quickly.

Sure, sometimes I make the wrong decision, but that happened before as well. We all get it right in some instances and wrong in others, but I think the number of wrong decisions I make has declined significantly.

Successful people don't play the victim

I had an unusual childhood: I grew up as an orphan, living with a host of different people during my formative years. Some of these people were great, some not so great; I had a lot of violence inflicted upon me. I was in situations where I trusted people that I shouldn't have. There were many people with whom I developed close bonds who died. But not once have I ever felt like a victim.

Life throws different blows at all of us and we can choose to either focus on these or focus on the good things that happen. I choose to focus on the good. I am not saying for a second there haven't been times when the going got rough, but focusing on the good got me through a lot of situations and a challenging start to life that many others may not have survived. As a result, I am compassionate with anyone going through a rocky patch.

Some people, though, wallow in the role of the victim—everything bad is someone else's fault and they are going to wear the title of 'victim' with pride. Victims attract other victims and the cycle becomes self-perpetuating. Ironically, I have found that the people who may have the most right to wear a 'victim' badge rarely do. They are too busy getting on with life.

The easiest thing for me to do would be to store anger and resentment against a host of people who either hurt me, abandoned me or used me. But without those people I wouldn't have turned out to be who I am today—and I am pretty darn happy with who I am today.

Late last night I happened to be watching a television show in which a man was getting a tattoo of his son, who was killed in a freak accident a few years back. Clearly he was very emotional, but he said something which I think needs to be shared: 'We all have hard things thrown our way in life; it's up to us to either get bitter or get better.'

Powerful words. How many of us get better when faced with adversity? Or even more importantly, how many of us get bitter? We really do have the choice and this applies to every challenge that comes our way. Who would have thought a show about tattoos would have provided such exceptional words of wisdom? Inspiration is everywhere if you choose to look.

We all face trying times, family problems, relationship problems, money problems and health problems—that's life. But playing victim won't make them go away. Focus on the good things in your life, learn from your experiences and move on. Keep people who play the victim out of your life and you will soon find that positive and enthusiastic people will replace them—and your life will become a lot better.

Back yourself completely

Recently I had the honour of being the MC at an innovation awards night, where local inventors and creators were identified in the community and acknowledged for some pretty amazing inventions. These extraordinary folk often toil away for years, usually with little or no financial resources, to pursue a dream or a passion and make it a commercial reality. But I realised as I was doing my research for the event that they all shared one thing in common: they backed themselves and their products 100 per cent.

There is real passion in each and every inventor I meet and it manifests as a sense of pride in the product or service that they have painstakingly developed over a long period of time.

On the night I referred to one great example of how backing yourself fully can be the real difference between success and failure: that example is the world-famous Zippo lighter. In 1933, the first Zippo lighters went on sale in the USA at a cost of $1.95. A wealthy oil man named George Blaisdell owned the company, and he was devastated by the dismal early sales of his revolutionary lighter.

Looking for some way to get people's attention and show just how good his Zippo lighters were, George offered a lifetime guarantee on every unit, something that had never been done before. Sales went through the roof. Zippos were bought in bulk for the US army, one famously stopping a bullet meant for one Sergeant Martinez. They later reached iconic status in movies like *Die Hard* and the James Bond series, and they have become highly sought after as collectables, with a solid gold Zippo likely to set you back about $10,000. Today, some 450 million Zippos have been sold around the world, all as a result of George believing in the product enough to offer a lifetime guarantee.

We have to be the number-one fans and believers in our business. If we are not our own biggest fans, it shows. And if you don't believe in what you do, how can you expect others to? We need to be passionate about our business, we need to be excited to tell people what we do, and most importantly, we need to give them a solid reason to buy from us.

This might sound like a simple concept, yet when you ask the vast majority of people what they do for a crust, they respond with very little spark, energy or enthusiasm—it is almost as if they are apologetic about it.

So if you are looking for that special 'thing' that can be the difference between success and failure, it really might be as simple as backing yourself. Be prepared to offer money-back guarantees, use your own products whenever you can, and get excited when you tell people what it is you do and why you do it so well. If you can't back yourself because you don't believe in what you're doing, it's time to have a long hard look at your business.

Remember to celebrate your victories

One of the best things I have ever done is to put a whiteboard in my office where I list the things that I have achieved during the year that I consider milestones for my business and for me. On the first of January, the board gets wiped clean (but I do take a picture of the previous year's victories) and as I achieve something significant, it gets put on the board.

It is amazing how this list of milestones and achievements makes me feel during the year. The things that I forget about, the victories from months ago that would have been lost in the day-to-day of a busy life, are up there in black and white. It adds a sense of perspective that is particularly important on those tough days when nothing seems to be going right. One glance at my victory board and all is better.

We need to celebrate our victories whenever we can. Look for ways to encourage other people around us to celebrate theirs too. The more we create a culture of celebration, the more we find to celebrate, and this has a constantly rejuvenating effect on you and your business.

It's not that serious—have some fun

I am a very firm believer that business should be fun. Sure, there are plenty of times when this is easier said than done, but some businesses just seem to lack any joy at all. I can't imagine working in an environment like that for hours on end, day after day, month after month. I think some people confuse professionalism with seriousness. It is not unprofessional to have a workplace where people like to laugh and enjoy themselves. As a customer it is much more enjoyable to walk into a light, friendly, energetic environment than one that is serious, gloomy and uncomfortable.

Fun takes many different forms but I believe very strongly that it should be welcomed into all businesses. In many of the leading winning businesses I have observed, it is a key component. For me it is a real joy to see modern entrepreneurs who actively promote bringing fun into the lives of their staff and customers.

We all have stressful times, we all have to balance money, deal with unhappy customers, manage staff problems and a host of other everyday issues, but it really isn't that serious. Have some fun at work, encourage other people to do likewise, and you and your business will enjoy the benefits for many years to come.

2

What do the truly spectacular entrepreneurs all have in common?

Identifying the characteristics shared by the very successful is a passion of mine. I have been fortunate enough to meet many of the leading entrepreneurs of our time, work with some, interview others, be trained by a number and read about the rest. These are people like Sir Richard Branson, Jack Canfield, Zig Ziglar, Dick Smith, Anthony Robbins, Donald Trump, T Harv Eker, Brendon Burchard, Louise Hay and many others. And yes, I believe that they do share common characteristics. In fact, I see these common characteristics shining through in many entrepreneurs who have little to no profile but who are equally as successful on many levels as the household names above.

There is no need to reinvent the wheel when it comes to success. Find someone you admire, get to know them either personally or through their books, website, media coverage or seminars and learn from them. Success mirrors success—most of us just have to find the right reflection.

Here are twelve of the most common characteristics I have observed in many of the world's successful entrepreneurs.

- Absolute clarity of purpose
- Total belief in themselves
- A knack for finding needs and niches
- Ability to focus on the most important things first
- A contribution culture
- An open mind
- Incredible networks, which they foster and participate in
- Invest in themselves on all levels
- Challenge themselves constantly
- Believe in technology
- Resilience
- A millionaire mindset

Absolute clarity of purpose

Without exception, great entrepreneurs are totally clear on why they are here, their big-picture reason for existing. The particular reason varies among them: some have the purpose of making money, a lot of money; others aim to use their influence to change the world. There is no judgment here on the actual purpose, but the importance of *knowing* their purpose cannot be understated.

I think that passion and purpose go hand in hand. If you are struggling to figure out what your purpose is, look to your passion. What are the things you are passionate about? What are the things you love to do, that have you leaping out of bed as opposed to dragging yourself out?

If you struggle to find your purpose, look to people who have found theirs, but remember that it doesn't have to be curing cancer. The scale of our purpose is up to us. Unless you are clear on your purpose in life, true success will elude you.

Total belief in themselves

This is an interesting characteristic. Again, each and every one of the world-class entrepreneurs I've come across has an incredible sense of self-belief. They back themselves completely, even if no one else will.

To me this is the toughest of all the characteristics because it means overcoming doubt, fear, and self-worth and self-esteem issues and this—going against the tribe—is something that is very hard for most of us to do on a purely biological level.

But the ability to back yourself is a powerful tool. Many books are filled with stories of ordinary people overcoming incredible challenges to achieve amazing things. How do they keep going? They believe in themselves. Surely we need to devote a lot more time to encouraging this quality in our children instead of instilling fears of the world in them.

A knack for finding needs and niches

I sometimes think that successful entrepreneurs have a pair of 'opportunity glasses'. They are somehow able to identify opportunity in just about every situation, and this opportunity tends to be in the niches found between established businesses: as the old saying goes, the riches are in the niches.

This ability is becoming increasingly important as the world becomes more cluttered. There is so much information around that for many people it has actually become overwhelming. Smart entrepreneurs find ways to stand out from their competitors, to make life easier for their customers and to respond to people's needs.

They may do this in one of two ways. First, establish a business and do it better than their competitors. Or second, invent a completely new way of doing business, which others will ultimately copy.

Ability to focus on the most important things first

In hugely successful business author Brian Tracy's excellent book *Focal Point*, he explains his technique for getting focused and staying focused. I think that successful entrepreneurs have a similar ability to control their thoughts and actions and be totally present and focused on whatever is in front of them at any time.

Clearly these are very busy people, who have huge numbers of opportunities, distractions, staff and commitments, all of which eat into their time and focus. Yet they appear able to put all of the clutter in the background and bring into the spotlight the most important item that needs attention and focus.

A contribution culture

Successful leaders all have an incredibly generous nature. It is what I call a contribution culture and it is their way of leaving a legacy, making a difference, sharing their success and much more. They use their networks and influence to give, often in huge ways. For many it becomes their purpose in being—I tend to think that it always was, but they now have the resources to do it.

Look at Bill Gates and Warren Buffett, the old-school entrepreneur and the new-school entrepreneur. Both give billions of dollars to charities around the world and if anyone can create change, they will. Anthony Robbins has established an organisation that delivers gift baskets of food to people in need; millions of baskets are given away annually.

This contribution culture also manifests in many other ways. I see it in the treatment of their customers and staff and their respect for everyone they meet. Contribution, or serving others, is an important reason for doing what we do, and I for one hope to make a lot of money in my life so I can give it all away.

An open mind

To me the most impressive entrepreneurs are at opposite ends of the age spectrum—the old-timer entrepreneur and the young entrepreneur. The oldest have achieved things way beyond what most people could dream of, yet they still have an open mind. They don't rest on their laurels; instead they are always looking for ways to learn more about what they are doing and, most importantly, how they could do it better.

The younger ones approach things from a different angle. They use technology and the media (social media in particular), and in many ways the old-school way of doing things must look archaic to them. But they treat the industry elders with respect and listen to their advice. This open-minded approach is a powerful tool in any entrepreneur's arsenal, because information is generally the commodity that makes or breaks a business.

Incredible networks, which they foster and participate in

Clearly these entrepreneurs have incredible business networks, but in talking to them it is interesting to note their attitude towards these. Without exception they treat their networks with absolute respect.

They have built these relationships over many years, developing contacts who are highly influential and have the ability to grow each other's business in leaps and bounds. They invest time and energy in their networks, always giving more than they take and acting without expectation of reciprocation.

So what do they end up with? A proactive network of like-minded, influential people, who all share an attitude of contribution and a strong desire to support others.

Invest in themselves on all levels

This is a very important point and one that I cover in more detail in Chapter 4. Elite entrepreneurs understand that they need to grow their skills, take care of themselves physically and mentally, and take time out to recharge their batteries on a regular basis. This is not an optional activity—it is essential.

They realise that their body and mind are their most important assets, hence the need to invest time, money and effort on these areas of their life. You will often hear them saying that this is their best investment—ever.

Challenge themselves constantly

Great entrepreneurs are big learners in every way possible: they do things that are way out of their comfort zones, they push themselves physically, they work hard, and they play hard by living life to the full. This attitude makes them strong and better able to deal with whatever life throws at them. It also keeps their minds active, their bodies fit and their emotions positive. I think we can all take a leaf out of their book on this one.

Believe in technology

Interestingly enough, many of these incredible entrepreneurs are techno neanderthals, but that doesn't stop them believing in the importance of it. Nor does it stop them investing vast sums of money into technology to do what they do better, and it is this belief that is more important than their own individual skills. As new technologies become available, smart entrepreneurs will try them, invest in them and see how they can use them to achieve what they want in their business and their life.

Resilience

We all face ups and downs in our lives. Some unlucky people have a seemingly endless supply of downs that would break most of us. All of the high-achieving entrepreneurs I have studied have had incredible challenges in their lives, ones that they could easily have hidden behind while playing the victim. Some even did, for a while, but all made the decision to become 'better not bitter'. They used the challenges of the past to make them better human beings in the future, and that is a very smart way of dealing with the challenges that life throws at all of us.

I am not sure that you can teach someone to be resilient, but I do think we can learn how to manage challenges in a more proactive way. Sometimes we need to get upset and have a good cry, but at some stage we also need to pick ourselves up, shake off the dust and get on with whatever it is we are trying to achieve in our world.

A millionaire mindset

How is it that Donald Trump can go from being a billionaire to being broke, to being a billionaire again, all within a few years? As author T Harv Eker explains, it is because he has a billionaire mindset (not just a millionaire mindset). Trump believes 100 per cent that he should be a billionaire and that he will always be a billionaire.

How can someone win $50 million in a lottery and be broke and in debt a few short years later? Well, put simply, their mindset is to be broke and in debt. Until they change this they will always stay in the same place, regardless of how much money comes into their world.

Having the right mindset, one that embraces abundance and opportunity, is often the difference between a rich entrepreneur and a poor entrepreneur. I see many people struggling in business; they always have and they always will, simply because their financial home base is to be broke. It isn't about how hard they work or the uniqueness of the product, it is about how they think. Anyone stuck in this zone needs to start reprogramming their brain and that's what T Harv Eker's book is all about. It starts with working out what your current financial mindset is, how you formed it and then how to change it. Any limiting belief can be changed; we simply need to have a strong enough desire to change.

3

The boss is the business barometer

Business owner, manager, partner, boss—whatever the position, there is no doubt that the person (or people) at the top set the mood for the entire organisation. I tend to think of them as the business's barometer.

If the leader is stressed out, angry, exhausted or bored, before long this attitude will permeate through the entire business. It will be reflected in the staff, and in their attitude towards the business, the customers and each other. On the other hand, if you are positive, energetic, considerate and supportive, this attitude will also permeate through the business and likewise be reflected by pretty much everyone who works with you.

For this reason alone, the wellbeing of your business is intrinsically linked to your state of mind. How we manage ourselves is vitally important and something that needs to be considered on a daily basis.

Whenever I am asked to evaluate a business to determine what is going wrong or what needs to be done to get it back on track, I start with the business owner. What is going on in their world? What is their state of mind? What are they afraid of? What needs to change? Normally this is hidden below the surface and it can take a bit of digging, but once you get to the root of the problem and address it, the business undergoes an energetic transformation.

In this chapter I look at some of the common issues that bring people down and impact on their attitude, and provide strategies to help overcome these challenges. This section includes some really practical ideas that can have a dramatic impact straightaway.

- Reschedule your day to suit you and the way you like to work
- Schedule time to do nothing but think
- Outsource or delegate the jobs you really don't like doing (and probably don't do well anyway)
- Gossiping, moaning and complaining—end it today!
- Identify the people who cause you problems and do something about them
- Get rid of unfinished business
- Make the hard decisions—stop procrastinating
- Encourage change and reward everyone who embraces it
- Learn to let go
- Compliment others, be positive to others, be supportive of others
- The grass is not always greener

Reschedule your day to suit you and the way you like to work

Often we end up working within a schedule that suits everyone but ourselves. It doesn't have to be that way. Some people work better in the morning than in the afternoon, while others are the opposite. Some people like to exercise in the middle of the day and flourish if given a couple of hours off to go to the gym. It is better to work in the manner that suits you rather than try to fit your life around your work. Often all it takes is a change in mindset.

Many of my clients plan their trading hours and the days they work around their lifestyle. It is very empowering to do this. The counter-argument for many people is that they have to be open for their customers —and yes, this is very relevant for some businesses, but not for all. And even if your business has to be open at certain hours, do you personally have to be there at those times?

A big part of this tip is about letting go of perceptions. Many business owners live in a state of near terror over changing anything that may affect their relationship with their customers. They don't want to change a thing: not the business name or the logo or the brand, or the hours the business is open, or the products or services being offered. But while I am an advocate of consistency when it comes to delivering a product or service, customers are much more open to change than most business owners think. In fact, they like it—because it shows that the business is getting better.

Think about it for a moment. If you are working like a dog and you're exhausted, lacking in enthusiasm and not really having a jolly time, do you think that your customers can't see or feel this? If you change the way you work so that it suits your lifestyle and needs better, you will be much more energetic and engaging at work, and your customers will get a far better level of service and a more enjoyable experience. You simply need to be brave enough to do it.

The first step in the process is analysing how you actually like to work. If you aren't a morning person, then arrange your business so you don't have to be there in the morning. If you find it hard to get anything done at work because you are constantly being distracted by the demands of staff, suppliers and others, work from home one day each week and give clear instructions on who can contact you and for what. I have found I get more done in one day at home than I do for the rest of the week at work—amazing.

The traditional way of doing business is often not applicable in the modern world. Set up your business to suit you. If you are reading this book in anticipation of going into business for yourself, think long and hard about this before you make your move. Buy or start a business that suits the way you want to live. If you are a night person, don't buy a milk run. If you are a recovering alcoholic, it probably isn't a good idea to buy a nightclub. If you are afraid of sharks, don't become a commercial diver. You get the drift, as silly as my examples might be. Make your business work for you, rather than you working for it.

Schedule time to do nothing but think

It took a good friend to give me a little guidance on this topic. A few years ago my typical work practice was to get to the office at around 6.30 every morning when I would set about making my to-do list for the day, which typically had about a million items on it. Of course, it would be impossible to get everything done on the list in a month, let alone a day, but I didn't know any better.

One morning I was having coffee with this friend and I happened to jot down a few things in my notebook. She saw my to-do list and, with a look of shock, asked, 'When do you find time to just sit and think?' Now that was a powerful question because I didn't allow *any* time to just sit and think. In fact, from the minute I got to work to the minute I left, I pretty much ran like a madman all day, fuelled by coffee and sugar, often not even bothering to stop and eat properly.

From that day on I made a point of putting aside some time each day to do nothing but think and reflect. Sometimes I might allocate 30 minutes; if I had a lot on my mind I might allocate an entire morning. I fly a lot these days, and I use this as 'thinking time'. It is perfect; there are no phones, emails or meetings to interrupt you. I can completely lose myself to my thoughts. I put on a set of headphones, take out my notebook, close my eyes and just let my mind go to wherever it wants to go. If there are certain issues that need my attention, I let these roll around in my brain until I get some clarity.

I am amazed at how empowering this feels and how it has reduced my stress and the sense of being overwhelmed. Our brains need time to process information, and the more information coming in the more time they need to process it. If you don't give your brain time to work through things it keeps them in a holding pattern—when more items are added every day, it leads to a sense of exhaustion and being overwhelmed.

Give yourself some quiet time to simply think things through. Don't try to fill every minute of every day. There are so many benefits in doing this, not the least of which will be a feeling of control and calmness instead of feeling thrown into the fray every time you walk through the door. Make sure your 'thinking time' is in your diary, change your work practice to suit and find a place that is conducive to letting you reflect.

Outsource or delegate the jobs you really don't like doing (and probably don't do well anyway)

As a marketing consultant, I encounter a lot of people at their wit's end with marketing. They know they have to do it, but they don't know how or what to do, so in the end it becomes an irritation rather than an opportunity. There are many facets to running a business that we don't like—not surprisingly, these are the same things we are generally not very good at.

In my business I am the ideas man. I love to come up with new ways to do what we do, develop creative concepts for my clients, write books, give keynote presentations and train people. But give me a profit-and-loss statement or an operations manual and I have the attention span of a flea.

Several years ago I realised that my business was getting a little out of control. I made up a list of all the general groups of tasks that needed to be done, who was doing what and, overall, how well they were being managed. It became glaringly obvious that the jobs people didn't like doing were all being done badly. So the first step was to work out which particular tasks people in my team did like to do. From here we matched up the tasks with the people, as much as we could. The tasks that nobody liked or that could not be done effectively needed to be outsourced rather than mismanaged.

In the end we outsourced all our computer maintenance, bookkeeping, graphic design, writing of business plans, and buying of flowers for the office—an eclectic list, but it worked very well for us. Now all of the above are managed magnificently by service providers, instead of having me or one of the team bumble through something that we are not good at or don't like. And if you ask me, the cost of most of these tasks has been reduced both by having an expert manage them and by freeing my staff's time and energy to focus on what they're good at—delivering quality work and making money for the business.

Getting rid of those jobs that drive you crazy is normally much easier and less expensive than you think. If you are unconvinced, pick just one and start there.

Gossiping, moaning and complaining—end it today!

When you are feeling overwhelmed, out of control, depressed or negative, your conversation tends to be less than positive. This is when gossiping, moaning and complaining slip into the conversation. Unfortunately, after a while they become the norm.

I have a client I used to meet with once a week. He would spend the first half-hour of our meeting moaning about the company he works for, a habit I found very depressing. My advice to him was always the same—leave, find a new job where you will be happy; life is far too short for ongoing misery.

There is absolutely nothing to be gained from gossiping, moaning and complaining; on the contrary, it has a long-term negative effect on those around you. It can also start to create a corporate culture that revolves around this mentality. And remember that gossip only works if it is passed on, so don't play a part in the process.

Creating a positive, nurturing environment is so important, and the rewards are great. But it takes an effort to break the cycle of complaint if it already exists in your business—and you may be the main culprit.

Every time you find yourself starting to complain, stop yourself in your tracks and rethink what you were going to say. If you have staff gossiping, moaning or complaining to you, let them know that you are simply not interested. Some people won't like this, but tough.

I once saw a company put out a 'no moaning or talking about people behind their backs' policy. It was great. Everyone in the business pulled up people who started to moan. When someone started to gossip they were advised to go and share the story with the person they were gossiping about. It took a while, but eventually this negative behaviour finished and the mood and culture of the business improved dramatically.

Remember that if you are the boss, you have to drive this process. Your staff will copy you. Every time you find yourself sliding into bad habits, take note—it is costing you big-time.

Identify the people who cause you problems and do something about them

Just as we develop negative thought patterns that are reinforced by negative language, there are often people in our lives who further reinforce negativity and literally bring us down by what they say and do.

We all have friends who, within five minutes of walking in, have us completely depressed by tales of their desperate, sad or boring lives, and odds-on you have a sympathetic ear so they keep coming back to tell you more.

Do you know why? Because it makes them feel better. They make you feel like jumping out the nearest window, but they leave whistling and smelling the roses.

If you are surrounded by people like this, it's not going to be hard to cleanse your life of negativity—it's going to be near impossible. It may be difficult to get them out of your life because they're your biggest customer, a relative or your business partner. But whatever else you do, you really do need to draw a line in the sand. If the majority of the people you mix with are negative rather than positive, you have a problem which will only get worse over time and keep you trapped in the cycle of feeling overwhelmed.

I made a very conscious decision a number of years ago about the type of people I would have in my life. I want to be surrounded by energetic, enthusiastic and positive people who are getting on with their lives. I don't care what they do for a living, how much money they have or who they know. All I care about is their zest for life. These people inspire me and motivate me to be the best person I can be; they are supportive of any decision or change that will help me to achieve this goal. If I fail, they are the first people to pat me on the back and say that at least I gave it a go.

If I listened to those negative folk who find the world so difficult I wouldn't do anything. There is no malicious intent in these people, it's just a reflection of where they are at in life at the time. And that's sad, but we all need to decide if we want to be equally sad. I made the decision not to be and that was that.

I suggest that you develop a way of keeping such people at arm's length. Some of them won't like you for it, and they may tell you so. Be prepared for some repercussions, but stay resilient because the pay-off is big. If you don't know where to find positive, energetic, enthusiastic people, try looking around for the busy people who are getting on with life.

Get rid of unfinished business

One of the biggest causes of stress in my life is that never-ending list of unfinished business. This includes half-completed projects, personal goals that I never seem to find the time to attempt, complicated problems—either personal or professional—that are just plain difficult to sort out, things that keep breaking (specifically, door handles around my apartment), and trying to catch up with the people I haven't managed to connect with in too long. I used to have a pile on my desk which was virtually nothing but unfinished business, and once in a while I would shuffle through the mess without really achieving anything.

About two years ago I decided that I had had enough of this pile, which seemed to mock me every time I looked at it. I realised that to get it sorted once and for all, I had to give it some attention.

First I got a notepad and started to work through that pile. I made up a very comprehensive list of unfinished-business items and what I needed to do to get every single item off the list.

The prospect was daunting, but I set a four-week timeframe and made a commitment to myself to completely clear my unfinished-business list—and I did. It felt fantastic—the relief was amazing. Emboldened by my success, I applied this technique to the other piles in my life. I highly recommend trying this for yourself.

Today I still have an unfinished-business pile on my desk, but it is much smaller and I make a point of not letting it get away from me. I allocate time each week to unfinished business. Most of the items in the pile really just need me to sit and focus for a few minutes on how best to handle them, and think about who might be able to help.

Go through your unfinished-business pile and make a list of what you need to do to get every single item off your desk. Set yourself a timeframe and start working your way through the list.

Make the hard decisions—stop procrastinating

Procrastination is another common cause (and effect) of being out of balance or overwhelmed in your business. Some decisions are just plain hard—especially the big ones like sacking a staff member, trying to placate an unhappy client or making a major equipment purchase. Often we need to work ourselves into the right frame of mind to make a big decision, and we know that knee-jerk reactions are not a good idea.

The typical cycle that becomes self-perpetuating is that the longer we delay the decision-making process, the more decisions need to be made. Then we start to feel a little overwhelmed and, in struggling to find the time or the energy to make the right decision in the right manner, we procrastinate further and even more decisions then need to be made.

I try to set timeframes around my decision-making processes. Let's say I have to decide if I want to work on a specific project or venture that someone has offered me. I make a point of telling the person on the spot how long I need to make my decision, and then set my mental timeframe and write it in my diary ('AG must respond to Bill Smith by 10 a.m. Thursday'). So then it is in my mind and in my diary, and I have to make the decision on time. It normally works; if the deadline arrives and I am still undecided I tend to say no—if it is that hard to decide, then I probably shouldn't do it.

The process is really no different when you have to make hard decisions such as whether to terminate a non-performing member of staff. Set a timeframe, spend some time in the build-up to the deadline to make sure you know how you will handle the situation, and then stick to your decision.

It's amazing how your mind gets accustomed to making decisions once you get the decision-making process moving again. The worst place to be is in non-decision-making mode where issues back up, you get more stressed and overwhelmed and the cycle continues.

Start setting timelines for your decision-making processes. You have to get decisions flowing no matter how hard it feels. The fewer decisions you make the more back-up there will be, and the more pressured and overwhelmed you will feel.

Encourage change and reward everyone who embraces it

Constant change is a given in the modern business world. Everything changes all the time, and at a fast and furious pace. The ways that I communicate, travel, manage, market and run my business are completely different today to what they were, say, five years ago, and I can only imagine what things will be like in another five years. Mamma mia!

Now, when it comes to change there are two types of people. The first are those who love change and really embrace it. They thrive on it, they are up to speed with technology or at least willing to try it, and they are open and flexible to new ideas and better ways of doing business. Then there are those who simply can't stand change. The mere mention of the word is enough to make them break into a cold sweat, and trying to introduce them to new ideas is like pulling teeth.

So how does this affect you and your business–life balance? This question is best answered by my own story. My business looks and feels very different today to what it did five years ago. It is dynamic, evolving and technologically dependent. We have clients throughout Australia so I travel often, meet a lot of people and have countless opportunities and projects sent my way. If my team were not proactive about adapting to changing markets, new opportunities and new work practices, I could not do what I do. At times I drive them crazy with changes of direction and demands to always be striving to do what we do better than anyone else, to embrace technology and offer new products and services.

Luckily for me, most of them can cope, although occasionally as I look around the boardroom table I can almost hear them thinking, 'Not more change!' But to their great credit they support me 100 per cent and help me to achieve my goals and objectives. Best of all, they have a can-do attitude.

In return, I realise that I have to restrain myself a little at times and not overwhelm them with too much change too fast. Not everyone copes well with such momentum, and I have had a few people resign simply because the pace of the business was too fast, with too much change to suit them; I admire them for admitting it and moving on.

Some people simply don't seem to be able to 'do' change. The best advice I can offer is to enter into an open and honest dialogue with your employees about change and what it means to you. Try to nurture people through change or at least provide an environment where it can be discussed. If necessary, get professional help—change-management experts can be very valuable when dealing with organisational changes at every level.

My message is that change is here to stay. Decide what your philosophy is towards change, take a few moments to write it down, then sleep on it. When you're happy with it, put it in a place where you can see it often and your staff can see it too. Once you introduce the concept of change you can start to gauge people's feelings about it.

Learn to let go

I have a friend who was always successful in business and became very wealthy. Then, through a series of misfortunes, his business failed and he went broke. He has never got over it. Although at the time of his business failure he was quite young and easily had the ability, the resourcefulness and the ideas to start again, he turned into a bitter and angry man who blamed the world for his loss.

Holding on to past failures and mistakes takes a lot of energy. One of the best lessons I have learned, not only in business but also in life, has been the art of letting go.

It's hard to find a new lover if you are eaten up with anger and resentment towards the ex who broke your heart. You might not even realise that you are still holding the flame. How can you build a successful business, then, if you are still bitter and twisted about losing the last one? You struggle on day after day, trying to make it work and wondering why it doesn't, and all the while this very struggle to succeed reinforces and perpetuates the bitterness.

A long time ago I had a business partner who took literally everything I owned. He left me with a pile of debts and a battered and bruised ego. I spent a year feeling really angry with him, thinking about how to get revenge. Then one morning I woke up and realised how much energy it was taking to hold on to this anger so tightly. I was physically suffering from my rage—I had boils all over my body, I wasn't sleeping, I was short-tempered and unhappy. That morning I decided to just let it all go, to learn from the situation, and to put a little faith in the universe and the law of karma. The change was amazing—my boils cleared up within a few days, I started to sleep like a baby and my whole disposition lightened so I could enjoy life again.

It's easy to find reasons to be bitter and twisted; I know I have plenty. My parents abandoned my sister and me when we were infants. It would have been easy to harbour anger towards them but I learned to understand why they did it, to empathise with a young couple—no more than kids themselves—who found themselves in a bad relationship. They did what they thought was best at the time—they left us with someone more able to look after us. If they hadn't done so, would I have gone on to become a bestselling author, successful entrepreneur and leader in my community? Somehow I doubt it. So I am actually grateful that my parents left us.

The realisation that my parents' actions had enabled me to succeed was life-changing. Instead of struggling with feelings of resentment and abandonment I could simply be grateful. But this required me to look long and hard at the issue and think about it from a very different point of view, and then to simply get over it.

Identifying the issues you are holding on to that are draining you of energy is the first step to letting them go. Then you have to ask yourself two questions. First, what have you got to gain by holding on to this issue? And what have you got to gain by letting it go? For example, if you have been hurt in a previous relationship you can choose to hold back and never get close to anyone again. The upside is that you won't get hurt. The downside is that you will be really lonely, living a shallow and joyless life without the highs and lows of a close and intimate relationship.

Or, in a business context, if a member of your staff steals from you, it's easy to decide that you will never trust another employee. Worse still, you might start to imagine that everyone is trying to steal from you. You could become paranoid and spend all of your energy worrying about this issue. But how can you grow your business if you don't empower people and trust them to do the right thing?

Learning how to let go is a valuable lesson in life. It takes so much energy to hold on to negative issues.

Compliment others, be positive to others, be supportive of others

One of the greatest books I have ever read is *How to Win Friends and Influence People* by that master of human interaction, Dale Carnegie. This book has been my bible for almost twenty years and I make a point of reading it again every year, at least once.

Written over 70 years ago, in 1936, the book shows, in very simple terms, how to get the best out of people, and the concepts Carnegie describes are as relevant now as they were then. His underlying theme focuses on the power of being genuinely positive and encouraging of the people we deal with on a daily basis.

The importance of being supportive of others, of listening to and being interested in people can't be overestimated. The most amazing and truly wonderful aspect of this is that the more you support others, the more you listen, the more interested and encouraging of other people you are, the more these same characteristics flow back to you in your daily life. While that should never be your reason for offering support and encouragement, it is a beautiful reward.

Something as simple as offering a compliment to the person serving you in the grocery store on the way to work can change their entire outlook for the day, and yours as well. The best time to be like this is when you are feeling the most out of control or out of balance. Take your focus off yourself and put it onto others.

Have you ever noticed how, when you are in your own world and someone compliments you, perhaps saying how nice your shirt is, for instance, you are forced to take a step back and stop for a moment to take the compliment in? It certainly makes you feel warm inside, doesn't it?

I try to be positive and complimentary to every single person I meet. Sometimes that is pretty hard, in fact it can be downright impossible at times, because some people are just too angry to even register a compliment. But in return, my life is filled with people being incredibly supportive, loving and nurturing to me, especially when I need it the most.

The grass is not always greener

I get to meet many business owners who seem to have lost any passion for their business. They have the perception that every other business is better than theirs—by this I mean every other business is easier to run, more profitable, less time consuming, less stressful and generally far more appealing than the business they currently own and run.

Apart from being wrong, this 'grass is greener' mentality can make a business implode simply because the business owner spends all of their time finding fault rather than fixing issues.

From my experience, there's no such thing as an easy business to run. I have seen so many people buy a restaurant or coffee shop because they think it will be a breeze; in fact, the food industry really is tough. If you don't think so, watch one episode of *Hell's Kitchen* with Gordon Ramsay—that should be enough to scare anybody away from ever running a restaurant!

There are times when we all forget about the things we really love about our business: the freedom it gives us, the satisfaction we get from a job well done, the people we work with, our relationships with our customers, and the blood, sweat and tears that have gone into doing something we are really proud of. It is nice to be reminded of the things we love about our business rather than the things that bug us.

To do this we need to take some time out to think about our business and what it really means to us. At the same time, think through the 'dream' business that you imagine will be so wonderful. Be honest, be realistic. You may come to the conclusion that what you really want is what you already have.

I love keynote speaking and I am very active in generating quality jobs of this nature. But one day I was thinking about what it would be like to do five keynote jobs a week. Sure, the money would be good, but what would my life be like? I can tell you it would be a blur of airports, taxis, hotels, big rooms filled with a never-ending sea of people, bad coffee and not much time left for my family or friends. So I limit how much keynote work I do for this reason.

Maybe all your business needs is a little tweaking to make it closer to being perfect for you. If after doing all of the above you still think the other business is what you want—well, go for it. But be careful what you wish for. Focus on what your business gives you as opposed to what you think it doesn't.

4

Invest in your greatest asset

I have written a lot in these first few chapters about the value of attitude and how it fits into the success model of most entrepreneurs. A big part of having the right attitude is the importance of realising the value of investing in yourself. All too often entrepreneurs are so busy working in their business, putting all of their energy into growing, or in many instances surviving, that they have none left for themselves. They are the first in the office, the last to leave. There is never a good time for a holiday, so they stop taking them. They are too busy to eat well or exercise. And the business has become so all-consuming that they have actually disconnected from their friends and their family.

I will cover business–life balance in Chapter 17, but right now I want to examine the concept of looking after your number-one asset—yourself—by investing in yourself. My advice in the following sections will help to ensure you are a super-successful small business owner for a long time to come.

- Accept and believe that you are the number-one asset of the business

- Put a financial amount on your investment
- Investing in ourselves is as much about what we *don't* do as it is about what we *do* do
- Increasing your own knowledge
- Do you take your health and wellbeing for granted?
- Have a holiday—it's when you will get your best ideas
- Invest in yourself on a daily basis

Accept and believe that you are the number-one asset of the business

This is the place to start, as many business owners tend to put themselves last, abusing their number-one asset until they are exhausted, burnt out and completely devoid of any passion for what they are doing. It is very hard to come back from this place—believe me, I have been there, and sadly I encounter a lot of people on a daily basis who are there now.

Everything changes when we understand the fact that the better we are, emotionally and physically, the better our business will be. And of course that means more income, more success, more of the rewards that you want and expect.

When I finally started to treat myself as my number-one asset, my life changed dramatically. I lost a pile of weight, I got much healthier (even climbing a mountain or two) and I cut my working hours in half. The end result? My income doubled.

Today I actively and passionately encourage people to treat their number-one asset with total respect. It will pay off in far more ways than you can imagine.

Put a financial amount on your investment

I recently went to a seminar in the USA run by a man named Darren Hardy, the publisher of *SUCCESS Magazine*. He is a living example of the philosophies promoted in the magazine. One of his most interesting comments was that he has always invested 10 per cent of his annual income in himself. This investment includes training programs, books, CDs, DVDs, personal training, health retreats and anything else that can be considered a positive investment in his own wellbeing and personal growth and development.

Darren has no doubt that his success is due to this investment. Today he is worth some $200 million, so clearly his investment is paying big dividends.

Investing in ourselves is as much about what we *don't* do as it is about what we *do* do

Speaking of Darren Hardy, something he stopped doing fifteen years ago was watching or reading the news. His view was that there was too much negativity in it, and he preferred instead to focus on more positive ways to spend his time or engage his brain. As mentioned in the last tip, clearly his ability to generate wealth has not been overly affected by this lack of current affairs knowledge.

The point here is that when it comes to investing in ourselves, it is just as important to know the things we should be avoiding. To me, this can be summed up in one word—negativity. Rest assured I will discuss it throughout this book.

Increasing your own knowledge

In straightforward terms, I believe that if we are not growing we are dying, simple as that. The really successful business owners and entrepreneurs who I encounter have an insatiable thirst for knowledge. They look for it, they crave it, they are open to it and, most importantly of all, they learn from it. But they are selective about where they get their knowledge from.

Learning takes many different shapes. It might be a course or a seminar of some kind. It might be a book or DVD. Knowledge comes in magazines, it comes through websites and attending industry-specific conferences. It comes from having an open mind and observing the world around us.

For me, this translates into a house full of books, CDs and DVDs. I subscribe to the best business and personal development magazines I can. I use my car as a classroom, with six audio books loaded in the CD player at any time. I go to at least two or three seminars a year. I observe businesses all over the planet—looking for ideas, ways to do what I do better and benchmarking information so I can evaluate what I do. I only subscribe to e-newsletters that give me short, sharp pieces of advice. I have notebooks full of my own musings and gleanings from all of this and I refer to them often. Most importantly, I commit time every single day to learning and growing my knowledge.

Do you take your health and wellbeing for granted?

For many years I would have answered this question with a resounding *yes*. I didn't think about my body or my health terribly much, and it showed. My main focus was always on my business—how to work more, achieve more, get more done and earn more money to make ends meet. All of my energy and attention were given to my business, and very little was spared for my own health and wellbeing.

While today younger entrepreneurs are generally more aware and in tune with health issues, I still believe that a large proportion of the small business community really doesn't look after themselves very well. We need our bodies to be strong and fit to help us achieve our goals. So why do so many of us treat our bodies so badly?

When you are in business survival mode, you block out most things except the need to make ends meet and get as much work done as you can. This can often go on for many years. It becomes habit-forming, and these habits are hard to break. Life becomes so full and busy, with so many demands from so many areas, that finding time for yourself is impossible, or so you think.

But you can only take your body for granted for so long. Abuse it and you will ultimately pay the price. The healthier you are—mentally, physically and spiritually—the better every aspect of your life will become.

From my own experience it is simply a matter of adjusting your priorities. Is your health and wellbeing a priority or not? For those times that I forget or lose focus, I have a list of the five most important things in my life which I keep at the front of my diary and in my wallet. Treating my body with respect is at the top of the list.

This translates to eating well, exercising, relaxing, recharging and also having fun. Now, I don't always get it right, but I get it right more often than I get it wrong. I feel that every year I hopefully get a little healthier rather than less so.

Have a holiday—it's when you will get your best ideas

At conferences and seminars, people often ask me what is the best thing they can do to build their business and make it more successful. My advice is very simple—have a holiday. In fact, I give this advice so often I am thinking about opening up a travel agency! From my experience, to have a truly successful business you need to work less on the business and more on yourself. Having regular holidays is certainly a key aspect of that concept.

But when is a good time to have a holiday? There is never a good time, or enough money, or enough staff to cover you, or a quiet time with clients, et cetera . . . My view is that the more reasons you can come up with for not having a holiday, the more important it is that you have one.

The years slide by, and one year without a holiday becomes two, which becomes three, which becomes never. But investing in yourself enough to take regular holidays is vital. When you remove yourself from your daily working environment, your brain functions differently. Instead of living in fight-or-flight mode, for those of us battling a challenging working environment, we actually get to relax. Our brain patterns change, our outlook on life changes, our priorities are refocused and we make better decisions with many more positive long-term effects.

If you really can't take a long break, take a long weekend. I coached one couple to simply start by having a coffee together, outside of the business, twice a week. This led to a day off, which led to a long weekend, which of course ended up at last count as their seventh international holiday to some exotic destination. And how is their business? Booming. How was it before? Struggling.

To be at your best you need to be well, physically, mentally and emotionally. The high-stress life of a business owner is not conducive to this, so you need to work on it daily.

Invest in yourself on a daily basis

This attitude towards investing in yourself needs to be a daily commitment. There are bound to be a host of obstacles that keep coming up to make you stray from the path, but if you truly believe that you are your greatest asset and that you need to treat yourself accordingly, it becomes much easier to avoid those obstacles.

Every morning I take about 30 minutes to plan out my day. I have developed my own activity sheet, which clearly lists the things I need to get done. But at the top of the page, I have five 'to dos' specifically for me. They are my investment in myself today. These are always at the top of the page, because they are the *most* important things for me to do today. Maybe I need to read part of a book, go to the gym, buy some fresh fruit, book a weekend away, make an appointment to see a doctor or naturopath, catch up with a close friend, and so on. They are all tasks that make me feel better about myself, broaden my knowledge, make me healthier, motivate me more and relax me. And it is great to have these at the top of my list, as it makes the day ahead seem far less daunting, while putting my priorities into perspective.

5

If you lie down with dogs, expect to get up with fleas

One of the surest ways to succeed in whatever it is you do is to surround yourself with positive, motivated and like-minded people. This doesn't happen by accident; it requires a very clear desire to achieve your goals, whatever they are, and resolve to distance yourself from anyone who tries to crush your dreams.

I travel a lot and get to meet many people from all walks of life. Some are building massive empires, others are building small businesses from home. Yet a common topic of discussion is always the importance of having good people in your life to help you achieve your goals.

So what do I mean by good people? Put simply, it means those people who will support and encourage you to achieve your dreams no matter what. They will not try to talk you out of your dreams or let their own fears and insecurities come to the surface. Having people like this in your life is incredibly empowering and I believe they can help you to do anything you want.

When I wrote my first book, *101 Ways to Market Your Business*, and I was toying with the idea of trying to get it published, there were two kinds of people in my life. The first said, 'Go for it'—they believed in me and my passion. The second said, 'Don't waste your time—there are so many marketing books published already, you will never get yours published and it will only lead to disappointment.'

For a while the dream-crushers had an influence on me, but luckily I didn't listen to them in the end. Sadly, not everyone wants to see you achieve or grow. For those closest to you it can be a little scary. They may be afraid that they will lose you or that you will outgrow them. Others may feel resentful that you are achieving your goals when they are not.

From my experience, and from the amazing diversity of people that I am lucky enough to meet on a regular basis, I have come to believe in this above all else: surround yourself with powerful, dynamic and loving people who support you and your dreams, and your chances of achieving them will be increased dramatically. Otherwise, get yourself a good flea collar!

This chapter covers the following concepts:

- The Tao of the hot dog stand
- Do a relationship audit
- Some customers have fleas
- Listen to your gut instinct—about everything
- Always check references of potential suppliers

The Tao of the hot dog stand

Recently I heard a very powerful story about a hot dog stand. This particular stand was run by an old man who had started it many, many years ago. He loved his business and his customers. He used the best buns money could buy and his sausages were made to his own special recipe by his friend, a butcher. He took great pride in every single hot dog that he made and word of mouth had spread far and wide. As a result he had many customers coming back time and time again for over thirty years.

One day, the man's son came by to visit his father. His first question to the old man was how he was coping with the challenges of the global financial crisis. The old man said he had no idea what this crisis was and he certainly hadn't seen any downturn in his business. But the son went on about how the old man needed to change his business, cut his costs, get smarter and do whatever he could to protect the hot dog stand.

The old man respected his son as he had got himself a good education and was very smart. So he started to look for ways to cut his costs. He started buying smaller hot dog buns that were one day old. That saved him a lot. Then instead of getting hot dog sausages specially made by his local butcher, he bought them in bulk from a supermarket. He also started to charge extra for condiments like sauce and mustard. And last but not least, he cut down his working hours to save on electricity.

The old man told the son what he had done and the son told him that he had done the smart thing.

Over the next few weeks, the old man noticed that many of his regular customers started to complain about his hot dogs—they had never done that before. Business got slower and slower, until finally the old man was forced to close down his hot dog stand. He was very sad that his business was gone after so many years. As he was taking the last sign down, a regular customer came up to him and asked him why he was closing. The old man paused for a moment and then replied, 'The global financial crisis sent me broke.'

Hmm . . . kind of makes you think, doesn't it? I think there are a lot of great hot dog stand owners out there who listen to what people have to say as opposed to the facts in front of them. My advice is simple: remember the Tao of the hot dog stand whenever someone starts to tell you what you 'have to do'.

Do a relationship audit

Often we don't take the time to really think about our relationships with people outside of our immediate family and close friends. By this I mean the relationships we have with staff, customers, suppliers, professional advisers, and so forth. Often we spend more time with these people than our families, yet we don't really think about the health of these relationships.

A while back I made up a list of the key people in my professional and personal life. It was a long list, but I narrowed it down to the twenty most influential people. The list included family members, workmates, friends, suppliers, and so on. Next to each name I added three columns. In one column I wrote what I liked about the relationship, in the second column I noted problems in the relationship, and in the last column I described how I would like the relationship to change.

This exercise had a very significant impact on me, and on these relationships. First, it made me take the time to stop and actually think about each of them. Second, it made me appreciate the aspects of the relationships that I liked. Importantly, it also let me put into words what I didn't like. And finally, it enabled me to clarify how I would like these relationships to evolve.

The end result has been more open and honest relationships with virtually everyone in my life. It is amazing how much stress can be removed from your life when you can fully express yourself. There are far fewer frustrations, confrontations and 'sticky moments'.

Often this simple act of analysis will solve many frustrations that you may be experiencing in a relationship. It works because your brain now has a way of understanding and translating the issues that have been causing you grief.

After some practice, you may find that you can do a relationship audit in your head, without the need to write it down. It is a quick and effective tool for clarifying why some relationships aren't working and what you need to do about it. Then you can start working towards making it happen.

Some customers have fleas

I came across a great story about a psychologist who had a few business problems. Her schedule was fully booked all the time, which was very good, but her income was not where she needed it to be. Added to this, half of her patients were wonderful and half were a nightmare.

The good patients always arrived early, they respected her time, gladly paid their accounts on the spot and offered sincere appreciation for the advice she provided. The nightmare patients arrived late, if at all, they never paid on the day, instead forcing her to chase them for money. They complained about the cost and they complained about her advice. So one day she decided to do something about it.

The psychologist's rather radical plan of attack was to double her rates, which she did overnight. The impact was immediate. Within a day of the letters going out she had lost half of her patients. But there was a huge upside. For starters, she was only working half as much for the same amount of money. Second, the patients she lost were the nightmares. Third, because she now had appointments free, her 'good' patients could recommend their friends to the psychologist. Of course they shared the same quality characteristics as the referring 'good' patients, so she won again.

The moral of the story is that sometimes we have customers who have fleas, and they tend to be the ones that run our businesses. They don't appreciate what we do, they are difficult, they don't pay or they try to negotiate you down all the time and, worst of all, they refer to you other people exactly like them.

I recommend that you figure out if any of your clients have got fleas and then work out a strategy to send them on their merry way. Increasing prices certainly sorts out the good from the bad.

Listen to your gut instinct—about everything

I read a fascinating newspaper article recently that claimed scientists had now proven we do have a sixth sense. The article explained how a completely blind man could navigate his way around a room simply by sensing pieces of furniture blocking his way. They could show the same man a range of photographs of people with various facial expressions, from angry to happy, and he could sense the emotions in each picture. Truly amazing.

I believe that we all have this sixth sense, but we tend to use it less these days, preferring to rely on data that we can actually see. In other words, if we can't see it, we don't tend to believe it.

We have all had those strange experiences that make us scratch our head in wonder. Like when we are thinking about a person and the phone suddenly rings and—surprise, surprise—it's them. Or perhaps when you have been thinking of someone who you haven't seen for a while and you literally walk right into them on the street.

I have had so many of these situations I don't know where to start. This sixth sense, or gut instinct if you prefer, is both incredibly complex and incredibly simple at the same time. We all get certain feelings when we first meet a person. We often form very strong opinions about them in a matter of minutes. Certainly a lot of the formation of this opinion will come directly from their body language, what they say and how they react to what you say. But there are certain feelings and situations that cannot be as easily explained.

My sixth sense has saved my life many times, particularly when I was a commercial diver. But I had an experience a few years back that was altogether different.

I had just released my third book and was basking in the success of my new-found writing career. I was starting to get enquiries from all over the world for speaking opportunities and media interviews. It was all very flattering and I got caught up in the moment (with more than a little ego).

Out of the blue I received a phone call from a man in Africa. He was setting up an adventure tourism company that was going to operate ballooning trips, whitewater-rafting safaris and mountain-climbing expeditions. It all sounded very exciting and he was passionate and compelling. He told me that he had read my books and was very impressed, and he wanted me to come to Africa and set up the marketing of his new business venture.

We chatted for about an hour and I felt that this was a great opportunity, but my schedule for the rest of the year was completely full and, as much as I would have liked to do the job, I would have had to let too many other people down, so I said thanks, but no thanks.

Then he said the magic words, 'Money is no object.' He told me how his family had made lots of money mining diamonds and he had a big budget to get this business off the ground. I said I would think about it and get back to him with a quote.

The initial project required me to go to Africa for three months. I really couldn't go but I went through the motions of doing background research. I checked his website, which was fantastic, and I rang his office several times for more information. After about a week I sent him a quote—$250,000 for the three months, plus expenses. I thought this was outrageous and he would certainly say no.

Within five minutes of me sending the email he had responded and agreed to the fee. I was flabbergasted. I'd expected him to at least barter. Then he asked me for an address to send a bank cheque for a deposit of $50,000 and the airline tickets.

I reminded myself that I was very important and successful (nothing like a gorilla-sized ego to block the sixth sense from working) and I told myself he was simply a man who knew what he wanted and that he wanted me. But as I was emailing him my postal address I got a little shiver down my spine. Something wasn't right. My head and ego were busy telling me to shut up and take the money, but my sixth sense was hitting me over the head with a shovel.

I started to think a bit more about this whole scenario. A complete stranger was asking me to go to Africa for three months, he was sending me $50,000 and he hadn't even met me. I like to think my books are good, but really, why would someone commit so much without even meeting me, or at least getting some testimonials from other clients of mine?

So I decided to do a bit of homework. I rang the Australian Trade Commission in Johannesburg and spoke to a very helpful lady. I explained the situation; she was immediately alarmed and cautious, and she advised me to be the same. I gave her all the information I had and she promised to get back to me. Within an hour I had the South African Federal Police on the phone warning me of the sting that I was caught up in.

Basically, this is how it unfolds. The criminals trawl through the internet looking for individuals who are experts in their field and, specifically, those who look financially successful. Then they build a business scenario that will attract their victim. From here they set up an office in a dodgy area where it is hard to trace numbers, but if someone was sent to check it out, they would find a legitimate-looking office with all the right signage and even company vehicles. They go to the extent of setting up a website, printing brochures and business cards, even making corporate DVDs.

Once the trap is set, they make contact with the individual with an offer that is too good to refuse. They will even send the money and tickets, which would convince even the most sceptical of people that the whole thing is legitimate.

Once the victim arrives, they are met at the airport and kidnapped. If the family of the victim doesn't pay a multimillion-dollar ransom, the person is never seen again. Simple as that.

All of a sudden I was smack bang in the middle of an international conspiracy. The police asked me to make contact one more time, to confirm with the criminals when the cheque and tickets were sent, and they would then work out a way to track them down, possibly with me meeting them at the airport and the police swooping to arrest (something I was not overly keen on).

So after much communication and correspondence with a range of government bodies, I rang my contact but the phone wasn't answered. The website had disappeared and the whole operation was gone. The police told me that there were many leaks and the criminals were probably tipped off by a contact on the inside.

I had been ready to take that ticket and get on the plane for the trip of a lifetime to a remote part of Africa. How lucky was I that my sixth sense stepped in just when I needed it most? And, even more significantly, how fortunate that my sixth sense spoke up loudly enough for me to hear it.

Today I put a lot of credence in my gut instinct—I employ it in my business, in my personal life, in my health and wellbeing: everywhere. I have found that the more you listen to your instincts, the more evolved they become.

Whenever I am considering doing a joint venture or evaluating a deal of some kind, I always take time to see how I 'feel' about it. Everything might look great on paper, but what is my intuition saying? I don't get it right all the time, but I get it right more often than I get it wrong.

I think that many business owners have a heightened sixth sense, simply because they have to use it so often. I suggest tapping into yours when it comes to potential partners, deals, opportunities and people in general.

Always check references of potential suppliers

Good suppliers are an important part of the overall running of a successful business. Having a strong relationship with them is important, and a good start will help the relationship grow in a positive manner.

When setting up accounts with suppliers it is very likely they will want to do a check on your business to make sure you are able to pay their bills. You will probably have to supply a lot of your personal details, trade references verifying your business is good at paying invoices and a personal guarantee from the business owners or directors, which means if the business goes bankrupt they will be personally liable for any outstanding monies owed.

I think it is equally important that you know that your suppliers are reputable and, most importantly, that they will deliver what they say they will. Clearly you don't have the same financial risk as the supplier does when dealing with your business, but it is important for you to do some homework and establish that this will be a good relationship for your business and, ultimately, your customers.

Based on this, I recommend that when setting up accounts you ask the supplier to give you the names of some of their customers who can verify they will deliver what they promise when they promise it. Many companies will not do this and that often makes me wonder, why not? What are they hiding? They want all of your details but they won't give you any of theirs. Not a fair transaction if you ask me.

If your suppliers let you down, you will probably end up letting your customers down. Your customers won't blame the supplier, they will blame you, and this can affect the long-term success of your business.

Remember, there are mangy dogs with fleas in many different shapes and sizes.

6

Learning from the anti-businesses of the world

I spend a lot of time observing businesses, specifically looking for both good and bad characteristics. So I like to think I can learn from these observations and, even more importantly, share my findings in my books or when I'm presenting at a conference or advising a client.

After much research and even more frustration, I have discovered that there are ten types of really bad businesses out there or, as I like to call them, anti-businesses. These anti-businesses seem to have mastered the art of doing whatever they can to scare customers away through a mix of nonchalance, bad habits and bad attitude, most of which have evolved over time. And the better we get at identifying the anti-businesses that are out there, the more likely we are to make sure that we don't make any of the same mistakes. Running a really successful business is as much about what we don't do as it is about what we do.

Looking around the room whenever I am presenting on this topic, in among the laughter I see some uncomfortable squirming as people realise that they have actually become an anti-business and they didn't even realise it.

So what are the ten typical anti-businesses, and how can we identify them and learn from them?

- The 'I'm too busy to serve you' business
- The 'no, no, no' business
- The 'that's our policy' business
- The 'we hate our business so we hate you' business
- The 'schoolteacher' business
- The 'we'll get right back to you' business
- The 'we just don't care' business
- The 'smarty-pants' business
- The 'how can we make everything really complicated?' business
- The 'we have no idea what we're doing' business

The 'I'm too busy to serve you' business

These are the businesses that have mastered the art of making the customer feel completely insignificant. When you walk into the business you will be completely ignored while the staff (and often the business owner) are extremely busy doing other really important things (like chatting to their friends on the phone). Generally they don't acknowledge you with so much as a nod of the head, or a simple smile; instead you have to stand there, waiting to be blessed by their presence.

The 'no, no, no' business

These businesses are extremely frustrating. The standard response to every question the poor unsuspecting customer asks is 'no'. Do you have this? No. Can you get one in? No. Do you have something that could do the job? No. Do you know where I could get something like this? No. Do you give a damn? No. And so on.

The 'that's our policy' business

I just love these businesses. One day someone made the smart move of developing some policies for the business to follow (good on them). Now, though, they are totally inflexible and just plain dumb when it comes to enforcing them. In other words, we have a policy and we are not afraid to use it—always. A lot of big businesses fit into this category as well. Logic is completely replaced by policy, which tends to be driven by a pedantic Policy Nazi somewhere in the bowels of the business.

The 'we hate our business so we hate you' business

Some people have simply stayed in their business for way too long—and it shows. They take their frustrations at feeling stuck and channel them towards anyone considered a part of the problem, including the customer. There is a wonderful Chinese saying that goes something like 'A man without a smile should never open a shop'—so why are there so many miserable sods out there that do?

These businesses are instant energy drains—you walk in and feel depressed. The business looks fatigued and worn out, the person behind the counter looks to be deciding whether to serve you or jump under a bus, and the hairs on the back of your neck are telling you that this interaction is not going to be any fun at all.

The 'schoolteacher' business

These are the businesses where you get chastised for being a naughty customer. I have had people tell me (yes, tell me, not ask me) to stop talking, to be quiet and read this, to take some time and learn how their business works. Typically this is done in a sanctimonious voice by someone hiding behind a cash register or telephone. It is the height of ignorance to talk to customers like this, even if they are wrong.

The 'we'll get right back to you' business

Typically the 'we'll get right back to you' business translates into 'you will never hear from us again'. How many businesses do you have to stalk to get what you want out of them? This is one of the areas of greatest dissatisfaction for customers and, tragically, it is so easy to overcome. If a business can't follow up or get back to you when they say they will, it sends a message that they are either totally disorganised or completely lacking in respect for their customers.

The 'we just don't care' business

These are the businesses with a zero care factor and they go to great lengths to show it. Everything to do with this business reinforces their mission statement: 'Proudly not giving a damn.' There is no attention to detail, no attention to service, the products and services are shoddy and generally the business looks like it could easily disappear overnight.

The 'smarty-pants' business

These really bug me. You walk in and ask a pretty standard question and get a smarty-pants answer. Okay, sometimes as customers we do ask dumb questions, but we don't do it on purpose—we do it because we have a legitimate desire for more information. Generally there will be someone at this business who thinks they are pretty smooth and will look down their nose, snarl a response and then have some kind of in-joke about you with any of the other staff who may be close by. The smarty-pants business makes you feel stupid and embarrassed.

The 'how can we make everything really complicated?' business

I think the people who run these businesses have special meetings on a regular basis to work out exactly how they can make every single encounter with their customers really, really difficult—from making it impossible to find them in the first place, to making it hard to give them money, to never carrying the right stock (or any stock) and so on.

The 'we have no idea what we're doing' business

Typically this business falls apart the minute one customer walks through the door. They can't find anything, nothing seems to work, and they don't even have a pen. You leave feeling very certain that these guys have no idea at all about how to run a business, let alone satisfy a customer, and you can't help but wonder what happens when more than one customer walks in.

The moral to the story is there are many anti-businesses out there. Every time you encounter one, make a mental note of what type it is and do a quick internal audit of your business, just in case.

7

Question everything—often

An open and inquisitive mind is probably the most powerful asset any budding entrepreneur can have. Business is not static these days—it is exciting, challenging and changing constantly, and we all need to strive to keep up and hopefully lead the way in this environment.

To truly stand a chance at becoming successful you need to be able to honestly appraise what you are doing every day and look for ways to do it better. You can't sit back and be content that your business will be just as successful in the coming years as it has been in the past few years if you don't review and modify what you do.

Question everything you do, regularly. One thing I love about experienced entrepreneurs is that they are not afraid to ask anyone for an opinion about what they do or for a suggestion on how to make their business better. In this chapter I will share some ideas that will help you to ask the right questions in your small business.

- Be open to feedback
- Question your business partners—ask them to be honest

- Walk around your business and really look at everything
- Go to successful businesses and find out *why* they are successful
- Mystery shop your way to success
- Do you charge enough?
- If it doesn't feel right, it probably isn't—the business owner's sixth sense
- Talk to your staff
- Don't be afraid to be a manager
- Write your own operations manual as a way to question what you do

Be open to feedback

We have to be able to question and review everything we do in our business. If we are not prepared to accept what we find out or do something about it, don't bother asking the question.

Many business owners are rigid and set in their ways. They think they want to hear about their business from their customers, but all they really want to hear is the good stuff—negative feedback can often make them quite hostile.

It is a real sign of business maturity to be able to take constructive criticism on board and use it to make your business even better. Think about it: how grateful should you be if someone's honesty gave you the opportunity to make your business better?

Businesses that operate as though set in stone are dinosaurs, and many won't survive in the modern business environment where we all need to change and evolve. Quiz the people you deal with on a regular basis about their experience with your business. But if you ask the questions, make sure you have an open mind about the answers. You have to make the final decision about what you will do with the information.

Do you have an open mind to constructive criticism? How do you respond if someone tells you something not so flattering about your business? If you do have an open mind, great—ask more people for their opinions and recommendations and use the information wisely. If you don't, it's time to work on opening up and becoming more flexible. Think of constructive criticism or feedback about your business as an exceptional opportunity and be sincerely grateful to the people giving it to you.

Question your business partners—ask them to be honest

In this instance I would consider business partners to mean anyone you have a professional relationship with—your professional advisers (lawyer, accountant), your suppliers, friends in business, your business mentors and really anyone else who is in a position to know about your business.

Just as we have discussed the importance of asking your customers for their feedback and their recommendations to improve your business, your business partners can offer excellent advice from a different perspective. An open-minded business owner has access to a lot of good information and advice from their network of business partners—all you have to do to access this is ask.

Question your network about ways to run your business better, successful marketing ideas, new products and services and ways to attract more customers. Just one good idea from a business partner could be a significant turning point for your business, but you have to be big enough to ask.

Often it can be interesting to see the different perspective your business partners bring to your business. Their views and ideas will have developed through being involved in their own industries and businesses, and their suggestions really may be things you would not have even considered.

Sitting down with a business partner and asking them how you could make your business better is a little tough and it puts them on the spot. I suggest making a small list of topics to discuss—this might include things such as customer service, product range, sales, advertising, business appearance and so on. Use the list to guide the conversation. This also gives you an opportunity to write down their responses. If you do this exercise with ten business partners, you might start to see some common themes emerging. Most will give their opinions freely, but remember: if you ask for them, be prepared to listen.

Start by making up a list of the areas of your business that you would like to discuss and then pick one business partner per day for the next week to ask for their opinions and feedback on how you could make your business better.

Walk around your business and really look at everything

When you visit the same place every day, year after year, it is very easy to walk in and out with blinkers on. Throughout this book I recommend that you stop what you are doing and go and look closely at certain aspects of your business—whether it is your front entrance, your signage, your staff, your customers, whatever. Well, the aim of this tip is to reinforce that message.

You need to become more observant in your business. You need to not only look more closely at every aspect of your business but also be able to make changes that will improve the business.

As a business grows, it is easy for the owners to lose touch with a lot of the everyday events going on. While it becomes impossible and in some ways unproductive for the business owner to know all of the nuts and bolts, it is important for them to have a clear understanding of how things work. The more they understand, the more they can look for ways to make things run better.

Get out of your work space and just walk around. Clear your head, open your eyes and try to look at the business without your normal blinkers on. The habit of walking in and out of your business with blinkers on has probably formed over many years.

Talk to your staff, talk to some customers. Go across the road and look at your business from there, have a good look at your website, read through your own brochure and look at the products that you have on display.

There are so many aspects of the business that need to be reviewed on a constant basis that it can be daunting. The first step is to remove the blinkers and open your mind to becoming an observer. After a week of doing this it will become second nature.

Once you become a keen observer you can start to make the business even better—and that can take it from mediocrity to magnificence.

Go to successful businesses and find out *why* they are successful

Again, the theme here is to become an excellent business observer. Whenever you find out about a really successful business—perhaps they have won an award, or your family and friends are all talking about them, or there may have been an article in the newspaper—I suggest you pay the business a visit. What they sell really doesn't matter; how they run the business does. What makes it so successful? Why do people keep coming back? Why does it win awards?

Venture in armed (metaphorically speaking, of course) to find out their secrets and to see if you can apply any of them to your business. Often discovering why a business does so well is not easy on first inspection. From my own experience, it is more often the way they do business in general rather than any one specific detail: the attitude of the staff, the attention to detail, the inviting and welcoming feel of the business. Rarely is it their pricing, a misconception that many business owners are far too preoccupied with.

Becoming a good observer of anything takes time and training. A quick walk around a successful business might give you a few clues, but you really need to go a little deeper. Give them a call and make an enquiry about their product. Consider how they handle it. Most importantly, after the call, did you feel like going to this business? Take the time to get to know that business, listen to their sales staff, make a purchase and see how the transaction is handled, or ask a few difficult questions.

After you get a good picture, make a list of what you feel makes this business so good at what it does, and beside each of the points indicate if they could be applied to your business. Then set about implementing them.

Mystery shop your way to success

Mystery shoppers are being used by more and more businesses every day to provide an independent evaluation of what the business is doing well and what it could be doing better. They are not witch-hunts trying to find the underachieving employee who can then be thrown to the wolves. They are mechanisms for giving an honest appraisal of a business.

Companies that offer mystery-shopping services can be found in most cities, usually through marketing companies and training organisations. In more recent times, firms have been set up that do nothing but offer customer service evaluations, utilising mystery shoppers as one of their key resources.

Ideally no one, not even the business owner, will know when a mystery shopper will be dropping by. They will appear to be just like any other customer, and that indeed is the aim. A short while later a report will be issued and the overall performance of the business can be measured. Periodically the mystery shopper evaluation can be repeated to determine if the business has improved or worsened.

Normally, the first mystery shopper visit is the toughest. It highlights the most glaring weaknesses and can be quite confronting for both business owners and staff. Often the initial response is to point the finger at someone, which is not the best course of action. What is needed following this first report is a clear and level-headed plan to rectify any problems and to work at improving the business in any of the areas that need improving.

Mystery shoppers can be used to evaluate the following:

- service and selling skills over the telephone
- how easy the business is to find
- how appealing the entrance is
- general layout of the business

- first impressions
- overall cleanliness of the business
- overall ambience of the business (smells, sounds, etc.)
- appearance of the staff
- selling skills of the staff
- perceived value for money
- general level of customer service
- response time to internet enquiries
- quality of the products or services sold.

Many other related and specific areas of any business can be evaluated. While the feedback can be a little confronting, the end result is that your business will have the opportunity to rectify problems that can be losing you customers. Another bonus is that if your staff know you are having regular mystery shoppers they tend to try a little harder, never knowing if the customer standing in front of them is the one. Because of this, it is important to share any mystery shopper findings, good and bad, with your staff. Show them the information that is collected and that you are doing something with it.

It takes a strong business to use mystery shoppers, but they are a great way to work out the difference between mediocre and winning.

Do you charge enough?

Pricing is a tough subject—do you charge too much or too little? There are a lot of businesses that simply don't charge enough, making it really difficult to ever make the business successful.

I received some excellent advice when I was starting out in my business life: a very successful entrepreneur friend sat me down and said, 'Someone has to be the most expensive and it may as well be you. But if you are going to be the most expensive, you have to be the best at what you do. Your business has to shine in every way.' An interesting concept, and one I have tried to adhere to in any business I have run.

I believe customers are less concerned with pricing than they are with service and value for money. Sure, there are a lot of businesses that operate in price-conscious markets. But even in these markets I believe the same principle applies—people will pay more for quality.

Running your business on tight margins makes it harder to be magnificent as so much energy has to be focused on just making ends meet. If you can gradually build your prices up so as to offer better service and a better experience to your customers, in general it will pay off.

Charging what you are worth is a hard concept for a lot of people. They usually charge what they think their customers are prepared to pay, and often the two are a long way apart. If your business doesn't make enough money it will not be successful, simple as that. If you are just scraping by and not really getting ahead in your business, maybe you are simply not charging enough. Winning businesses are not afraid to charge what they are worth because they can back it up by being the best at what they do.

Today is a good day to review what you charge. Look at all of your pricing and see if you can charge more and deliver a better product and a higher level of service.

If it doesn't feel right, it probably isn't—the business owner's sixth sense

I have spoken about the business owner's sixth sense with a lot of entrepreneurs and I have experienced it myself many times. It is the ability to be able to tell intuitively that something is not right in your business, perhaps to sense that something is wrong with a proposed deal or that the person sitting across the desk from you is saying something you don't quite believe. It most certainly exists, and those aware of it use it to their advantage. They encourage this sixth sense to grow and they listen when it needs to be heard.

This sense develops over time and it is just as relevant in life as it is in business. We need to learn to listen to this little voice at the back of our mind. Any time I have ignored it, it has either cost me money or caused me grief.

While I am sure some readers will find the idea implausible, I have no doubt many others will know exactly what I'm talking about. There are many intangible aspects of running a business that have as much impact and bearing on your success as the more tangible aspects.

Have you ever been in a situation in your business when something just didn't feel right, but you ignored the nagging feeling and went ahead anyway, only to find out it was a bad decision? Well, that tingling wasn't your spider sense, it was your business owner's sixth sense trying to get out and be heard. It is a priceless tool that will help you as an entrepreneur to be far more successful and enjoy your business.

From today on, try to listen to your business owner's sixth sense. When you have nagging doubts, try to decide whether it is just fear or natural caution, or more of a gut feeling. The more you listen to your sixth sense, the more it will talk to you.

Talk to your staff

Many business owners take an us-and-them approach to their staff, but for most of us, life without staff would be pretty hard. Our businesses would never be able to grow, our workloads would be enormous and there would be a hollow feeling when it came to sharing the trials and tribulations experienced in our daily business life.

Involve your staff in your business. Ask them for their ideas and their opinions—after all, they often know your business almost as well if not better than you. Most certainly they will know the specific jobs they do better than you. The more you let your staff play an active role in your business, the more they will grow, the more ideas they will come up with and, ultimately, the better your business will run and the more successful it will be.

Involving your staff means not just asking for their opinions and thoughts but also taking these opinions and thoughts seriously and being appreciative of the fact that your staff members are prepared to be involved. Just because you give them a weekly paycheque doesn't mean they have to open up; it is a real trust situation and it needs to be well handled.

Give your staff the same level of respect as your customers. Sure, there will be times when you drive each other crazy, but never forget that you are working on the same team.

Get your staff involved in your business. Ask them for their thoughts and opinions and build a strong relationship based on mutual respect.

Don't be afraid to be a manager

Being a manager is a big task. It covers an enormous amount of constantly changing ground. Being a manager means being a leader, it means being a decision-maker and it means being committed to what you do.

Business owners often fall into the role of manager by default and sometimes that can be the hardest part of running your business. You know how to do your business but you may never have had to manage people before, so it is a whole new ball game.

Being a manager can mean making tough decisions. Some decisions affect the lives of others, for example when staff just don't work out and have to be dismissed. There has to be a balance between what is best for the individual and what is best for the business.

Becoming a better manager starts in your head. Understanding and accepting the complexity of being a manager is one part, but realising you are not expected to know everything overnight is the real key to becoming a good manager. Sure, you will make mistakes, but as long as you learn from them your skills will improve.

Read books on management styles and ideas—there are an amazing number of these around. Do a management course and ask your mentors for their ideas and advice. You will become a better manager for it, which is very rewarding personally, and your business will benefit from your increased ability as a manager.

Write your own operations manual as a way to question what you do

An operations manual is simply a written description of how your business operates on a daily basis. Every business should have one, regardless of the size of the business. Operations manuals put details in black and white, and writing one is the perfect way to examine why you do things in a particular way.

An operations manual can be as complex or as simple as you want it to be. It is going to be used internally by other members of your team, not put on display for the general public to read. It should outline how any situation should be processed within your business, for example:

- opening procedures
- expectations regarding staff appearance and conduct
- customer service procedures (including a complaint resolution process)
- processing sales
- ordering stock
- paying accounts
- company policy on staff entitlements
- use of company vehicles
- cleaning.

Writing a manual like this really does make you investigate every part of your business in a detailed manner. Having written a few and advised my clients to write them, the same feedback comes out every time—writing an operations manual is a work in progress. As you start writing a section, you begin thinking about how a procedure works and come up with better ideas on the spot. So while the end product is helpful for making sure everyone knows what to do within your business, the writing process itself is great for questioning what you do and coming up with ways to do things better.

If you haven't got an operations manual, today is the day to begin. First, make a list of all of the operational aspects of your business and then start filling in the details. Accept that the manual will be a work in progress. If you have an operations manual already, determine whether it is current and still accurate. Pull it out and read it cover to cover; I'm sure you will make changes for the better.

8

Bad things happen to good businesses— be prepared *now*

'm probably the most optimistic person in the world, and proudly so. There is nothing that bugs me more than being around people who zap my energy, who live life with their glass not even half empty but absolutely bone dry, and who seem to be able to find the negative in the very best of situations. But for a moment or two, I have to play the role of devil's advocate.

Bad things really do happen to good businesses, and sadly I see them happen all the time. Many are outside the control of the business owners and most lead to financial disaster. But the good news is that you can take steps to reduce your risks and to make your business as bulletproof as it can possibly be.

Believe me when I say it is so much easier to make your business bullet-proof than it is to try to bring it back from the brink of disaster. The big problem is that most business owners wait until they are standing on that brink to take action. Getting your business into shape in the good times will dramatically increase your chances of survival in the tough times. The smartest economic minds in the world can't tell us exactly when the economy will turn, but they all agree that it *will* turn because it always does. Good times come after tough times, and vice versa.

The suggestions I make in the following pages will certainly make your business stronger and far better able to deal with challenging times, no matter what causes these challenges. And some of the suggestions are so important that they warrant their own sections throughout this book, as they fall into my category of 'Highly Important Themes'.

Planning for the worst and hoping for the best may sound pessimistic, but I think it is more a matter of being well prepared. Those businesses that have been through hard times unprepared but survived will tend to avoid making the same mistakes again.

I guarantee that if you focus on the following ten aspects of your business, you will be well on the way to being around for a very long time, all the while watching your ill-prepared competitors come and go.

- Take responsibility for your business
- Have all the information at your fingertips
- Understand your business
- Have the best advisers you can afford
- Without customers you don't have a business
- Build a large network
- Commit to constant and never-ending improvement
- Treat marketing as a priority
- Cash is what makes or breaks any business
- Get a life

Take responsibility for your business

Some time back I had a bit of trouble with the taxation office. I was behind in my business tax payments and I was struggling to find the money to pay the growing bill. Things reached a head and I had to have a mediation meeting to explain why I was behind in my taxes and, most importantly, what I was going to do about it.

There were a number of reasons why my taxes were overdue, but they were mostly normal business issues including slow-paying customers, a failure to project-manage as well as I should have, and not being tough about collecting money. However, I prepared my story for the meeting along the lines of how tough it was to have a small business, especially when the economy was sluggish, as it was at the time, and how various other issues were affecting my business.

I turned up for the meeting and proceeded to tell my tragic tale. I went on for about twenty minutes and there were lots of nodding heads but, sadly, no tears. Then the taxation officer said slowly, 'This is a very sad story, Mr Griffiths, but we really don't care. You are the company director; you are 100 per cent responsible for your business. We want to know when you will be paying the money you owe the Australian government. If we don't get a firm answer on that from you right now, we will be taking further legal action which will, in all likelihood, mean making you bankrupt.'

Up until that moment I had taken a bit of a loose approach to rules and regulations, particularly those concerning tax. But right then I realised that, yes, my name was on the bottom of the page and I was 100 per cent responsible for every single cent my business owed. I left that meeting feeling a little like a naughty schoolboy who'd been caught out. I knew that from that day on I would take full responsibility for every single aspect of my business; as I did so, my attitude changed markedly.

Before the stern words from the taxation officer, I had been easygoing with my staff, and not overly concerned about deadlines or performance. If someone was going through a tough spell I would cut them some slack for months, even though they were not contributing to the business. Now I realised that their lack of performance was costing me money and, while I was never unkind about it, from then on I certainly reacted quickly and made it very clear that the situation had to change.

I made a point of setting budgets and targets for my staff and, most importantly, if they were not met I wanted to know why straightaway. I became much more careful about where and when I spent money. It was almost like an awakening for me—this might sound strange, but I had spent most of my time and energy focusing on the work that I did, not on the business itself. That led to all kinds of problems, and the only way to solve them was to take the time and energy to address them one by one.

So, without doubt, the first step in bulletproofing any business is to step up and take responsibility for everything that the business does, and I really do mean everything: bills, products, staff, legal obligations and liabilities, taxes, ethics, services and anything else that falls under the banner of your business. This is not a responsibility to be taken lightly. If the crunch comes, you can blame other people or circumstances that are out of your hands, but it won't matter one bit. If your signature is at the bottom of the page, the buck stops with you.

Have all the information at your fingertips

I have never been much of an 'attention to detail' kind of person when it comes to financial figures. In my early days as a business owner, my record-keeping would involve literally taking a shoebox full of receipts and cheque stubs to my poor accountant once every few years (not hard to imagine why I had issues with the taxation office, is it?).

I had no idea about cash flow, account reconciliation, profit and loss or balance sheets. I bumbled my way around these things for almost twenty years. I never had accurate figures; my accounting entailed simply adding up the money in and the money out in my bank account or seeing how much was in the till at the end of the day. Of course I couldn't budget—I had no way of managing money and I never knew how much anything cost.

I didn't realise how important all this really was because my attention was always on the front end of my business: focus on making money and as long as you make enough, you won't have any problems. This is so wrong for so many reasons that I hardly know where to start!

To be successful in business and to make your business as bulletproof as possible, you must have access to accurate financial figures that are as current as they can be. Ideally you need to know at the end of each day exactly what the financial position of your business is. You need to have complete faith in any figures being given to you, either by an accountant or your bookkeeper. You have to know your debt position and what all your liabilities are. Nothing is worse than getting a huge bill you didn't know was coming.

Having accurate reports is great, but they are of no value at all if you can't read or understand them. I make a point of getting my accountant to explain all financial reports to me. I read a lot of books and ask a ton of questions. I get copies of the annual reports of public companies and read through page after page of figures to form my own opinion on the financial state of the business. I took the time to learn how to make cash-flow forecasts based on the payment history of my clients, and so on.

My biggest realisation was that none of this is all that complicated, it just takes some effort and time to learn what the numbers mean. It won't be long before you will be able to see mistakes in reports or pick up on issues that will affect your business.

Knowledge really is power, especially knowledge about figures. Numbers tell you so much about the state of your business: whether or not you are making money (something that is surprisingly hard to work out at times), how long your cash reserves will last, whether your business is growing, how quickly you collect money, and so on.

A business with great records is always worth more than one with poor records, for obvious reasons. My first recommendation in the process of bulletproofing your business is to take responsibility. So here I suggest that you take total responsibility for the financial figures for your business, no matter how much you may dislike that part of things.

Any business that does not have accurate accounting nor an owner who understands the figures is destined for doom at some stage. I guarantee that even the most flamboyant of entrepreneurs, like Richard Branson, who don't seem to have the slightest care about things as dreary as spreadsheets, actually have incredibly accurate accounting systems and on any day know their exact financial position. I believe that it is impossible to bulletproof your business if you don't have accurate figures that you can understand delivered to you reliably and regularly.

Understand your business

Many years ago a friend who became a business mentor posed a question that literally stumped me: he asked how much it cost to open my doors every day. I had no idea. I now ask this question of my clients all the time and I am constantly amazed at how little people know about their own business. If I ask this question in a room with a hundred people in it, I am lucky if five people put their hand up with an answer.

We all need to know about every aspect of our business. I am not saying that we should become micromanagers, but we need to know certain basics. The profit and loss of a business is not something that we want to learn about months down the line. After all, what if you don't have enough money to cover the loss?

Whether we are making a profit or a loss is something we need to know straightaway. Using a very simple formula, I add up the net cost of products and services, the fixed costs like rent and wages, and all other expenses and come up with the daily sales target that is needed to cover these costs and make a profit. For example, if it cost $1000 a day to run a business and we sold products with a 50 per cent mark-up, we would have to sell $3000 worth of products each day to break even. But who wants to just break even? Surely the objective is to make a profit. Ideally we would want to make at least double our cost for the day, so we would have to sell $6000 worth of products or services.

Imagine this equation if we were not selling anything. Our cost just to open the doors would still be $1000 per day, so if we sold nothing in a week, we would be $5000 down the tube. I think every business, big or small, needs to know whether or not it has made money or lost money that day. I know of enormous businesses, operating in thirty countries, that get daily figures which are just more complicated versions of my simple formula—without doubt they know if they have made or lost money that day.

We also have to know what is normal for our business: for example, which products sell and which don't, and what changes in customer patterns, trends and costs are to be expected. If unexpected changes or increases in cost occur, we need to find out why. So much money slips between the cracks in a business that it is ridiculous.

I once ran a reasonably large marketing company where my receptionist ordered all our printing and stationery supplies. While we were moving office I came across a huge stockpile of printer cartridges that would have cost about $10,000. I couldn't believe it. The receptionist had since left so I had to cop it on the chin, but I found out from the supplier that she had made these big purchases to receive the gifts that came with buying larger quantities. Mamma mia—how much had this cost me? But I learned some very valuable lessons from the experience.

I now watch out for any anomalies in the bills. Things like phone bills going up unexpectedly, an increase in stationery spending, or even an increase in petty cash spending always activate my Sherlock Holmes synapses. But how can you recognise anomalies if you don't know what is normal?

I make a point of signing every invoice that comes into the business. I want to know exactly what we are buying and how it is being used. I don't want to sound like one of those anal retentives who get uptight about someone taking a pencil; I don't actually care, but if they take it, I like to know. While I am in fact a very easygoing boss, over the years I have realised that the difference between paying attention and not paying attention can be tens of thousands of dollars a year. And let's be honest— surely that money is better off in your pocket rather than tied up in a ten-year supply of printer cartridges.

Any business owner who knows their business inside and out—and I mean all parts of the business, not just the parts that they are most interested in—is way out in front of the competition. The sad reality is that very few business owners have even the slightest idea about any part of their business other than selling the products and services that they specialise in.

Being bulletproof means being aware, informed and disciplined.

Have the best advisers you can afford

Having cheap advisers is like buying a cheap motorbike helmet. Why would you? I am not suggesting that you pawn your house and your kids to pay for the greatest legal mind to write up the new lease on your shop, but I am suggesting that, generally, when it comes to professional advice from accountants, financial planners, solicitors, marketing consultants and so on, you get what you pay for.

This may not always be the case, but my experience tells me that more often than not it is. If we were sick, we would want the best doctor we could get and worry about how to pay them later. Yet when it comes to business, all too often there is a fear of cost, so the business settles for second best and gets second-best advice.

In my field I come across countless businesses that want to do all their marketing themselves. I understand that and I wish them luck, but often they have no idea what they are doing. So they waste a pile of money on things that don't work, execute it poorly because they don't really have the time to do it properly, and when they don't get the results they want, they blame marketing as a concept. If they used a professional to at least develop a plan that they could work by, they would be miles out in front financially because at least they would be on track towards doing something that works.

This fear about fees is generally unwarranted. When it comes to choosing professional business advisers, spend some time recruiting them rather than just engaging the first one you encounter. Talk to friends and associates, then interview prospective advisers to make sure they can give you what you want. Be upfront and tell them that you are concerned about being hit with big bills and come up with a way to resolve that issue by working with each other. It is all about communication. If you can't communicate effectively with your newfound adviser from the start, they are probably not for you. If you like to have specific recommendations explained to you in detail, find an adviser who will do this.

Sometimes you might have to go through a few advisers until you find the right one. But that is why you do the recruiting when you are bulletproofing your business, not when you are in crisis. In fact, the point of having exceptional advisers ('good' just doesn't cut it) is that they will play a huge role in preventing you from getting into grief.

I once paid an incredible adviser $130,000 to help me restructure a business I owned. I had got into trouble due to a messy partnership. If I hadn't used him, I am sure I would have gone bankrupt, or at the very least would have had to find the best part of half a million dollars to get out of the horrible mess I was in. So was he worth it? Absolutely—every single cent. And at the time I didn't have that kind of money, but I found it, because I knew the cost would be far more if I didn't use him.

Over a lot of years, after dealing with many complex financial issues, legal issues and every other issue imaginable, I have found that when I go down the cheap route, I get nothing but trouble. So what I learned was to get better advisers and become more commercial in my dealings with them. That is, I ask them hard questions about their fees upfront, I give them a budget or I negotiate. I want our relationship to be win-win but I don't want the fear factor operating when we are working together.

As well as paid advisers, I strongly recommend the value of having good business mentors around you. I have one very good friend, Neville Burman, who constantly amazes me, even in the darkest of times, with his words of wisdom. Whenever I have had challenges, Neville and I have sat down and spent a few hours talking through every single option, many of which I wasn't even aware were options, until we found a solution.

This kind of sounding board is priceless for any business owner. There are always people around who have been in business for a long time and who are willing to take a novice business owner under their wing. You can learn from their mistakes, but please remember that if you ask for their advice, it's a pretty good idea to take it. I have been in business for many years and have had a lot of mentors going back over twenty-five years. Today I have more mentors than ever before, simply because my decisions have more riding on them than they ever did.

Regardless of whether your advisers are paid or free, get the best people you can. If you invest time researching them and build relationships whereby you both benefit, these people will help your business to grow for many years to come.

Without customers you don't have a business

A business that is not absolutely committed to its customers is one that is going to get into trouble somewhere down the line. When times get tough and customers start to question their relationship with a business, the quality of this bond will soon become apparent.

When we start our businesses we bend over backwards to not only meet but exceed our customers' expectations in any way possible. Nothing is too much trouble and the slightest hint of an unhappy customer has us begging for forgiveness (well, not quite, but you know what I mean). But over time the business grows, and the person who started the business and had such a passion for their customers now spends less time dealing with them face to face while they attend to their staff and all the other aspects of running the business. As time goes on, they probably don't even leave the back office. The only time they hear from a customer is when there is a problem, so they start to dislike their customers, whose only function seems to be to disturb them with complaints.

Anyone finding themselves in this situation needs to change their attitude dramatically. Our staff mirror our actions and our attitudes, so if we have a bad attitude towards our customers they will pick up on this in a second. I often stand in shops waiting to be served and watch the staff. I can tell in a second if the owner has lost their passion for the business and the customers because I can see it and hear it in the voice of their staff. Everyone adjusts their mood and their attitude to yours. Clearly there is an issue if you are not in a positive, customer-service-focused state of mind.

Customers are everything to a business. We should all be looking for ways to service them better, to listen to what they need, to build strong relationships and to do whatever we can to make life easier for them. However, some businesses seem to go out of their way to make every interaction difficult. It's hard to find the business, then it's hard to park.

It's cluttered and dirty inside, nothing has a price on it, and there is one bored staff member behind the counter to serve five waiting customers. When the customers get to the counter they are told that credit cards are not accepted and so on. More businesses make it hard to buy from them than we realise.

There are many great books, websites and training services that show you how to improve your overall level of customer service. However, none of the advice will work if the person who owns the business isn't committed to treating their customers as their number-one priority every single day of the year.

Build a large network

We live in a world where it is getting harder to make our business stand out from the crowd. In the future it will be even harder as more advertising mediums appear, as customers' habits change and become harder to understand, and as competition increases. This is where networking can prove invaluable.

As consumers we are becoming more driven by word-of-mouth recommendations simply because we trust what a friend tells us much more than we trust what an advertisement says. Because of this it is vital for any business owner to have the biggest possible network of friends, associates, fans, followers and fanatics.

I live in Cairns, a relatively small city. If my business is a bit slow, all I have to do is go for a walk to the post office and I will bump into someone who needs some marketing done. It happens all the time and over the years I have built a big network both in my hometown and around the country. This network provides referrals, it provides advice, it gives me opportunities and it is a kind of insurance policy against tough times.

I often hear people say that they hate networking, it feels false, and it is awkward and embarrassing. Well, it can be. I don't like going to cocktail parties and standing around looking and feeling like a sore thumb. But there are many ways to network and build up a client base. Let me share one example.

For several years I had a courier who used to make deliveries to my office several times a day. His name was John and I knew him enough to say a friendly hello, but nothing more. John had been to my business thousands of times and I realised one day that I knew nothing about him. I felt awkward that he was such a familiar part of my business yet I knew nothing about him, so the next time he came in I asked him if he had time for a coffee. He said yes, so we wandered down to the local coffee shop and had a short but very enjoyable chat. He had moved to Cairns from Sydney, where he had had a big management job that was slowly killing him. Now he started early and finished early and he had lots of time to spend with his kids. We really connected and I was glad that I had suggested we talk.

Over the next couple of weeks my business became incredibly busy, so I didn't have a lot of time to think about John. The work kept piling in and I realised something strange was happening. I asked my consultants where the work was coming from and they told me it was all the result of referrals from John.

His job meant that he spent all day going from business to business, chatting to people. They would say that they needed some marketing done and John would tell them to use my business. He also suggested to firms that looked a bit run-down or as if they were doing it tough that they needed professional advice from a company like mine. John became our very own personal sales rep and he was amazing. I couldn't tell you how much work he directed our way but it was a lot—all because I had a cup of coffee with him.

Today most of my work comes from word-of-mouth referrals. I am very proud of this fact because it must mean that I do a pretty good job if people refer me to others.

Likewise, the people who refer clients to me are my sounding boards. They offer advice if I need it, and they help me to see through complex situations when I am too involved.

To bulletproof your business, you have to build a network of people who protect and promote you, and provide information. To build this network you have to meet people, honour the relationship by being honest and ethical in your dealings, and make it a two-way street. If they support you, you must support them however you can.

Building a network takes time, but it should certainly not be written off as a waste of time. I don't go to a lot of networking functions, but I make a point of introducing myself to people, getting my existing network to introduce me to their contacts and so on. In other words, you can make networking suit your personality. If you are a one-on-one type, make an appointment and go and see a person. If you like the social scene, go to networking functions and meet people—but make sure you don't just stand in the corner talking to the same person you talk to at every event.

From my observations and personal experience, a network of good people will help to make any business bulletproof.

Commit to constant and never-ending improvement

Any business that is constantly trying to improve what it does has to be well on the way to success. This attitude is one that any customer notices the minute they walk into a business, just as they notice a business that doesn't care.

So how does a business constantly improve? There are so many ways. We can improve the way we communicate with our clients; we can make it easier for people to buy from us; we can keep working on the appearance of our business, ensuring it is always clean and tidy but also fresh and modern; we can train our staff better; we can keep our product knowledge up to date. Most importantly, we need to have an open mind and look for new and better ways to run our business.

When you are committed to constant and never-ending improvement it really does show. This attitude rubs off on staff who start to look for ways to do things better as well. Customers are more likely to come to you with ideas to improve your business because clearly you care. Suppliers note this attitude and are more likely to want to help you grow your business. Competitors will respect you.

But the most important thing that needs constant and never-ending improvement is you. As business owners, we need to learn new skills, to look for ways to do what we do as individuals ever better, to research our industry and be a leader in it, to read and broaden our knowledge on a range of subjects that will help our businesses to grow, to be trained in ways that make us better leaders, and to always be open-minded enough to find new ways of doing things.

With this learning and improvement comes a degree of flexibility that is a key component of the overall bulletproofing strategy. Any business that isn't committed to constantly becoming better is ultimately going to perish. Any business that is too rigid, too lazy, or too bored to change will not survive. Committing to constant and never-ending improvement adds an air of passion and excitement which is the fuel that powers any business to success.

Treat marketing as a priority

Marketing is what we do to put money in our cash registers. We market our businesses to keep our existing customers coming back and at the same time to attract new customers.

Marketing isn't an exact science. It isn't that complicated, either, even if many marketing people try to tell us that it is. Having run my own marketing companies for years, I certainly feel that the simpler you keep it, the more effective it is.

The aim of this tip is not to tell you *how* to market, as there are plenty of places where you can get that information (and I will give you my top tips on marketing later in this book). It is to implore you to make marketing a year-round activity, to commit time and resources to marketing and business development every single week. One of the most common traits of truly successful businesses is that they treat marketing as an essential part of their business, not just as something to do every once in a while.

Marketing takes time to work. I feel that the marketing we do today actually benefits our business tomorrow. I encounter many business owners who don't market in the good times because they don't see the logic in it. Then when it does get tough, everyone else starts to market aggressively and it costs a lot more money and takes a lot more time for their business to stand out from the crowd.

Often business owners don't know how to market their business. I understand this completely. But there are plenty of fantastic books, websites and specialist businesses that can help (in fact, visit my blog and you will find hundreds of ideas to help market any business—www. andrewgriffithsblog.com).

Another comment I hear all the time is 'I don't have any money for marketing'. I believe that you should spend as much money as you can on marketing. If you don't have much, well, you will have to use some elbow grease or hit the pavements. The days of waiting for customers to come running through the door are over. We all have to go out and get them, remembering all the while that there are lots of other businesses chasing the same customers.

Bulletproof businesses market all the time. They try new ideas, they do big things, they do small things, but they are always actively looking for new customers.

Cash is what makes or breaks any business

We've all heard people say how important cash flow is to every business. Well, I am going to say it again. You must manage your cash flow. If your eyes glaze over and you start getting bored when you hear these words then you are heading for trouble.

There is no doubt that cash is the lifeblood of any business. If you can't manage cash flow in good times, how on earth are you going to survive in bad times? If you have excellent systems in place for collecting and managing your cash, your customers will be used to following these processes and procedures and will be more likely to continue doing so when times get tough.

Cash flow is about much more than chasing people for money down the end of the phone. Sure, that is a part of it, but it is also about building relationships with people in the accounts departments of your clients' businesses so that you know firsthand when you will be paid. It is about being careful when considering doing work for customers who don't have a track record with your business. It is about making sure you have enough money to pay all your bills when they are due. It is about being tough enough to make policies and stick to them.

Whenever I get a new client, I always charge them 50 per cent of the fee upfront. If they don't want to work this way then I politely tell them that we can't do business together. Once they have proven their ability to pay they can go onto a monthly account.

So how do you get better at managing your cash flow? If you haven't already I suggest that you first and foremost make this a priority. Then find a good accountant or even a business coach with considerable experience in this area and get them to teach you how to become a cash-flow management rock star.

A sure-fire way to lose customers is to have a rude or aggressive person doing your debt collection. Good customers soon leave when they are bullied by someone who has no idea about the history of their relationship with your business. A person who can chase up your outstanding accounts in a friendly and professional yet unrelenting way will be worth their weight in gold. Remember, though, that they are ambassadors for your business and you need to give them clear guidance on exactly how hard you want them to chase and any exceptions to the rule.

One last point I would like to make regarding this subject is that the longer a bill remains unpaid, the less likely you are to get the money. Once I learned this I made it my mission to get money in from clients as quickly as possible, paying particular attention to those accounts that were getting into the red zone, the area where I was unlikely to get my money.

At the beginning of this section I spoke about taking responsibility for your business. Nowhere is this more important than in the management of your cash flow. Businesses that have a very good handle on their cash flow are much more likely to survive and succeed than those that don't. It isn't a glamorous part of running a business, but without it there is soon no business.

Get a life

I wrote a book a few years back called *101 Ways to Have a Business and a Life*. I often joked that this was my first work of fiction and that trying to have a business and a life was the Holy Grail of most business owners.

I wrote that book because actually I needed to read it. I have been a workaholic and serial entrepreneur most of my working life. I was completely driven in every way to build my various businesses and to make them successful. That often meant working up to eighteen hours a day, seven days a week. In hindsight, I know that was crazy. Really, how productive can any person be with a schedule like that? I was always exhausted, I was 50 kilograms overweight and my marriage was not in a good place.

So I set about changing my life completely. I lost a pile of weight, I made exercise a part of my life, I started eating much better food, I refused to work on weekends and I spent more time doing the things I loved.

As a result, my head was much clearer, my body was in much better shape and, of course, my business became more profitable. I worked about half the hours I used to work and my income doubled. I admit it wasn't as easy as I perhaps make it sound, but I did it, and even though I stray from the path from time to time, I know I have the ability to get back on track and I do. I believe that the single most important part of a business that needs to be cared for is ourselves. Be the happiest and healthiest you can be and everything else becomes so much easier. The more relaxed, fit, energetic, passionate and in the present you are, the more successful your business will be.

I see many business owners who are completely burnt out and exhausted, somehow dragging themselves through another day. If business owners work crazy hours and live with way too much stress, then when the challenging times arrive they are already at a disadvantage. It is really hard to do everything you need to do to survive when you barely have the energy to get out of bed.

Having a balanced life means something different to each of us. I don't want to be sitting on a mountain picking fluff out of my belly button all day. I like stress and I do my best work with impending deadlines, but what really wears me out is being overwhelmed, waking up at 2 a.m., my mind racing with all the things I have to do in the day ahead.

You have to determine what balance between work and life is best for you, and then you have to have the courage and tenacity to make it a reality. Anyone can do it. It is just a matter of getting rid of all those bad habits that have crept in over the years and making a balanced life a priority. Like anything, it can be achieved if you want it badly enough.

9

Does your business look the part?

I don't know that the old saying 'appearances are everything' is necessarily 100 per cent correct, but I have no doubt that it is way up towards the top of the list of things that matter. In my dealings with successful entrepreneurs, they generally look the part. They have an air of confidence about them that screams success. So do their businesses.

I had this drummed into me from an early age. If you want to succeed at what you do you need to look the part: dress for the occasion, be well groomed, drive an appropriate car and so on. If you are trying to portray yourself as a successful business owner, make yourself look successful.

Think back to the last time you walked into a business that looked like it was on the skids. Not very inspiring, was it? You certainly don't get a feeling of confidence from a business like that. The same can apply to an individual. If you want your customers to have confidence in you then look the part. And this applies not only to you but to anyone representing your business.

Uniforms should always be neat, well ironed and spotless. Company vehicles should be well maintained and clean. Crumpled, worn-out uniforms and beaten-up company cars send a clear message: business is either struggling or the owners just don't care—both normally go hand in hand.

I recently pulled up at a set of traffic lights and waiting next to me was one of the most beat-up and filthy cars I had seen in a long time. Clouds of smoke were billowing out from the exhaust and the driver was choking back a cigarette. All over this car were signs promoting a business, which I gather owned the car, that was selling the virtues of filtered water as a means of living a healthier life. There is no way I would ever buy filtered water from this company. If their vehicle was like this, what must their end product be like?

We all make these assumptions based on appearances. To succeed at what you do, look the part and your customers will know that you take your business seriously. In this chapter I am going to cover what I consider the basics of looking good in your small business:

- Is your business name telling the right story?
- Do you have a logo and is it the right one?
- What is your tagline?
- Consistency and the power of branding
- Who controls your corporate image?
- There comes a time when you need to review your corporate image
- When it comes to visual images, invest in the best

Is your business name telling the right story?

Choosing the right name for your business is a tough decision. For many new businesses this is often a major stumbling block. Before we look at choosing the right name I want to spend a few moments on changing a business name.

Over time all businesses evolve. The name you started out with may no longer be applicable to what you do, but many business owners are very hesitant to change their business name if they have had it for a while because they feel they will lose their current customers. I have done a lot of corporate makeovers and have recommended businesses make quite dramatic changes, often including changing the business name. Not once has this had a negative impact, in fact, quite the opposite: customers like to see that a business is changing and evolving, showing that it is progressive and energetic. Large corporations reinvent themselves regularly and their customers almost expect it.

Don't underestimate your customers' ability to cope with change. From my experience they are better at dealing with it than most business owners are. From here you need to decide if your business name really does represent what you truly do. If it does, excellent; if it doesn't, it might be time to make a change.

So what name do you change it to? There are lots of options. You can choose a clever name, you can choose a simple descriptive name or you can choose a combination of both. Some people like to invent their own word. All are fine options but remember that if you choose a clever or a non-descriptive name, you will need to spend more money promoting and branding the business to let prospective customers know exactly what product or services you are selling.

An example of this is a florist I worked with recently. The business was well known and established but it had a similar name to other florists in the same region, which all mentioned the word florist, flowers or bridal in their names. It was really difficult to pick any one name out of the Yellow Pages because they were all basically the same. After a creative session we came up with 'Buds', a short, simple, modern name that reflected the owner's style and beliefs perfectly. They now had a name that was easy to remember, distinctive and fresh. Their business never looked back.

The decision you need to make when choosing a name is this: do you want to be more interesting or more functional? I am not really advocating either, just explaining the choices. Ideally, coming up with something in the middle, a creative name that is still easy to get the gist of, is the simplest to build a brand around and the best to let customers know what you do.

Whatever your business name is or whatever name it is going to become, getting customers to know and use the business quickly is the difference between losing money over a short time or over a long time.

Do you have a logo and is it the right one?

A logo is simply a graphic image used to promote your business. For some businesses it is a symbol of some sort, for others it is just the name in a stylised font and for others it is a combination of both. Logos are excellent tools for carrying a unique theme through your business and this is the very essence of a good corporate image.

Logos need to be distinctive and unique to your business. In one of my businesses I use a 'splat' in lime green. Ironically, getting a good splat, like a paint splotch, is quite difficult, but the end result is a very memorable message: if you use us, we will make an impact on your business. All of our promotional material, stationery, signage and websites use the logo to carry through our corporate image.

One of my major gripes with many modern, smaller businesses is their lack of a quality logo or, worse, logos designed at home by someone who really has no idea what they are doing. If you are starting a new business, allocate a budget to developing a good logo. If you are in business and you either have no logo or a pretty ordinary one, today may be the day to commission a graphic designer to come up with one that is memorable and distinctive.

Smart businesses have good logos and strong corporate images because they know how important they are. Think about the logos of companies you deal with. Look through newspapers or magazines and check out the logos of larger organisations. There is nothing stopping a business of any size from having a strong corporate image. Those that do will reap the rewards.

When deciding on which graphic designer to use, contact a few. Most have websites where you can check out their past logo designs. Try to find one whose style you like and ideally show them what type of logos you like. Negotiate a price upfront so you know how much it will cost. Remember also that you will need to incorporate the new logo on your stationery and promotional material, so you may wish to plan the introduction of a new logo when your current stocks are low.

If you are changing your existing logo, make a big deal of it. Let your customers and suppliers know, take ownership of it and be proud of your new corporate image.

What is your tagline?

A tagline is basically a few simple words that make a statement about your business. All businesses can use a tagline and the best advice I can give about choosing one is that it should answer the customer's question, 'Why should I use your business?' And keep it short and sharp.

Trends come and go, and likewise taglines go in and out of fashion like colours, but I think they have considerable merit. Taglines can be altered as your business changes or as the market in which you do business changes. Like choosing a name for your business, trying to decide on a simple tagline is not an easy task, but the two should go hand in hand.

Spend some time researching corporations and other businesses online and see what their taglines are to get a feel for the concept. Some are emotive, like Nike's 'Just do it' and Qantas's 'Spirit of Australia'. Others are more functional and tend to relate to a term like 'the biggest', 'the oldest', 'the widest range' and so on.

Whatever direction you take, it really is of benefit to have a good tagline for your business, one that gives potential customers a clear and distinct reason to use your business.

Consistency and the power of branding

Branding is a concept we hear a lot about: 'developing a brand', 'building a brand', 'brand value' and so on. Most people think branding is applicable only to large corporations but it isn't. It is equally important for small businesses.

Any business can build a brand. Put simply, this means that when a consumer sees your company name (and logo) they already have a positive perception about the business. This is one of the most appealing aspects of buying a franchise—you are purchasing an accepted brand name that consumers will hopefully already know and have a positive opinion about. Clearly it takes time to build a brand and to develop brand awareness, but we all need to do it.

The real key to branding is consistency: sending a consistent message through your advertising, corporate image, the look of your business— wherever your business interacts with consumers.

Consistency is controlled by systems, so having the right mechanisms in place to ensure all aspects of your business are consistent is the starting point. In the next tip I discuss how to control your brand and assign an individual to this task, but maintaining consistency across all aspects of the business needs to be driven from the top.

We've already examined how change is a good thing in corporate imaging but I would like to clarify this point. Having a current, relevant and impressive corporate image is essential to making a winning business, so if yours doesn't achieve these goals then it needs to be changed and your customers will adapt. But when the change is made, you need to build your corporate image and your brand with consistency in all that you do.

Who controls your corporate image?

Believe it or not, there are companies that specialise in controlling corporate image. These are generally used by large organisations, such as hotel chains, and their role is to be a central point of reference to approve promotional material and advertising for the individual operators within the chain, ensuring all material is consistent with the determined corporate image. This creates a very professional and consistent public face and makes sure consumers are being sent the right message.

On a smaller scale, keeping control of your corporate image is equally as important. Over time it can easily start to erode as different fonts are introduced, the colours of the logo start to vary and the layout of promotional material differs each time it is produced. Ideally, one person should be used to control all aspects of your corporate image. Their job is to:

- make sure the logo appears in the right format every time
- make sure the colours used are correct and consistent
- ensure the same font is used in promotional material
- check wording to ensure the tone is consistent
- sign off on all proofs for advertising and promotional material
- keep copies of all promotional material and advertisements to form a historical library
- control the use of images—for example, always sending copies to printers to avoid losing originals.

There comes a time when you need to review your corporate image

Corporate images thrive on consistency, but sometimes they need to change. Over time they become dated, they lose their impact and, to be honest, they can often start to look amateurish. There is no set period of time between corporate image changes—it is more a matter of realising when the existing image has had its day and no longer truly represents the business.

A lot of businesses struggle with making changes to their corporate image—I see this in my work every day. There is an underlying concern that if they change their corporate image they may lose customers. I am not sure if this is a general resistance to change or a genuine belief that their customers will go somewhere else simply because the business introduces a new logo or even a new name. The key is to ensure you tell your customers about your new name or logo and why you are changing.

The reality is that customers like to see businesses changing their image—it shows the business is innovative and keeping up with the times. It also shows that the business owners are proud of their business and they are prepared to reinvest in it. I have never, ever instituted a new corporate image that hasn't been a very positive step in the history of a business. A new corporate image reinvigorates everyone—the business owners, the staff and even the customers. It is in its own right a sign of business success.

Another common mistake I see is the business owner who has developed their own logo and corporate image on their home PC—and they think it is sensational. Sure, sometimes people can develop great logos at home, but more often than not the end result is a long way from professional, and the business's corporate image looks second-rate as a result.

Spend some money and get a professional logo developed, and get the right advice on the use of colours and design of promotional material. Saving a few dollars on the design of a strong corporate image is not a smart move, and in most cases it ends up being a false economy as the business struggles to attract customers from the start.

When it comes to visual images, invest in the best

I often see businesses that have invested in a great corporate image but then let it down by using poor quality photographic images or, even worse, bad clip art.

Look through any glossy magazine and you will see extremely high quality images being used by corporations. Why? Because they work. Quality images are within reach of any business owner today. There are plenty of 'royalty-free' photographic sites where high-resolution professional images can be downloaded for a very reasonable cost.

Don't let your corporate image down by scrimping on the use of great images. After all, a picture tells a thousand words, so hopefully your pictures are saying the right things about your business.

10

Use every opportunity to build rock-solid relationships

To succeed in business you are going to need strong relationships with a lot of different people and organisations. These relationships will help your business grow, they may guide you through difficult times and they will certainly bring a lot of enjoyment to your business life. Like any relationship, they need to be built over time and with mutual trust.

This chapter deals with building relationships to help you succeed in your entrepreneurial life. The topics we will cover include:

- Who do you want to have a strong relationship with?
- Building relationships takes time and energy
- Loose lips sink ships—and sometimes businesses
- Never let a long-term relationship be destroyed over a petty issue
- When it comes to referring, be a giver, not just a taker
- Partnership pitfalls—how to avoid them
- Build a relationship with your suppliers
- Build a relationship with your landlord

- Build a relationship with your professional advisers
- Build a relationship with people in your industry

Who do you want to have a strong relationship with?

A distinct observation I have made of successful businesses is that the owners are generally very good at building relationships with everyone they deal with. This includes their staff, customers, suppliers, landlords and bank, and professional advisers, such as lawyers and accountants. These people clearly understand that to create a successful business takes more than one individual—it takes a team or a network with many components, each equally important.

Often entrepreneurs can overlook some relationships or not really give them the attention they need. One example that comes to my mind in this respect is banking. Like most people, I assumed that the days of having a relationship with your bank manager were long gone. I had been with one of the big banks for many years and never really considered changing because I thought all banks were the same. This caused me many problems: I struggled to get an overdraft, I didn't have a personal contact who could advise me on various financial matters and I really looked at banking as an irritation rather than a relationship-building opportunity.

That all changed when I was approached by a small boutique bank in Cairns. This bank had been operating for over a hundred years but I didn't really know much about it. My firm was commissioned to develop a strategic marketing plan and a new logo and corporate image for the bank, which we did. During this process I learned a lot about this impressive business and before long I had moved my accounts to them. All of a sudden I had a bank manager who not only knew my name, he also took an active role in my business and continues to do so. He is one of my unofficial mentors—an honest and open man who has helped my business to grow—and I will be grateful to him forever.

The point I am trying to make here is that we shouldn't necessarily believe everything we hear—in this case, everything we hear about banks. They are certainly not all the same and the opportunity does exist to forge a relationship if you can find the right person. The same applies to virtually everyone you deal with, but you have to be open-minded to let a relationship form—it takes trust and effort. Every time a customer comes into your business they are putting their trust and faith in you, that you will meet their expectations. If you do, they will keep coming back. If you work with your suppliers to develop a mutually beneficial relationship, they will reciprocate.

As important as it is to try to build relationships, there are bound to be some people you just can't deal with or whose expectations you can't meet. In this case there will be no relationship and that is okay. Let it go and move on; hopefully these situations will be few.

Make the effort and put some energy and thought into the cogs that make your business go round. You'll soon see the benefits both to you and to them of your relationship being stronger.

Building relationships takes time and energy

Most people know that building better relationships requires a commitment of time and energy. But when you are stressed out, working really long hours, under financial pressure and struggling to stay on top of things, the idea of taking time out to build relationships just keeps slipping down your list of priorities.

One example of this is delegation. Clearly, if you can delegate some of your responsibilities life will become a little easier, but it takes time to delegate and to teach other people the skills or the systems required to take on particular tasks. In the midst of a typically crazy day you probably think, 'It will be easier to do it myself.' So that is what you do, taking on more and more responsibility every day until you reach breaking point.

I know firsthand how easy it is to prioritise tasks over people. I tend to start work earlier than everyone else in my business. It gives me a little quiet time before the phone starts to ring and the demands of the day kick in. From about 8 a.m. my team arrive. They like to drop into my office to say hello and have a chat about the day ahead. This used to drive me crazy—I had already been working for at least an hour and was trying to beat the clock to get things done. I came to dread the sound of the front door of the office opening because I knew that it meant I would spend the next hour being distracted.

I looked at this hour as a waste of my time, but I also knew that the people I worked with needed the interaction, some social chitchat and a chance to ask questions and plan for their day. In spite of this, I was getting more and more frustrated, until one day my frustration reached overload. At this point I knew that I had to change my attitude and I decided to look at this one hour as an opportunity, not an irritation. Every day, from 8 a.m. till 9 a.m., I wouldn't plan anything other than meeting and greeting my team, planning the projects for the day ahead and generally getting to know everyone a little better. I decided to enjoy this time instead of resenting it, and what a change this has made. Now that I look forward to everyone arriving, communication works at a much higher level, projects run more smoothly, issues are sorted out faster, and we all feel much closer.

Again, the shift required is a mental one. Look at the time spent building relationships as an investment, not a chore. The stronger your relationship with your customers, the more loyal they will be. The stronger your relationship with your staff, the more likely they will be to do the extra things that will make your life easier.

Regardless of the desired outcome, a relationship of any sort is like a flower: it takes time and the right environment to grow. Look at the time and energy spent building relationships as an investment in you.

Loose lips sink ships—and sometimes businesses

Building relationships is important, but there also need to be very clear boundaries established. In most business relationships, limits are required around what information you pass on or talk about—there is always the possibility the person you are talking to is going to walk out of your business and into your competitors' and tell them everything. I don't want to sound paranoid, but I have personally experienced this.

At a meeting with a supplier about a project I was tendering for, I discussed prices and the outline of my tender. I later found out that a last-minute submission by a competitor got the job because they were cheaper. After a little research I discovered that a relative of my supplier worked at the competitor's business. I learned a valuable lesson from this and moved on, but since then I have been much more cautious about what I tell people and the confidential information I share.

The other side of the coin is that a lot of people confide in me about their business. What would happen to my good name if I didn't honour their trust and started giving away their trade secrets? This is a quick way to develop a reputation for being unethical.

So, in short, build relationships but keep your cards a little close to your chest. No matter how secure the relationship appears to be, there are some things that should not be shared—it's your integrity on the line.

Never let a long-term relationship be destroyed over a petty issue

All too often a strong relationship can be ruined over a very small issue. Things can go wrong in business, we all know that, but don't let a perfectly good relationship suffer or end because of something that in the scheme of things is quite petty.

If you have a fabulous supplier and they mess up on one shipment, they deserve another chance. After all, everyone makes mistakes and while they are embarrassing they are generally not the end of the world.

I deal with a lot of printers and this seems to be a trade where things can go wrong. I have been working with one firm for over ten years, and nine out of ten jobs run perfectly. Every once in a while I have to sit them down and read them the riot act, but they handle that very well. Any problems are sorted out quickly and efficiently and we get back to business. If the problem is their fault, they will always cover any costs or print extra quantities to give to my clients as a way of apologising for what has gone wrong.

On a similar note, we buy a lot of stationery and I have been dealing with the same small stationery company for many years. I could probably get my supplies cheaper elsewhere, but in this case the exceptional service they offer is more valuable. I have competing stationery suppliers calling my office every other day trying to get my business but it would take a lot more than cheaper prices to move me away from my existing supplier.

I believe this is an important point to pass on to your staff; often people get a little crazed when they are promoted or are new to a position and try to flex their muscles. This can result in good relationships built over many years being destroyed without the business owner even being aware that it is happening, so make sure employees are clear on the value of these relationships.

Life is too short to get stressed and bent out of shape every time something goes wrong. Work with the people you have good relationships with and your business will enjoy the benefits.

When it comes to referring, be a giver, not just a taker

Most successful businesses get that way through word-of-mouth referrals. I think that if people are willing to go to the trouble of referring us we should try to do the same. This is particularly relevant for business-to-business relationships, of course.

I know that when I refer a lot of people to a business, I sincerely appreciate it when they send me some business in return. And it certainly strengthens the relationship and motivates me to keep sending them customers.

On the flipside, if I refer a lot of customers to a business and I know that they could refer business to me but they don't, my motivation and desire to refer them lessens over time.

The moral of this story is to be a proactive cross-referrer, not just a taker. It will pay off in the long run.

Partnership pitfalls—how to avoid them

Having a partner in business can be both a blessing and a disaster. The sad reality is that partnerships have a high rate of failure due to problems between the partners themselves, not with the business. I have had several partnerships, but only one that has really worked. In that case, the other partners were silent and very supportive.

The biggest problem with partnerships is that the partners spend a lot of time planning the honeymoon and no time planning the divorce. What I mean by this is that everything is peaches and cream in the early and exciting stages of the business. Then one day, you may find that your business partner is driving you crazy and you no longer want to be involved with them. The honeymoon is now well and truly over.

If you have a written plan and agreement on what to do in this situation, you just pull it out and implement it; it's like the business version of a pre-nuptial agreement. But if you don't have an agreement, things can suddenly turn ugly.

If you have a partner, there is always a chance that the relationship simply won't work—regardless of how close you are as friends or relatives today. If it reaches the stage when you need to part company (and you will know that time when it arrives), you need to have what is commonly referred to as an exit strategy. This is simply a plan that outlines how you or your partner can get out of the business with minimal damage and loss.

I strongly recommend that you budget some money when setting up your business to have a lawyer draw up a partnership dissolution agreement, which is the legal form for an exit strategy. It is in both your and your partner's interests to have such an agreement, and all parties must be fully aware of what it means and the implications of signing it. Basically, an exit strategy document normally allows the remaining partner the first option to buy out the departing partner at a price determined in a pre-agreed manner.

I have painted a pretty grim picture of partnerships, and you may now be looking across your desk at your partner with some trepidation. However, like any relationship, a successful business partnership can also be emotionally and financially rewarding. It's all about communication and working together. If you are lucky enough to have a strong partnership, congratulations; if you are involved in an awkward partnership, try to work things out.

My pool of advisers all made the same comment: partners are often a necessary evil. You may need their money, their expertise, or a combination of the two. Ensure that everything is in writing and plan for the day that you hope never comes.

Build a relationship with your suppliers

Suppliers are an important part of any business. Having a good relationship with your suppliers will help you to get through the hard times. Most of these relationships start off somewhat tenuously, with both parties kind of checking each other out. How you treat your suppliers will have a big impact on how they treat you.

People often complain about how slack or unreliable their suppliers are, always letting them down. Sometimes I find this quite amusing, having seen the companies of those doing the complaining treat their own customers the same way. Like any relationship, the ones we create with our suppliers need to be built on solid foundations. If you are always phoning up to complain about this or that, your suppliers will soon become sick and tired of hearing from you. Be professional and courteous, and try to develop a rapport with individuals within the company.

It's much easier if you can give Steve the sales manager a call and ask him to courier you an urgently needed part as a personal favour rather than go through a sea of anonymous faces who will probably say 'no' as a reflex action.

Likewise, if you are having a lean month and cash is short, your suppliers need to be onside. If you are a bad payer as a rule they may not want to deal with you anymore. But if it's just a temporary situation and you have a good relationship with your suppliers, business will likely proceed as usual. You need your suppliers, and they need you. Why not work together and make everyone's life a little easier?

I had a client who always required their printing to be done urgently, a message I had to pass on to the printers. However, when *every* order seemed to be urgent, the printers stopped treating them as such. Then when I really did need another job done urgently, it was a struggle to get the printers to take me seriously. I had to sit down and explain to the client that they needed either to review their ordering timing, or to order larger quantities to help alleviate the problem they were inadvertently causing.

Now I ask my clients for realistic deadlines for their printing requirements. I mark the job accordingly, and I have a contract with my printer that states that they will do everything in their power to complete the jobs according to my deadline. Where possible I allow as much time as I can, and the really urgent jobs now get done very quickly. Everyone wins.

A lot of people regularly use the word 'urgent' on orders, telephone messages and emails. Only do this if it really is urgent, otherwise people will stop taking you seriously, and the last people you want in this category are your suppliers.

Build a relationship with your landlord

Love them or hate them, landlords play a big part in any business. So if you are planning on buying a business or renting a space, do a little homework first on the landlord.

I once had an office with communal toilets shared by six other businesses. As public toilets, it was up to the landlord to clean and maintain them. We received a letter one day saying that as a group we were using too much toilet paper and from now on we would have to supply our own. This, of course, was a ridiculous suggestion, so I asked the landlord if we were supposed to hand our clients a roll of toilet paper on their way to the loo. Shortly after, I moved out.

If you have a good relationship with your landlord, your business life will be made much easier. Our business was located in a high-rise building owned by a prominent Japanese company. I had heard all sorts of rumours about how difficult the company could be, so it was with a degree of trepidation that I started negotiations for renting an office. From day one, the company and their representatives were fantastic— 100 per cent supportive, friendly, pleasant to deal with and understanding. They even sent me flowers during a recent stay in hospital, and now our company works on a lot of their property marketing projects. It's a two-way street. We pay our rent on time (well, most of the time) and we spent a lot of money fitting out our offices. We attract customers to the building and have added an air of professionalism to a part of the building that was starting to look empty and run-down.

In another case I was evicted at short notice because I didn't have a legal lease, only a simple letter of intent, and the landlord wanted the space for themselves. This very traumatic and expensive experience highlighted the importance of having a lawyer read over any lease documents.

It's essential that you know and understand your rights as a tenant. My last lease document was over 150 pages in length, with so many clauses and techno-legal talk that most people would have no chance of understanding it. While there was no intention to mislead in the lease, my lawyer identified a number of points that could have been of concern down the line. By spending $500 to have the lease reviewed, I was reassured and my landlords made several amendments that kept us both happy.

Many organisations out there can offer excellent advice on your legal rights as a tenant, and if you need help a quick surf on the internet will find details for some of these. Prevention is always better than a cure, so ensure that all of your homework and legal advice is completed before you even think about signing a lease document.

Your landlord has a vested interest in your business succeeding— it means that they get a rent cheque each month. If you go broke, no one wins, so it pays to do your best to work together as a team. It also pays to shop around when it comes to leasing a premises. Everything is negotiable to a degree, and even if your landlord won't negotiate on the rental price, perhaps there are other areas where they could be more accommodating.

Build a relationship with your professional advisers

I encourage everyone reading this book to use professional advisers, including accountants, financial advisers and solicitors. In fact, I believe strongly that you should call in professional advice whenever you need help outside your field of experience. Most importantly, do it as soon as possible; don't wait for the problem to get worse before calling in the cavalry.

Building a relationship with your professional advisers is important. Don't just look at them as people who are billing you by the hour. Where possible, get to know them and how they think. We can learn much from Asian cultures, where a lot of time is spent getting to know people. A friend of mine is currently working in Korea, setting up a tourism venture. He has travelled widely and conducted many sales trips to Korea in the past but had very little success. Having now spent some time there, he has come to the realisation that it's all about building relationships— Koreans like to get to know you before doing business with you. In the past, my friend would try to visit as many companies as possible; now he realises that his time would have been better spent visiting just one company on each trip, investing as much time as possible getting to know the key people and letting them get to know him.

As someone who charges by the hour and falls into the category of a professional adviser, I have to say that I am fussy about who I do business with. If I don't click with a particular person or business, I will do my utmost to avoid working for them. All of my clients are friends, and while I don't socialise with them much, I would go out of my way to help them in any way I could and I know they would do the same for me.

Treat your professional advisers as people, not the hired help, and your business will be enriched. Odds on they also won't bill you for all the work they actually do and, if they like you, the ink will normally be a little lighter on the invoice. Develop a long-term relationship with your advisers and make sure that they know where you are going and the role that you want them to play in getting you there.

Build a relationship with people in your industry

There are two distinct groups within most industries: those who are willing to share information, and those who want to guard everything, treating all knowledge as top-secret. From my experience, those who are willing to share information often end up being far more successful because they get back as much information as they give out.

I am a firm believer in exchanging information. It can be very beneficial to talk to other industry associates who are open-minded to see if they share your thoughts on current industry trends, new methods, new products, and so on. This is, after all, what makes any industry grow and expand.

I work very hard to establish a strong rapport with my industry peers. This is made somewhat easier by the fact that I live in a small regional city, because I tend to know the other players through the course of my everyday business dealings. In larger cities it can be more difficult, but often industry groups here are quite organised with larger member bases, allowing for more functions, meetings and conventions.

Working with your industry peers enables you to share both successes and failures. If sharing an experience helps to prevent an industry associate from making the same mistake, you are doing more than a good deed—you are establishing your own credibility as a professional.

It's also a great feeling to be able to sit down with your peers, regardless of whether you are a florist or a flautist, and be able to openly discuss problems that you may be experiencing. It's reassuring to know that you are not the only one having these problems (and the chances are that you're not).

Successful business boosters aren't afraid to be open and frank with their industry peers. They may keep specific details close to their chest (and that makes sense), but they are secure enough in their own abilities to be willing participants in a fair exchange of information.

11

Smart marketing is simple marketing

Marketing is a complicated topic these days and there appear to be plenty of people lining up to make it even more complicated. I tend to look at it in simple terms: marketing to me is anything that puts money in your bank account.

Marketing covers a host of topics including customer service, advertising, selling, the internet, networking, being a great corporate citizen and much more. I have provided my best pieces of advice for each of these topics in later chapters, but here I want to talk more about the philosophy behind marketing. If you get this right, everything else will fall into place.

There are an overwhelming number of books, websites, magazines, seminars and even television programs that will give specific marketing advice, and I am certain that anyone could come up with a hundred ideas suited to their specific business within a fairly short period of time. But generally none of these ideas will work if the philosophy behind them is not sound, so here goes, let's talk about simple marketing ideas for your small business.

- The marketing you do today is an investment for tomorrow
- Stand out from the crowd

- If your budget is small, put in some elbow grease
- Commit quality time to marketing
- Ask people to send you business and they will
- Giveaways will promote your business
- The power of the testimonial
- Let others help with marketing ideas
- Look to big business for big ideas
- Treat the internet as a marketing priority
- What are the things you have stopped doing in your business, and how much is this costing you?
- Can you generate more income with only a little extra effort?

The marketing you do today is an investment for tomorrow

Many business owners stop marketing when their business gets busy simply because they don't have enough time to devote to it. Then, when their workload eases, they start marketing again. Another common mistake is that businesses stop marketing when things get quiet, a tendency related to cash flow more than anything else. But stop/start marketing very rarely produces results, in my experience.

The best approach to marketing is to be consistent and always have something on the go, even if you are already very busy. For some people this is a hard concept to put into practice. I use the momentum principle when it comes to marketing: getting it going takes a lot of effort and it takes a while for the results to pay off, but to keep it going doesn't take as much energy. Stop/start marketing ultimately requires that you put more time, energy and money in to get the results you need.

When planning your marketing, you are not planning for today but for tomorrow. Personally, I like to know that I always have about ten proposals being considered by clients at any one time as this means that my business's workload for the coming month will be on track with my forecasts. If I have more proposals pending I know that I am in for a very busy month and can subcontract some extra help to accommodate it. If less than ten proposals are in the works I know that I have to get out and look for some more projects.

Sure, if times are tight financially you might have to cut back on a few marketing activities, but take advantage of having extra time on your hands, roll up your sleeves and do more of the marketing that takes time and energy, not money.

Taking a longer term and more consistent approach to marketing your business will smooth out a lot of the peaks and troughs that cause all kinds of problems with cash flow and staffing. Your business workload will become more manageable and you will feel much more in control.

Do you tend to do stop/start marketing? If so, start to think in a more long-term way about your marketing, because the work you do today will get you customers tomorrow. A change in philosophy towards your marketing is the first step in ending the stop/start marketing cycle. Consistent marketing brings consistent results.

Stand out from the crowd

Before you can even think about marketing you need to be committed to making your business stand out from the crowd. But what does this really mean?

It means that every part of your business has to be better than your competitors'. The way the business looks, the service you offer, the products or services you sell, your staff, your corporate image—the lot.

The threat of ever-increasing competition impacts on all businesses around the world; it is here to stay and it will keep increasing. For a business to truly succeed it needs to be better than its competitors in every way, and this requires commitment and dedication from everyone involved. Every tip in this book will help your business stand out from the crowd in a host of areas, but unless the commitment to do what needs to be done is there, nothing will really get it off the ground.

A lot of businesses set out with the goal of being average and they achieve it perfectly. But the real gems, or the winning ones, know they want to be better than everyone else. By aiming to stand out from the crowd, they do, and they enjoy the rewards as a result.

If your budget is small, put in some elbow grease

Many business owners have the perception that building a successful business requires a lot of money. From my own experience, having helped literally thousands of businesses to grow, it's rarely about how much you spend but more about how much energy you put into growing your business.

There are countless examples of businesses that have had big cash injections to get started and then failed miserably. Likewise there are countless examples of businesses that started on a shoestring and ended up as huge corporations. Money can help, but it is by no means the be-all and end-all when it comes to building a successful business, and this is particularly relevant when you talk marketing.

The simple reality is that if you haven't got a big budget to spend on marketing your business, be prepared to roll up your sleeves and do some hard work yourself. High-profile advertising—full-page ads in newspapers, prominent television and radio slots—will certainly get the phone ringing or customers coming in the door, but it costs a lot of money. If you are planning to spend every penny you have on a 'do or die' campaign, I would strongly suggest you rethink your strategy: more often than not, the return is nowhere near what you expect.

So what sort of hard work do you need to do? Well, first you need to accept that there is no single silver bullet that will solve all of your marketing needs and expectations. Rather, be prepared to take on lots of smaller strategies.

Commit quality time to marketing

One of the biggest reasons for businesses failing to market themselves is that they don't allocate enough quality time to the process.

Successful businesses are normally good marketers. They know it is important and they make sure they devote the time necessary to market their business regularly. This time commitment is the key to their success, not the amount of money that they spend.

Marketing needs to become as important as opening the doors of your business in the morning. It requires the same attention as paying your bills or collecting money from your customers because it determines the long-term success of your business. But because it is less tangible and generally less demanding (if you don't do your marketing, no one rings and chases you) it is easy to put it off for another day.

Another factor is that the average business owner doesn't really know how to market. They are good at what they do but not at marketing, which is logical, but it is something you can learn. Start by using your network of business associates and mentors—if you ask, people will normally be happy to share what works for them. There are also plenty of good courses offering simple marketing skills for all levels of business experience, or you can pay for a marketing consultant to teach you. Regardless of how you improve your skills, the point is that you need to commit time to marketing.

So yes, we need to allocate a set amount of time to marketing each week, but it has to be good time, quality time, not just filler time. It is impossible to market creatively when you are exhausted and brain dead—it just won't work.

I had a client a while back who ran quite a large massage therapy business. While he was busy and successful, he was also frustrated because the business had grown to a certain level and then plateaued for the last three years. A big part of the problem was that he had become so busy during the day that he was trying to do his business development late at night, after a full-on day of running a very busy operation. It simply wasn't working.

I suggested a basic but fundamental change where he would take himself out of the daily schedule until 10 a.m. and use the first hour or two each morning to do nothing but work on growing the business. The results were amazing and instant. He finished important business development projects, he made plans, he thought through and actioned his marketing and literally gave the business a major boost. After several weeks of working to this revised schedule, my client was adamant that he would always spend his most creative and energetic time working on his business, as it was the best investment of time and energy that he could make in his financial future.

Ask people to send you business and they will

Often one of the greatest sources of new business comes from referrals. Winning businesses tend to get more than their fair share of referrals from happy customers, and this is a pretty good indication that they are doing what they do well.

Surprisingly though, many of us often forget to ask our customers to refer business to us. Sometimes they need to be reminded. If you have happy customers (and I certainly hope you do), take a few minutes to ask them to tell their family, friends and workmates about you. Often people simply overlook referring business because it doesn't occur to them. But if you ask them to do it they will go out of their way.

The end result can be a wonderful network of people, all spreading the word about how fabulous your business is. Imagine how much your business could grow if every customer you have today recommends you to just one other person. Potentially your business could double overnight.

How do you ask your customers to refer your business? There are a couple of options and it really depends on the type of business you run. A consulting firm might simply make it a closing statement at the end of the project: 'Thank you for your business and please tell your associates about the work we do.' It may be more formal, by mail, or a sign on the wall that says, 'If you are happy with what we do, please tell your friends.' Unfortunately, most of us are a little hesitant to ask for business and it really is something we need to overcome.

I recently advised a clothing retailer to ask for referrals from their existing customers by explaining that they are looking to grow the business and attract more customers. This would mean their buying power would be greater so existing customers could get even better value for money as prices might drop. This strategy worked well because not only did the existing customers take on the sales responsibility, they also had an incentive to promote the business—everyone wins. Winning businesses are built on word of mouth and that costs nothing. But you only get it if you deserve it.

Always be prepared for an opportunity

The potential for a new customer is always just around the corner and the astute business owner and entrepreneur knows this fact well. They are always ready for action. To truly take advantage of any opportunity, you need to be prepared: keep a supply of business cards and your promotional material handy and be ready to talk to someone about what you do.

Many business owners can be shy when it comes to talking about their business, almost embarrassed to say what they do. While the humility is nice, it really isn't a good strategy for building up a business.

Look for any opportunity to promote your business—and you will find plenty of them. Any chance encounter is an opportunity. A surprising number of excellent contacts and customers have come from people I have sat next to on planes, or been forced to wait with in a queue, or just bumped into for some reason. If you are genuinely interested in other people, you will find they will reciprocate and be interested in you.

I am not advocating stalking, just that you be prepared to tell people about your business and give them more information. And never judge a book by its cover; I have come across a lot of people who may at first glance look more like they need a job rather than being in a position to give me work, but always keep an open mind. A potential new customer could be standing right in front of you.

The starting point here is being able to explain what it is you do for a living, something a lot of people actually struggle with. Instead of responding with a mumble and downcast eyes, I recommend that when asked what you do, you stop, look the person in the eye and tell them loudly and proudly.

Giveaways will promote your business

This is the 'put your money where your mouth is' principle: if what you sell is as good as you say it is, be prepared to give potential customers a free trial or taste.

I recently worked on a marketing campaign with a health studio wanting to promote personal training, a good source of revenue for the business. We could have advertised special introductory offers to get new people in the doors, but at the end of the day we agreed that the best way to sell the service was to actually give potential customers a free personal training session. This was a big expense for the business but they felt their service and the overall personal training they offered was the best around, so they put their money where their mouth was.

It paid off incredibly well. By promoting personal training sessions to their existing members as well as to the general public, they literally doubled their personal training clients in a very short period of time.

This 'no risk, no commitment' trial is a good option for customers who can try a product or business without obligation, and it is up to the business to sell themselves. If they don't measure up, the customer can walk away.

I often recommend clients try this technique when looking for ways to build up their business, and I have seen it work very successfully in businesses as diverse as restaurants, dance academies, training organisations, bakeries, filtered water suppliers, cleaning product manufacturers and professional service-based businesses.

For my own business, I offer a one-hour free consultation which provides potential clients with the opportunity to assess the advice offered by my firm. If they like what they hear, they come back; if they don't, we never see them again. Nine out of ten people come back, and I put much of this high success rate down to the fact that the client has the opportunity to make up their own mind in a non-pressured way, with a clear understanding of what my business can offer them.

If you think your business is as good as it can be, try embracing the concept of a free trial. Analyse what it will cost you to make this offer and monitor the results. You may be pleasantly surprised.

The power of the testimonial

Testimonials are basically endorsements of your business from satisfied customers. Large companies use them all the time, most noticeably when high-profile celebrities endorse their products and services. Used to build credibility, testimonials need to be a part of any marketing material you produce, and there is no reason why small businesses can't use them just as effectively.

Testimonials help potential customers to make up their mind about using a new business because they are going by the recommendation of a third person. All businesses will tell you how great they are, but to have an independent customer sharing their experience is far more convincing.

Collecting testimonials is easy (assuming you have plenty of happy customers). Every business will have a number of loyal customers, and they are normally more than happy to offer a comment about your business. Asking for a written testimonial is fine; if they haven't got the time to write something down, get a verbal testimonial and transcribe it. But it's wise to make absolutely certain that the customer is happy for you to use their testimonial in marketing material. I like to actually ask them to sign a release simply stating that the testimonial can be used.

The types of comments you are after are ones that state how satisfied the customer is with your business, products or services. Testimonials are recommendations, so they are even more powerful if the customer mentions how long they have been using the business, why they use it and the fact that they intend to keep using it. This all helps to reinforce the message that your business, product or service is good.

Collecting testimonials can be time-consuming and, unfortunately, most of us wait until we need them before doing so. This makes the whole process a bit of a rush or, instead, it gets forgotten or is put in the too hard basket. I recommend you collect testimonials on a regular basis and keep them in a folder. That way, as soon as you need them they are at your fingertips, ready to be used.

Testimonials can be printed on brochures, listed on your website, hung on the wall of your business or used in your advertising. They are versatile, and very worthwhile.

Let others help with marketing ideas

Many people struggle with coming up with ideas for marketing and I really understand that. But don't worry: there may be more ideas out there than you realise, you simply have to be prepared to put up your hand and ask for help.

If you want an influx of ideas about what you need to do to increase your business, have a brainstorming session. A friend of mine rang me recently inviting me to lunch. She mentioned that there were a few people coming along and she was hoping to generate a few ideas regarding a Lifestyle Expo she was in the midst of planning. It was a free lunch—how could I say no?

There were ten people at the quiet and tasteful restaurant when I arrived: salespeople, managers, consultants and a few others. My friend started by explaining why she had invited everyone there, detailing some of the problems she was experiencing and asking for ideas that would help her expo be a success.

The lunch lasted for two hours and my friend left with a list of 44 excellent ideas. For a few hundred dollars and two hours of her time, she had a business plan full of fresh ideas donated by knowledgeable, intelligent businesspeople.

A slight variation to this theme is to get ten or so people together every month and take it in turns, brainstorming one business per gathering. Every brainstorming session will provide great ideas that can generally be applied to any business, so even if it isn't your turn you may well pick up a few tips that will help.

Look to big business for big ideas

Large corporations spend a lot of money on marketing. They understand just how important it is to add value to their brand, to keep them 'top of mind' with their customers, to show that they are good corporate citizens and to actually sell their products or services. Because of this they spend a lot of money on research and getting very high-level technical and creative marketing advice.

I know that most small businesses don't have big budgets to spend on marketing, but the good news is that you don't need to. By taking the time to look closely at what larger corporations are doing, you can get plenty of exceptional marketing ideas that are fundamentally sound, with all research paid for and the concepts ready to be adapted to your business. These marketing ideas have been tested and researched at a level that small businesses could never afford. I am not saying that the larger corporations get it right all the time, but when it comes to marketing they tend to get it right more often than wrong.

As an example, let's look at being a great corporate citizen, which simply means that your business plays an active role within the community where it operates and aims to make a social or environmental difference. Large corporations are spending a lot of money in this space and they are very active at promoting the good they are doing. Why? Because research shows that their customers (and shareholders) want to know that the companies they are buying from are good corporate citizens. So any small business needs to adopt the same principle. First of all you need to actually be a great corporate citizen, and then make sure you tell your customers that you are (there is more information on this in Chapter 18).

How about advertising? Look at fast-food franchises like McDonald's and KFC, now actively promoting healthy items like salads, skinless chicken, low-fat desserts and wholesome foods. Why? Because considerable research has shown that customers want healthier food choices. In my mind, this means that every food business needs to be heading down the same path. Source better quality and organic foods and make sure you promote this fact to your customers.

Take the time to research larger corporations: watch their television commercials, read their brochures, visit their websites and look at their print advertisements. Notice the consistency in their advertising. See how they use high-quality photographic images, generally only one per advertisement. Notice how they keep text in advertisements to a minimum, selling emotions rather than facts and figures.

The corporate world is a wonderful source of inspiration and information, ready and waiting for any business to utilise.

Treat the internet as a marketing priority

As a marketing tool, the internet is unequalled in many ways. It is cost-effective, convenient for customers to use, offers plenty of choice, and used by more potential customers every day. The role the internet plays in our everyday lives just keeps advancing. Ten years ago the thought of being able to pay all of your bills from your computer would have been a dream; now it is as normal as watching television. There is nothing that cannot be purchased over the net and businesses are becoming more and more creative about how to use it to grow their business.

But despite all this, I still encounter people who think the internet is a waste of time. No matter how much I try to convince them otherwise, they have formed their opinion and it is unlikely to change. Generally, these people don't use the internet a lot themselves or they have a bad website that doesn't really work and have based their opinion on the lack of visitors to their site. Building a website is only the start; directing traffic to it is the next and obviously the most important aspect of your online strategy. A web development company can advise you on how to increase traffic and while this topic is a whole book in its own right, I do explore it more in Chapter 15. The fact is that it can be done and it isn't necessarily complicated or expensive.

From a marketing point of view, the internet provides a very accessible way for customers to find out more about your business. At a time that suits them and without the added pressure of facing a salesperson, they can form an opinion of your business in the privacy of their own home. Customers will also use the internet to research purchases before taking the plunge, so if your business is not online and your competitors are, they have a distinct advantage.

Having a good website is the bare minimum for any business. It should be professionally designed, visually impressive and easy to use. Design your website from a customer's perspective: what information would they like to see and how would they need to navigate the site? If you need to include lots of information, arrange it in a way that doesn't make the site overly complicated or filled with page after page of detail.

Have easy-to-download information in PDF format, so the layout of the page doesn't change when it is downloaded. Include pictures of you and your business, but optimise them so that the site loads quickly—remember, we are all short of time and there is nothing more frustrating than waiting for what seems like an eternity for a website to load.

Successful businesses accept and embrace the internet as part of their overall marketing strategy.

What are the things you have stopped doing in your business, and how much is this costing you?

I met with a new client recently who was experiencing a pretty major financial downturn in her business. In fact, her revenue had dropped by almost 50 per cent in the past two years. This decline had been gradual, but the end result was that her business was now in big trouble.

We sat and chatted about the things she had been doing over the past couple of years to try to get a grip on what was going wrong. Sure, some of the blame could be placed on the economic conditions, but nowhere near a drop of 50 per cent.

The owner had built her business up to a very successful level over about five years before starting to expand two years ago, setting up some satellite offices and even a franchise or two. As you may have guessed, the expansion occurred at the same time that her main office started to go downhill. In retrospect it was easy to see that her focus was on the other new and exciting business opportunities, not on her core business, and that is what caused the problem.

Once we had figured out the lay of the land and where she was right now, it became clear that we had to put some serious effort and energy into the main business, and we had to do it fast. So I started to rattle off a list of things that I would do to get the cash register smoking, such as increasing communication with existing clients, developing more targeted and inspirational promotional material, following up sales religiously, instigating a refer-a-friend campaign, getting out into the community to talk about what is happening in the business, doing some media releases, and so on.

As I worked through this list, my client was shaking her head somewhat forlornly, so I asked her what was wrong. She said she used to do *all* of the things I was suggesting when she was building up her business, but she stopped a while ago—actually, about two years back—because she was too busy focusing on her expansion.

Sadly, this is a common story. Businesses often struggle financially not because of what they *are* doing but because of what they are *not* doing.

When we stop doing certain things, the effect is not always immediately clear. The impact is often gradual and it can sneak up on you, just as it did with my client. It can be hard to keep putting energy into your business day in and day out, but it is much easier to do a little every day than a huge amount to save a business that gets into grief.

So think about this: what have you stopped doing in your business and what effect is it having?

Can you generate more income with only a little extra effort?

My accountant recently introduced me to an idea that I believe has merit for many other types of businesses. He explained that, due to a general tightening up by the taxation department, a proportion of his clients were audited every year. It wasn't anything out of the ordinary, it was just the way things were going. It was fair to assume that if you were in business you would be audited at some time in the future.

When a client is audited there are many expenses, the main one being paying an accountant to spend a lot of time sorting out records and answering questions raised by the taxation department. So on top of any fine they may receive, the client is also hit with a bill for several thousand dollars from their accountant. All in all, it's not a very pleasant experience.

The idea my accountant mentioned was 'audit insurance', where a client pays a premium of a couple of hundred dollars per year so that all of their accounting bills will be covered if they are audited. With the increased possibility of being audited these days, this appears to me to be excellent value.

My accountant funds this insurance himself and deposits all of the premiums into a pool. If he has a lot of clients audited he may lose out, but if he only has a handful he tends to make a few dollars. In reality, everyone wins. As a client, I have the peace of mind of knowing that when I am audited I don't have to worry about being hit with a large accounting bill at the end of the process. It's a great service and if my accountant makes a bit of a profit from it, well, good on him for having the initiative to put the plan in place.

Perhaps there are ideas like this that your business could initiate, which not only generate extra income for your business but also offer a degree of peace of mind for your customers. Friends in the car hire industry often say that they make more money out of the insurance than they do from hiring the car. The key is to take some of the risk away from your customers and take that responsibility on yourself—for a fee.

I went on a whale-watching trip out of Boston in the USA several years ago. The company made a bold statement: if you don't see any whales you get half of your money refunded. This seemed a fair deal and as none of their competitors made the same offer, I went with them. We saw about 30 whales and I was later told they see whales every trip without fail, so it was a fairly safe offer on their behalf.

In Borneo I heard of a similar insurance idea where, on a hundred-dollar fishing trip, you could pay an extra ten dollars to guarantee your money back if you didn't catch any fish. I got to know the owner over the course of the day and asked him how many people had claimed on the insurance. He said only five people in ten years had claimed the refund ('they couldn't catch fish in a barrel with a bazooka'), yet around 90 per cent of his passengers paid the extra ten dollars. This smart entrepreneur had increased his revenue by almost 10 per cent for a very minimal outlay, and that doesn't even take into consideration those people who went fishing with him simply because of his novel insurance offer.

Still on a nautical theme, I once went diving in Vanuatu and took out clear-water cover: if the water visibility dropped below twenty metres you dived for free. This premium cost about twenty dollars extra per day, but how could a mad keen diver such as myself refuse this offer? Once again, the owner said that occasionally bad weather made them give away some free dives, but overall they were hands-down winners as visibility was normally well in excess of 50 metres. They had increased their revenue by almost 25 per cent simply by introducing this insurance policy.

The only real danger in this area lies in making certain that you are very, very clear about what situations the insurance covers and how you will judge these. Remember that if you are taking money from people they will be expecting something in return. Make sure you give it to them.

12

Customer service commandments

I used to promote the idea of 'under-promising and over-delivering' when it came to building rock-solid relationships with customers. Today I have set my sights much higher. To make our businesses really stand out from the masses, I firmly believe that we need to *over-promise and over-deliver*. And no, this is not a misprint. We need to make a big statement or offer and always deliver more.

Exceeding customer expectations is one of the greatest strategies any business can have for huge success, because very few businesses are able to do this consistently. The relationship between customers and businesses has become much more complex in the modern world, simply because there is so much choice. Customers hold the upper hand and they know how to use it. Word-of-mouth promotion (ideally, word-of-mouth *raving*) is the single greatest way to keep your customers for longer, increase the amount they spend with you and have them referring their family, friends and colleagues. Lousy service is the enemy so we need to get much smarter when it comes to engaging with our customers.

Start with the basics of customer service, something that very few people are really aware of, in my experience. Like virtually every business skill, these need to be taught (and there are plenty of us who need a refresher course).

You might feel a little bit embarrassed instructing a member of your staff in how to answer a telephone or greet a customer, but it's worth starting from scratch. If it's your business, your main focus needs to be on satisfying your customers and making sure that they have a pleasant experience every time they deal with your organisation.

Many of the customer service ideas suggested in this chapter are considered 'the basics'. I suggest that you encourage your staff to read them or, even better, sit down as a group and discuss the key topics, working through each tip and making sure everyone understands its importance. An open discussion provides a better learning environment than simply telling staff what you expect of them.

Customer service is a big issue and there is a lot to learn, so start at the beginning and work your way through the topics one step at a time. As every business has its own unique aspects, it is important to apply the principles of customer service in a way that is appropriate for your specific business. Sometimes it's difficult for people to make the leap from a theoretical example in a book to an everyday situation that they may face in real life, but the key here is to be absolutely committed to constantly improving your overall level of customer service.

One way to teach staff the basics of customer service is to team up new and impressionable employees with a senior member of the team who can teach them the ropes. Be aware, though, that this can also backfire. The experienced member of the team has probably developed their own style, and it's likely that they are confident, their product knowledge is good and they know a lot of your customers well. The new staff member might mirror their behaviour and become overly familiar with the customers, they may not learn about their products for themselves but simply repeat what the senior staff member says to customers, or they may learn bad habits and take short cuts without learning and understanding the basics.

For this reason, I suggest that all staff have a very clear understanding of your basic expectations when it comes to customer service. You should personally control and monitor this. Once the basics are clear, allow experienced staff members to present their own skills to new employees. The importance of their role in this process should be emphasised to the experienced staff members. It is often a good idea to have your experienced staff sit in on basic orientations as well, as it's very likely that they have forgotten some of the ground rules. We all need a reminder from time to time.

Regardless of whether you run your own business single-handedly or you have a team working with you, spend a lot of time thinking and talking about ways to build better relationships with each and every customer who makes the decision to use your business. This is a great investment in your future.

Ensuring the following tips are in place will help you take your customer service to a whole new level, even if some of them might seem obvious—it will pay to check that everyone in your business understands their importance.

- Treat each and every customer with absolute respect
- Make time to talk to your customers
- Always put yourself in your customers' shoes
- Take your staff to visit a business you admire
- Have regular brainstorming sessions
- Is it easy for people to visit your business?
- Are there ways to speed up your customer service?
- Beware of looking tired and worn out
- Ask a customer to come in and talk to your staff
- Make it easy for customers to pay you
- Eliminate all obstacles to making a purchase
- If necessary, go to them
- The sweetest sound is your own name
- Be one step ahead of your customers
- Make a visit to your business memorable
- Do something unexpected
- Remember to say thank you—and mean it

- Don't let customer service stop when you're busy
- Avoid the biggest mistake—not delivering on time
- Simplify your paperwork
- Always think about your customers
- Get it right the first time

Treat each and every customer with absolute respect

Here is a basic law of business: if you and your staff don't treat your customers with the respect they deserve, they will go elsewhere. From a business owner's point of view, this can be financially devastating. Staff members need to understand the importance of respecting your customers and the ramifications if they don't (for example, they may lose their jobs because the business goes belly up).

I often see businesses that have been fitted out at a cost of hundreds of thousands of dollars, situated in prime locations, and well stocked with competitively priced goods. Everything is in their favour when it comes to succeeding—except for the sales attendant behind the counter with a bad attitude. A staff member who ignores the customers or is disrespectful to them can cost a business a fortune in lost sales, both on the spot and in the future. The state-of-the-art fit-out and prime location are a complete waste of time and money if the person on the cash register has no idea how to care for customers.

It's unfortunate but a fact of life: bad experiences create far more word-of-mouth advertising than good experiences. As customers we have a very advanced and active underground propaganda network that identifies and singles out businesses that provide bad service with a bad attitude.

It's to a business owner or manager's benefit to sit staff down and explain to them the long-term effects of poor customer service. They need to be made very aware that their actions can also impact on others—namely, other staff who may lose their jobs if the business isn't performing financially.

From my own experience, explaining the ramifications usually brings a horrified response, with staff often not realising the impact of their action (or inaction). If you explain the long-term importance of treating customers with respect, most staff members will react positively and hopefully a change in attitude will follow. Any employee who continues to have a bad attitude towards customers should have a short life in any organisation that wants to grow and be profitable.

Remember that every time a customer walks through the door, the first word that should come into everyone's mind is 'respect'.

Make time to talk to your customers

As a business owner and operator, it's very easy to spend your time in the back office rather than standing out front talking to your customers. People love to talk to the owner of a business—it's a mark of respect for you and for them.

No matter how busy you are, always take the time to talk to your customers. Ask them how they are finding dealing with your business. Get to know them and why they use your business. A few minutes' conversation with your customers can give you a lot of information. I find that if I stop and have a chat with my clients, it not only strengthens our relationship but also inevitably leads to new business. Perhaps they know someone who needs some marketing advice, and maybe I should give them a call . . .

When the owner of the business is too busy to talk to the people who pay the bills, there is a problem looming. Always remember that without customers, there is no business. Spend time building relationships with your customers, show them that you value them, their feedback and their ideas.

Always put yourself in your customers' shoes

To be really committed to customer service you need to continually place yourself in your customers' shoes, which simply means viewing every aspect of your business from your customers' point of view. It can be easy to slip out of the habit of doing this and to revert back to an 'us and them' mentality.

Whenever you are making a key business decision that could affect your customers, stop what you are doing and think about all the possible ramifications. Write down the possibilities, both negative and positive, and then make your decision.

We all need to make difficult decisions in business from time to time, but there is a right way and a wrong way to go about this. Simply putting up your prices with little or no explanation to your customers is a good way of upsetting them. Taking some time to explain that your prices will be going up and why the price rise is necessary will help to defuse the situation.

Start looking at everything that your business does as if you were a customer. You'll be surprised by how enlightening this can be.

Take your staff to visit a business you admire

We all know of great businesses—everything they do, they do well. Just as it's a good idea for you to visit your competitors' businesses, it's also useful for your staff to visit a business that you really admire, regardless of what industry it's in.

Stepping outside your own industry is a useful exercise, as sometimes innovative ideas can become confined to what the competitors do. While it's important to compare your business with your opposition, there are many other excellent ideas out there that could be adapted and used in your own industry. For example, if you visit a beauty salon and they have a great promotional idea, with a little smart thinking you can usually change a few details and use the same promotion in a lawyer's office, a restaurant or a mechanic's workshop.

Before taking your staff on a field trip to a business that you admire, talk to them about the types of things you would like them to observe. Have a good debrief after the visit and see what points they have picked up that you may have missed.

I am always on the lookout for businesses that offer exceptional customer service. Sadly, they are few and far between, but when you do find one of the best, think of it as a university for you and your staff to learn from.

Have regular brainstorming sessions

One of the most important lessons I have learned over my years as a small business owner and manager is that some of the best ideas for improving your business can come from your staff. All you have to do is ask for their input.

Develop an environment that encourages input from all of your staff. One way to do this is to have regular brainstorming sessions. These should be conducted in an informal manner; seniority within the business should be put aside and everyone attending encouraged to have their say.

I recently sat in on a brainstorming session for a client of mine, whose business offered professional services to a large number of customers. The aim of the session was for staff to identify where the business needed to improve its customer service, and the person who offered the best input and suggestions was the receptionist. When you think about it, this is logical. The receptionist spoke to all of the firm's clients at some time, dealing with their frustrations, unreturned phone calls, documents not being sent out on time, unreasonable waiting times in reception, and the daily mail. She knew which departments in the business got the most complaints, which individuals were the slowest at returning phone calls, and what the most common enquiries were from customers, and she had opinions on a host of other day-to-day matters. Her opinions were welcomed by the group, and her suggestions and observations were taken seriously. The end result was that virtually all of the business's customer service–related problems were eliminated following the two-hour brainstorming session.

Every member of an organisation has the potential to provide excellent input in areas that will ultimately improve the overall level of customer service. Welcome their ideas and suggestions and thank them for being involved. If you belittle their suggestions, your staff will stop giving their input.

It's important that brainstorming sessions are well controlled, otherwise it's easy to get sidetracked or bogged down on a particular issue. I always assign someone to chair the gathering and, when it starts to go off the rails, their job is to keep it moving forward. Some ideas may need to be followed up, and complex issues may need more than one session to be resolved.

Is it easy for people to visit your business?

Physically accessing your business is an important aspect of customer service. If someone has made the conscious decision to visit your business, you have to make certain that it's as easy as possible for them to get there.

Make certain that your business is well signposted so your customers can pick it out at a distance, which means putting your name and street number in a clear and prominent position at the front of the business. If you are upstairs or at the back of a building, ensure that the signage reflects this clearly.

If your business is new, try to use a well-known landmark as a reference point. Don't be concerned about promoting another business by doing so. If it makes it easier for your business to be found then you are helping your customers who may not necessarily have time to consult a map or to stop and ask for directions.

Is it easy for your customers to park when they visit your business? If it isn't, look for ways to improve the parking situation. Encourage your staff to park further away so they don't take up prime customer parking positions. Ensure that the car park is easy to enter and secure where possible. Are the parking spaces too close together, resulting in car damage and customer complaints?

Including a map on promotional material and even business cards is another way to make it easier for your customers to find you. If you are thinking about opening a new business or relocating an existing one, ease of access should be a key consideration when surveying for possible sites.

Are there ways to speed up your customer service?

Serving customers quickly is very important in most businesses. Time is a commodity that many of us have in short supply, and it can be very frustrating to have our time wasted due to poor customer processing techniques. From my experience with customer service surveys, long delays significantly affect the overall level of customer satisfaction, and in many cases it's the number one reason for customers choosing to shop elsewhere.

Customer processing procedures often evolve over time. They may have worked in the past, but as a business grows the old system may no longer cope with the increased number of customers that the business may now be serving. I suggest that you spend some time looking at your customer processing area. The following suggestions could possibly be incorporated into your business.

- *Traffic control:* Is it clear where your customers should go for service and how they should queue? There is nothing worse than a mass of people jostling to be served.
- *Express service:* Are there lots of people waiting for simple services that will take only a few seconds? If so, you may need an express service lane, similar to those found in larger supermarkets. Banks now offer express boxes for cheque deposits and payments. There are many businesses that could offer similar express payment options.
- *The waiting area:* Is your waiting area inviting and friendly, or are your customers forced to dodge other customers entering and leaving the business? Do you need to provide seats?
- *Distract your customers:* Can you make the wait more interesting? I went into an insurance company recently to

pay a premium renewal and they had a video playing with a well-known comedian telling jokes. It was fun and relaxing, and it made a five-minute wait pass very quickly. Best of all, I arrived at the counter with a smile on my face. Some businesses insist on having big clocks at the front of the queue so that you can watch every excruciating second pass as you continue to wait in line.

■ *Review your signage:* Just because you have a sign telling customers where to go and what to do, it doesn't mean that everyone will see it or understand it. Look at your signage with fresh eyes. Some of your customers may have language or reading difficulties, or they may simply be distracted and not really observant of complicated instructions.

■ *Talk to people who are waiting:* When the queue is long, go out and talk to your waiting customers. Apologise for the delay and let them know that it won't be long. You might consider handing out a 'treat' of some sort.

Last but not least, the same principles apply in the online world, so speed up web transactions however you can. The most successful websites offer instantaneous delivery of products and services. Mirror what they do and the results will follow.

Beware of looking tired and worn out

Over time, the appearance of any business can deteriorate, often without the owners or managers being aware of it. When you go to the same place day after day, gradual changes are less obvious than if they occurred overnight. It's like looking at a photograph of yourself now and comparing it to one taken ten years ago: sadly, there will be a few more lines, possibly a few more kilos, and in my case a little less hair. If you woke up and saw that these changes had occurred overnight, you would rush to your doctor to find out what life-threatening illness you had suddenly developed.

The same is true of your business. The day you open the doors the business is sparkling, the uniforms are fresh, the company cars look smart and everyone has a bounce in their step. Over the space of a few years, however, the premises can become run-down, the uniforms fade, the company cars get dented and old, and the signage and carpets look worn, giving the whole business a run-down appearance. A friend of mine aptly describes this as 'business fatigue'.

Stop for a few minutes and take a good look at your business. Be objective. Think back to the day you opened your doors: how does it compare today with when you started? Are there areas that could be improved?

For most businesses, a revamp is required every five years or so. It may be necessary to get in a professional to give you a few ideas on what you can do to make your business sparkle again. An added bonus with doing a review of this nature is that, with technological advances, there will be many new and exciting options available when it comes to fitting out a business. Amazing new materials, communication systems, fabrics for uniforms and many other developments will help to freshen up your business's appearance.

The benefits to you are that this reinjection of enthusiasm and money into your business will be reflected in the attitude of your staff and the perception of your business by your customers. Customers like to see that a business is staying current and fresh. It shows a commitment to customer service that will pay for itself many times over.

My company recently did a corporate makeover for a recruitment agency. It was a very successful business, but their name stereotyped the type of recruitment that they offered. No matter how hard they tried to change this perception, their customers only ever used them for one aspect of their recruitment needs.

We recommended changing the company name and logo, and completely revamping the office, staff uniforms, signage and company cars. The overall process required a firm commitment from the owners and I can really appreciate their bravery in changing the name of this well-known company. As it turned out, the change worked fabulously. The entire business was transformed and there was a real transformation in the attitudes of staff and clients. The end result was a successful corporate makeover that will take the company into the next stage of its development. If this change hadn't been made, the business could have been overtaken by its competitors.

Ask a customer to come in and talk to your staff

This is an interesting technique that I have seen work very well. Sometimes just talking to your staff about what you are trying to achieve with your business may not have the impact you are looking for. After all, they see you every day, they might be a little afraid of you as the 'boss', they might not relate to you, or they simply may not grasp the importance of what you are trying to get across to them.

The best way to get everyone to sit up and take notice is to get a regular customer to come in and talk to your staff about what they like about the business and what they don't like. It may be hard to find someone to do this, but most businesses have a few customers who are very vocal and willing to give some feedback.

This feedback session is designed to highlight the areas where the business offers good service and those areas where it needs to improve. Your staff will listen with considerably more attention because (hopefully) they will have an instinctive respect for the customer. Issues that you may have been trying to resolve for months can be fixed almost overnight when discussed from a regular customer's point of view.

As always, if you are inviting someone to come into your business and to be open and forthright, you need to be prepared to take their comments on board. The areas needing improvement are equally if not more important than what the customer likes about your service. This is an excellent way to deal with issues that you may have been struggling with for some time.

Make it easy for customers to pay you

Some businesses just seem to make it really hard for their customers to give them money. I struggle with this fact and I have to shake my head when I come across a business that seems to go out of its way to make every transaction difficult (check out Chapter 6 on anti-businesses).

Here are some common problems in this area:

- *Long queues to make a payment:* We all hate having to stand in long lines to give someone our hard-earned money. Look for ways to speed up the payment process (face to face, on the telephone and online).
- *Not taking credit cards:* Any business that doesn't take credit cards is destined for extinction. It might do all right for a while, but I am sure that it won't last. These days passing on the bank fees for these transactions has become quite acceptable, so there really is no excuse not to take credit cards in any business.
- *Not accepting all payment options:* We generally assume that all businesses will offer EFTPOS or credit card transactions these days, but this isn't necessarily so. It can be very embarrassing to arrive at the cashier's desk only to find that they don't accept the card that you wanted to pay with (or the only one you have on you). Some businesses even seem to run into problems with taking cash off their customers. The more payment options that you can offer, the easier it will be for your customers to do business with you.
- *Complicated payment procedures:* Some businesses have complicated payment procedures that require a long time to process. The customer has to stand at the cash register waiting while personal details are filled in, credit card numbers are typed in manually, questions are asked, and so on. These businesses are dinosaurs; in the new electronic age, there is no excuse for long, drawn-out and overly complicated payment procedures.

Often payment procedures have evolved over time and the system in place is no longer efficient or relevant. Review your payment procedures on a regular basis to find ways to make the system work better and faster for your customers. Make it quick and make it simple, and your customers will appreciate it.

Eliminate all obstacles to making a purchase

I talk about cafés a lot in my work. There are two reasons: the first is that I spend a lot of time scribbling notes in them, and the second is that they often produce customer service anecdotes that can be applied to virtually every kind of business.

I visited a café recently that just couldn't seem to get it right. The shop itself looked fabulous, the location was great, and even the coffee was good, but they had absolutely no idea about customer service. To order your coffee you had to stand in a line that moved at a snail's pace. The staff working the till had to punch so many buttons I thought they must have been writing a novel. After they had taken your order you then had to wait by the counter with the rest of the crowd for your coffee. The silliest part was that there was no way to know whose order was whose. They put a cappuccino on the counter and yelled out, 'One cappuccino.' Of course, every second person had ordered one cappuccino, so whose was this one?

The whole process was a mess. People were arguing, the staff had no idea whose order was whose, and the whole time the owner sat at a table and watched the mess unfold. Who is ever going to go back to the counter to order a second coffee and go through all that again? How simple would it be to give people a number? I still don't understand the reasoning behind this café's service philosophy, but it's a great way to learn what *not* to do.

Like this one, many businesses inadvertently put obstacles in the way of their customers buying their products. It may be a cluttered counter, or a prerequisite that you purchase a minimum amount of a product. Perhaps you are made to wait on the end of the telephone for half an hour for the privilege of handing over your money, or it may simply be too hard to get served.

Whatever the reason, a key to customer service is to remove all the obstacles that make it difficult for your customers to make a purchase from your business. Every step of the buying process should be as smooth as silk.

If necessary, go to them

In recent years there has been a significant increase in the number of businesses that go directly to the customer, and I believe that this trend will continue. We're all busy, and so any business that can save us time will definitely be considered a customer service leader.

A friend of mine runs a home-based business and doesn't drive. The dry-cleaning business she uses picks up clothing from her home and delivers it, freshly laundered, to her door. She wouldn't consider using anyone else.

Are there ways that you could take your products or services directly to your customers? Here are a few other examples that I have come across recently:

- *Mobile car batteries:* the service comes to you when you get a flat battery.
- *Mobile mechanics* work on your car at your home.
- *Mobile dog washers:* no more wet dogs in the car.
- *Mobile finance brokers:* discuss your finance needs in your own home.
- *Restaurants:* home delivery is becoming more and more the norm.
- *Hairdressers:* many will now come to your home or office.

These are just a few examples of businesses that were traditionally run from a fixed location but realised the potential benefits of taking their products and services directly to their customers and have profited as a result. Perhaps there is some way that your business can go directly to your customers. I have noticed in the marketing and public relations fields that I now spend much more time in my clients' offices than I used to. I am more than happy to do this, as it gives me a better understanding of their business and helps to develop our relationship.

Making life easier for your customers is a key success strategy when it comes to customer service. Look for as many ways as possible to achieve this and your customers will be more than satisfied with your business.

Remember, though, that if you are going to offer this service, tell as many people as possible about it. There is no point in being a customer service guru and no one knowing it.

Just because a mobile service hasn't been tried in your business before doesn't mean that it won't work. Be innovative and look to be the first to establish a business that goes directly to your customers.

The sweetest sound is your own name

One of my favourite business gurus is Dale Carnegie. His observations on personal behaviour and self-development are legendary. In his most famous book, *How to Win Friends and Influence People*, he mentions a point that has stuck with me for many years: the importance of remembering a person's name and using it whenever you meet them.

This is no small feat, especially if you have a business that has thousands of customers. What you can do, though, is to encourage your staff to use customers' names after they have made a credit card purchase: 'Thank you, Mr Jones'; 'Is there anything else that I can help you with today, Ms Lee?' By using a person's name you are showing them that they are not just a credit card with a pair of legs attached.

There are many times during an exchange when a customer may give you their name. If it's a telephone enquiry, for instance, it's normal courtesy to say who is calling. The customer's name should be noted immediately and used throughout the conversation. I may be a little old-fashioned, but I encourage my staff to use formal titles such as Mr and Ms when talking to someone they are not familiar with. If the customer asks to be called by their first name, that's fine. Respect has been shown and continues throughout the conversation.

Some people have difficulty remembering names, but there are a number of techniques for making this easier. The one I use is called memory association. Whenever I meet a person for the first time, I put a picture of them in my mind and I think of another person that I know well who has the same name. For example, if I meet a man called Jamie, I associate him with a great friend of mine called Jamie. Whenever I see this man, the picture of Jamie comes into my mind and I remember the man's name. This technique works well for me and for many of the people I have told about it.

Another excellent technique is to use the person's name repeatedly in the first few conversations so that you get used to saying it. After a while, you will have trained your mind to remember that name and it will come automatically without you even having to think about it.

It can be embarrassing when you forget someone's name but chances are they have forgotten yours as well, so just get it over with and ask them.

Another technique developed some years ago when I did a lot of travelling overseas for work and was meeting a lot of people. After a sales trip I might have 100 new business cards in my folder—how on earth could I remember all of these people? I started to do something which has proven to be very valuable, even ten years down the track.

Following a meeting with a new person, I sit down for a few minutes and write some details on the back of their business card. It might be something about the person that will jog my memory—perhaps it's something easy, like their purple hair! Or it might be something in their office that I can associate with them, perhaps a picture or a trophy or a book. They might have said something memorable during the conversation. Then, when I go through my teledex of business cards, on reading the back of any card I know exactly who that person is and a few details about them. I feel confident that if they were to ring me or if I bumped into them, I would remember their name.

Do whatever works for you, but try to remember your customers' names. Encourage everyone in your business to get into the habit of respectfully calling customers by name and the end result will be happy customers.

I also think that customers like to know the name of the person serving them in a business so I am a fan of name tags, particularly in retail businesses. Some people really don't like the idea of name tags for one reason or another, but it's a detail that I believe can make a difference when it comes to stand-out customer service.

Be one step ahead of your customers

Have you ever been to a business where they seem to read your mind? Just as you have a thought, someone is standing beside you with the exact item that you had in mind. Or as you stand looking at shelf upon shelf of products, a knight in shining armour comes to your rescue and guides you to the product you need, with a smile on his face and a twinkle in his eye.

These businesses are excellent but, unfortunately, they are few and far between. If a family enters a restaurant with small children there is every chance that they will need a little assistance, but time after time I see families struggling to get seated and having to ask the staff for this and that, as if they were the first family ever to dine there.

Smart customer service is all about being one step ahead of your customers, knowing them so well that you can meet their expectations without them even having to tell you what those expectations are.

Rather than waiting for a customer to make their request, try to be one step ahead of them. If they have a lot of packages, ask them if they would like them delivered or help taking them to their car. If the customer is moving house and you are the removalists, offer to give them a printed inventory of their belongings for their insurance company or to call them the day before the furniture will arrive. If you run a clothing shop and a customer buys some items that will need alterations, offer to have them done before the customer asks. Wherever possible, try to predict your customers' needs and make suggestions or recommendations that will prove useful to them.

Make a visit to your business memorable

One of the great advantages that small businesses have over their large corporate cousins is the ability to form relationships with their customers. In a big firm, people come and go, accounts are passed around the business, and when customers call they rarely speak to the same person twice.

Small businesses have a much greater degree of consistency, which customers like. It's nice when you call the local butcher to place an order and he asks about your family or your plans for the weekend. Or when a small art gallery that you have visited contacts you to tell you of a new artist's work that they think you might enjoy. As small business owners and operators, we should all cultivate these relationships. Take a few minutes to get to know your customers and always use the personal touch.

Look for little ways that you can make a visit to your business memorable, too. It can be as simple as walking around and talking to your customers, perhaps giving out a few free samples or offering advice. I like to make my clients tea or coffee when they come in for an appointment. My receptionist feels that she should be the one to do this, but I enjoy making my clients a drink and I know that they appreciate it. It's a very small thing, but it's a personal touch.

The personal touch can extend to sending notes of thanks or congratulation if a client or customer has some good fortune or a reason to celebrate. If, in the course of a general conversation, you find out that it's their birthday, shout them a product of some sort on the spot. Be spontaneous and show the customer that you value not only their business but them as a person.

Some people struggle with spontaneity, but you will be surprised at how good it feels and how appreciated small personal gestures are. Encourage your staff to be spontaneous too.

Do something unexpected

Exceeding your customers' expectations is often really quite easy. I was purchasing a chocolate bar recently, looking for an afternoon energy boost. It was only about $1.50 and I took it to the counter. The man serving me asked if I was planning on eating the bar today and I said I would be devouring it the minute I left the shop. He suggested that I buy the same bar that was on special in a half-price discount box because it was almost out of date. As I was going to eat it straightaway, it made no difference to me. To make the deal even better, he said that if I wasn't completely satisfied with the discounted bar he would give me the original one for free. How could I go wrong?

All of this extra service happened over a $1.50 chocolate bar. I now go back to this shop on a regular basis simply because of the unexpected service that I received.

I also visited a bottle shop recently to buy some wine and beer for a dinner party. There was a new brand of beer on the market that I had seen advertised and it was being sold at a good introductory price, but I thought that I would play it safe and buy the usual product. The salesperson started up a conversation and I told him my concerns. He immediately offered me one of the new beers to try, which I did. I ended up buying a carton. This bottle shop is out of my way, it's not necessarily the cheapest and it's a pain to park, but I always go back because of the service that I get.

If the salesperson isn't too busy, he even carries my purchases out to the car. This is out of the ordinary and, in my eyes, very good service. While I feel special as a customer, I notice that he treats all of his customers in a similar manner. This is a very successful bottle shop that thrives with no advertising.

Good customer service is all about details and doing the small, unexpected things. The key to successful customer service is to meet and, wherever possible, exceed your customers' expectations. Look for ways to do the little, unexpected things to make your business stand out from the crowd. People will talk about the extra little things that you do and word will spread that your business is better than the rest.

Remember to say thank you—and mean it

We've already touched on the importance of a strong and confident greeting when meeting customers. The same principle applies to the farewell, but with one main difference. When a customer leaves your business after making a purchase, it's nice to say, 'Goodbye, hope to see you again soon,' but it's also very important to thank the person for their business.

Consumers have choices and they know that they can decide where to spend their money. Like any conscious decision, it's good to feel that you have made the right one. Assuming that everything else goes smoothly in the transaction stage of a sale, all of the benefits can be lost in the closing stage.

It drives me crazy when I make a purchase and the person behind the counter doesn't even say 'Thank you', let alone 'Goodbye'. They have moved on to the next customer and you have basically been dismissed. At this moment you know exactly how important you are to the person behind the cash register—not at all.

My advice is simple: stop for a second, look the customer in the eye, thank them for their business and say 'Goodbye'. The 'thank you' needs to be sincere and focused, not just a throwaway line delivered while studying your fingernails and wondering what to have for lunch. These days I stand at the counter and wait until I get a 'thank you', and on many occasions I have had to tell the shop assistant what I'm waiting for. Of course they look at me as if I'm deranged, and often they have no idea what the big deal is.

Poor service encourages more poor service. It's a cycle that makes staff lose their enthusiasm for being friendly and trying that little bit harder. We have all been to a supermarket expecting fairly ordinary service, only to be greeted by a bright and bubbly, young and enthusiastic checkout attendant who greets us sincerely, processes our goods, perhaps even engages in a little light conversation, thanks us for our business and wishes us all the best for the rest of the day. We leave these encounters feeling great. The same effort and energy needs to go into every sale and face-to-face encounter, but it can't be forced and it has to be sincere.

A friend of mine purchased two paintings at an exhibition marking the opening of a small commercial gallery. The gallery owners not only sent her a card thanking her for the purchase but they also delivered the pictures to her home, along with a bottle of champagne, and helped her to hang them.

Always remember to thank your customers for their business. If you find that your staff are forgetting to do this, pick them up on it immediately and don't let it become a bad habit. The same principle applies to telephone orders, internet orders, wherever the business comes from—say 'thank you' and mean it.

Don't let customer service stop when you're busy

We all get busy from time to time. The telephone rings non-stop, there is smoke coming out of the fax machine and the customers are charging through the door, all on the day that someone is off sick. It's great to be this busy, but it's also a time when customer service can really suffer. There can be longer than normal delays, tempers can become strained, you can run out of products, the rubbish bins overflow, and so on.

As consumers we understand and accept that when a business is busier than usual, the level of customer service tends to suffer. However, the real problem with businesses that face fluctuating numbers of customers is that the entire focus of the business revolves around the busy times, not the quieter, more normal times, so the entire level of customer service drops.

Several years ago I had a restaurant as a client. They were very busy during the tourism season, which lasted for about three months. For the other nine months of the year they were much quieter, only serving about one-third of the number of diners each day. A mentality had developed in the staff and management that revolved around the three busy months— the rest of the year wasn't taken as seriously. So, for nine months of the year the service was fairly average and for three months it was good. I had to work hard to change this mentality and remind them that it was essential that their level of service during the off season was the same as, if not better than, in the height of the busy season.

Just because you are busy today doesn't mean that you will be busy tomorrow. If a competitor moves in and their products or services are as good as yours, their prices are similar but their customer service is better than yours, you are heading into dangerous waters. Be constantly aware of increasing your level of customer service. Don't slacken off because last week was really busy and you want to take it easier this week. Don't stop doing the little things that make your business not just good but exceptional.

In my experience, when a business stops focusing attention on customer service, the overall level of service drops rapidly along with the level of customer satisfaction. The financial impact of this is soon evident and very hard to overcome. As with most business maladies, prevention is better than trying to find a cure.

Avoid the biggest mistake—not delivering on time

There are a number of reasons why businesses don't deliver on time, and most of us are guilty of them at some point. From my experience, the following are the main offenders.

First, in an attempt to keep the customer happy, the business agrees to deliver a product or service within a certain time. They know full well that they won't be able to deliver but are afraid that they will lose the sale if they admit they can't comply with the customer's timeframe.

Second, a disorganised business may have poor ordering techniques that cause longer than expected delays in providing goods and services. Perhaps orders only go through once per week, so if you miss the ordering day you are a week behind from the start.

Third, suppliers may be unreliable and inconsistent. This is a common problem and one that is hard to deal with, especially when you have to appease angry customers who see the delay as your fault.

Customers have high expectations in terms of delivery—everyone wants everything yesterday. So you may need to review your operations to ensure that problems like these don't occur. Be honest with your customers and don't make promises that you can't keep. If you find that there is going to be a problem with supply, contact the customer to let them know. There is nothing worse than making a special visit to a business to pick up your goods, only to find that they haven't arrived as promised.

Delivering on time is also relevant for restaurants and professional services. People have a patience threshold and they don't like to be kept waiting, so it's better to advise them of potential delays and they can decide if they want to hang around or not. Better to lose them this time around than lose them forever because you kept them waiting for three hours. I have a doctor that I visit and his receptionist rings me prior to the appointment to let me know if he is running on time. This is a great service and it ensures that I don't sit in his waiting room for hours on end. The surgery is only a five-minute drive away, so I can keep working until I get the call that he will soon be available to see me. How many hours have you spent waiting in a doctor's or dentist's surgery?

Time is precious for all of us. Showing that you respect your customers' time is a very important way of distinguishing good service from lousy service.

Simplify your paperwork

I am often amazed by how hard some businesses make it for people to deal with them. This is reflected in the use of over-complicated, hard-to-use and impossible-to-understand paperwork. Such paperwork and forms have often evolved over time. Things have been added but nothing has been removed, and no one has ever sat down and looked at ways to improve the system.

I recommend that every business should review its forms and paperwork at least once a year. Make sure forms are simple to use—give a sample of your new layout to a friend who doesn't really understand your business and see if they can fill it out easily. If they can't, how can your customers? Take out anything that is unnecessary or outdated, and if you have to add anything, keep it to a minimum.

We all need to be proactive about reducing complicated paperwork. For a lot of people, such forms are enough of a reason not to buy a product. Imagine how people who have difficulty with reading and writing must feel when they are handed a twenty-page application form.

Periodically review all of your business's paperwork and make it easier to use. Your customers will definitely appreciate it and so will your bottom line.

Always think about your customers

Show customers that you are thinking about them and their needs. Something that I have done for years is to cut out articles from newspapers that may be of interest to my clients. I have one who is a leading organic dairy farmer and manufacturer. This is an innovative field and at present there is a lot of information in the news about what goes into our food. By cutting out these articles and posting them to him, he knows that I am thinking about his business and helping him to stay in touch with world developments.

My lawyer often sends me articles about copyright law and copies of advertisements that are interesting or unusual. I always appreciate receiving these and I ring to thank him. It is excellent public relations for his firm and it costs only a few cents to do.

Recently I witnessed a charming example of this tip being put into practice. It was a very hot day and a woman arrived at a local café with a beautiful labrador and a small puppy. She tied them up outside, went inside to order a coffee, then came back out and sat at a table. The waitress brought out the customer's coffee and a large bowl of water for the labrador and a smaller bowl for the puppy. She wasn't asked to do this; she did it on her own initiative. The customer was very grateful (as were the dogs) for the waitress's thoughtfulness and I think it's fair to assume that this café has a loyal new customer.

Using your initiative to try to assist your customers wherever possible is a state of mind. Businesses with poor customer service tend to have staff who all appear to be wearing blinkers; it's virtually impossible to get their attention while you wait at the counter for them to finish their discussion about the weekend's activities—very frustrating.

There is a café in the high-rise building where my office is located, and we often hold meetings there, or have a meal or just a quick coffee to get out of the office. The staff are excellent. Not only do they know my name and the names of all the members of my team, but they make each coffee unique and a little bit special. In the creamy froth they make shapes such as hearts, stars, flowers or swirls. It may sound corny, but they bring the coffees to our table and explain that the hearts are for the women in the group and the flowers for the men. This always goes down well and shows that they haven't just made us coffee like every other café; they have put a little thought into what they are doing. The same business also delivers lunches when you request them, rather than keeping you waiting around. This business has gone from a struggling enterprise to a booming, very busy and, I would imagine, very profitable café in a relatively short amount of time.

Let your customers know that you are thinking about them. They will be both touched and impressed.

Get it right the first time

Every business, whatever its size, will have to deal with customer complaints at some stage. You may find yourself having to placate customers who are plain difficult and demanding, or you may in fact be 100 per cent in the wrong. Whatever the case, there is a right way and a wrong way to deal with customer complaints.

If you handle the complaint well, the end result will be an appeased customer who is satisfied with how their complaint was dealt with— these customers will most likely return. If you handle it poorly, they will never come back again and they will tell their friends not to use your business. The only real loser in this situation is you.

The real dollar value of losing customers due to poor handling of a complaint can be quite amazing. If I spend ten dollars a day on coffee from a local café, that makes me worth about $3000 a year to that particular business. Multiply that over a few years and the real cost of losing a customer soon becomes apparent.

The biggest complaint customers make *about* complaints is a lack of follow-up: if a customer goes to the trouble of making a complaint, either in person, over the telephone or in writing, the very worst thing that you can do is to ignore it. This only adds insult to injury.

A friend of mine recently complained to a sales assistant that she had received change for a twenty-dollar note when she had handed over $50.

The manager was called and he spent some time checking the till against the cash receipts tape. My friend was required to wait around while this was done.

The manager finally said that he would have to wait until close of business to check if there had been a mistake. He asked for a phone number to contact her, and she is still waiting for the call. This business has opened only recently and one wonders how long it will last if customer complaints are all handled like this. The manager lost a perfect opportunity to secure a loyal customer by showing concern for my friend's predicament and handling her complaint quickly and courteously.

A lot of the time, customer complaints aren't handled well simply because no one knows what to do. Often they are put at the bottom of the in-tray because people don't like to deal with conflict. In some cases it may mean that someone will lose their job and, if you are the person processing the complaint, others may blame you for it.

Whatever the reason, customer complaints cannot be ignored. Ensure that the right systems are in place so that complaints cannot be covered up or hidden in the system. Make it mandatory that any complaint received by your business should be brought to your attention.

When training your staff, emphasise the importance of handling complaints professionally and promptly. I once received a response a year after I had written a letter of complaint to a department. It's hard to believe that my complaint had been shuffled from desk to desk for all that time before someone finally wrote to me to apologise. While it made me a little angry, I have to admit that I was impressed that my complaint hadn't just been thrown in the bin.

The moral of the story is that the best way to handle customer complaints is to avoid having them arise in the first place. Make sure that you have systems in place and ongoing monitoring to reduce the chances of customer complaints. Most importantly, stay in touch with your customers, ask them about your business, and make certain that they are completely happy with the service that you are offering.

13

The lost art of selling

Sales skills today are generally pretty bad and, in my opinion, getting worse. There was once a time when much attention was put into training staff and improving sales skills, but somewhere along the line businesses have stopped investing in sales training and it shows. The part I struggle with is seeing so many businesses spending millions on building a business, filling it with stock, advertising and promoting it, but they will spend nothing in sales training to give the staff the tools they need to actually make the whole thing work.

For many of us, when we go to buy something we generally know we are on our own. Our expectations have been lowered considerably and we tend to look at sales staff as someone to give our money to, not someone to get good information from.

In this highly competitive world, I am a strong advocate for encouraging any business I meet to work on their sales skills. This means everyone in the business needs to be trained, not just the frontline staff. However, many people are resistant to sales training, afraid of turning into a 'used car salesman'.

I hear the words 'I'm not in sales so I don't need to know about selling' all the time. Well, I hate to burst anyone's bubble, but the reality is that we are all selling something. It might be our products and services, it might be the company we work for, or it might just be ourselves in a job interview or on a date. Today, no one is isolated from selling in some shape or form. If you are employed by a company, you share the responsibility of selling and promoting that business whether you think you do or not.

A lesson I learned very early on in my sales career was that if you don't believe in what you are selling then don't sell it. If you are selling something that you believe is not as good as it should be, or that is overpriced, faulty or defective in any way, it will always come back to haunt you.

We all need to get much better at selling, and businesses and individuals who master this process—and continually strive to get even better at it—will lead the way in the modern world.

Sales is such a big topic that I easily filled an entire book on the topic (*101 Ways to Sell More of Anything to Anyone*). Here are a number of tips that I think are the most important to consider when it comes to selling.

- Learn from the common mistakes that most salespeople make
- Decide what type of salesperson you want to be
- Believe in your product—it shows if you don't
- Honesty, integrity and passion—the three pillars of successful selling
- Never judge a person by their clothes
- Become a listening guru
- What is your attitude to money?
- To succeed at sales you need goals
- Product knowledge—a salesperson's most powerful tool
- Know everything about your competitors
- Rehearse your sales presentation
- Look the part or go home
- Be prepared and have everything at your fingertips
- Always be ready to make a recommendation

- Tell me in 30 seconds or less why I should buy from you
- How do you monitor your sales?
- What is the customer's main concern in the sales process?
- Always ask for the sale
- Be detached from the outcome—customers smell desperation
- Do what others won't do
- Do a public speaking course
- What to do when you hit a hurdle
- Beware of sales burnout
- Often the most difficult customers become your biggest fans
- Have an extraordinary amount of fun

Learn from the common mistakes that most salespeople make

Trying to narrow this list down was a challenging task. However, based on my observations and experiences, these are the top ten mistakes a salesperson can make:

1. Not being prepared when it comes to making a sales presentation, either face to face—as in a retail environment—or over the phone.
2. Not looking the part—either the salesperson is dressed inappropriately or the entire sales environment looks unprofessional and unappealing to the customer.
3. Not having enough knowledge about the products or services being sold. This is a big issue and, in fairness to salespeople around the world, the rate of product development is making it really hard to keep up. But we have to, because our customers not only expect it, they deserve it.
4. Not asking the right questions. Selling is about communicating and a big part of being a successful communicator is being good at asking the right questions so you can find out exactly what your customer needs.

5. Not listening to what the customer is saying. This goes hand in hand with not asking the right questions and being a poor communicator. Poor salespeople never listen to the customer.

6. Not getting back to the customer as promised—or in other words, over-promising and under-delivering. We all know how frustrating it is when we have to chase salespeople.

7. Not having clear, specific sales goals. Very few people set goals, but those that do tend to achieve them. The same is absolutely true when it comes to selling.

8. Not reading the customer. To do your job as a sales professional, you must be able to interact and connect with the customer and to see that you are indeed helping them.

9. Not being compelling. If you don't believe in what you are selling, don't sell it. Being compelling generally translates to being believable and salespeople already have that stereotype to overcome. If you don't believe what you are saying, your customers won't either.

10. Not caring about the sale. This is the situation where the salesperson really doesn't care if the person buys a product or not. They still get paid the same amount so their attitude towards their customers reflects this. This type of salesperson can cost a business a lot of money.

By being aware of where people tend to go wrong when it comes to selling, we have an excellent checklist of the things we have to make sure we never do.

Decide what type of salesperson you want to be

We all know the clichés about salespeople: smooth, silver-tongued, slick and basically dishonest sharks. Thank goodness the days of the smooth-talkin' shark are long gone, or at least well on the way out—no one wants this type of person selling to them, and who wants to be a pushy sales thug anyway?

It's up to you to decide what kind of salesperson you want to be. You need to make a conscious decision, upfront, then set the rules and abide by them. I realised long ago that I had my own 'sales philosophy', comprising the following key points:

- I can only sell something that is high quality and that I have total confidence in.
- I will always act with complete integrity in everything that I do.
- I will do everything in my power to ensure that my reputation is continually growing for all the right reasons.
- I will only sell for ethical and honest companies.
- I have to be passionate about what I sell.
- I want to be proud of every sales interaction that I have.
- I will be one of the best salespeople in whatever industry I am in.
- I will constantly invest in myself to become a better salesperson.
- I will be creative and innovative, learning from those around me but never getting stuck in the 'that's the way we always did it' headspace.
- I will always exceed my sales budgets.

I strongly advise that you decide what kind of salesperson you intend to be. Or, if you have been selling for a long time, decide what your philosophy is when it comes to selling. Defining these helps give perspective to what you do, regardless of whether you work in sales or own your own business.

Believe in your product—it shows if you don't

I find it impossible to sell anything I don't believe in, whether this involves doubt about a product not doing what it promises, the quality of the product, its value for money, or whatever. Any good salesperson needs to have absolute faith in the product they are selling.

If I am interviewing someone for a sales position and most of their questions relate to the product being sold, the quality control processes, the after-sale service offered by the business, and so on, I know they are a professional. If all they want to know is when and how much they will get paid, I generally get a different picture of their ability and their integrity in the sales world.

If you have doubts about a product or service that you are charged with selling you need to resolve them, and quickly. If you can't resolve your doubts, perhaps you should be looking for something new to sell—I would. Customers can tell if you are trying to sell them something that you don't believe in. If you own your own business and your salespeople lose faith in your business's products, sales will fall and a fast downward spiral could occur.

One of the best ways to build confidence in your own products is to talk to satisfied customers. We cover following up on a sale later, but if you spend some time talking to existing customers about what they like (and don't like) about what you sell, your confidence will grow. And if there is more bad news than good news, you certainly want to know about it so that you can do something pronto.

Honesty, integrity and passion—the three pillars of successful selling

If you can't sell a product openly and honestly then you shouldn't be selling it. Being honest doesn't just mean telling a customer the facts about a product or service and ensuring that all of the relevant and important information is communicated effectively. It also means being honest about when things will be done, when the product will arrive, what to do if there is a problem and so on.

Unfortunately I seem to encounter a lot of dishonesty in sales, not in what people are saying but in what they don't say. Most misleading information is in the small print and it's not until we want to get out of a contract, or return a product, that we find out exactly how misled we have been. It is easy to say buyer beware, but I think that is just a cop-out. The authorities in every country need to tighten up on the small print that we all have to deal with and try to decipher.

If your product or service has weaknesses when compared with your competition, your job is to figure out how to make the most of its virtues without tampering with the truth. Honest salespeople build long and prosperous careers. I know many; they are impressive people who enter every sale with the intention of building a relationship with the client that will last for decades. As a result, they sell a lot.

A great salesperson has absolute integrity. They know what is right and what is wrong—there are no shades of grey. Anyone who sells anything will at some stage of their career have their integrity tested. It may be by a boss, it may be by a supplier, it may be as part of your own business. You are tested at that moment when you know that what you are contemplating or being asked to contemplate is wrong. Which way will you go? Will you leave a job if your boss asks you to do something that you believe is wrong? Will you tell the customer about the flaw in the discounted product that they are buying?

My integrity, and subsequently my reputation, mean more to me than just about anything else in my professional world. There have certainly been times when my integrity has been tested. Had I gone down the dishonest path I could have made a lot more money, but I wouldn't have been able to walk down the street and hold my head high, or sleep at night. If you find yourself in a position where your integrity is being challenged, alter that position as fast as you can. Your job can change, the products or services that you sell can change, but your reputation is yours for life and you decide what that reputation is going to be.

Last but not least is passion. Personally I don't know how anyone can sell anything they are not passionate about. I know that some things are more exciting to sell than others, but luckily we are all different. There are people who are incredibly passionate about selling paper clips. There are people who leap out of bed in the morning to sell toilets. They are lucky; they have found their passion in the world of sales.

It is really hard to sell anything that you don't either believe in or feel passionate about. The wonderful thing about sales is that you can apply the fundamental skills to virtually any product or service. Become an exceptional salesperson and you will never be without a job. But having a job and loving your job are two different things. Perhaps when people say they aren't into selling, they just haven't found the right product or service to sell.

Passion is contagious. People love dealing with people who are passionate. We like getting excited about making a purchase and when you encounter a salesperson who clearly loves what they are selling it is very hard to say no to them. Added to this is the fact that passionate people go out of their way to find out as much as they can about the product they are selling. They don't find this a chore as they have a hunger to learn, which means that doing research never feels like work.

Honesty, integrity and passion together create a truly exceptional salesperson, whether they work in their own business or for someone else. If you want to be the best salesperson you possibly can, then be honest and passionate and show integrity—I guarantee the results will be astounding.

Never judge a person by their clothes

A few years back I was presenting a seminar to about a hundred people in Alice Springs, a desert city in the middle of Australia. The crowd was very warm and welcoming, and while I spoke to them about how to build a dynamic business I noticed a man at the front of the room who seemed very excited. He was wearing a pair of tattered shorts, a dirty old singlet and he was barefoot—none of which would be considered normal attire at a seminar even in Alice Springs—and I assumed he was a little strange. I also assumed that he had no money and that perhaps he was mentally challenged in some way. Subconsciously, I probably made many more assumptions about this man. We all do it. We form an opinion of a person in a matter of seconds. Sometimes it's right and sometimes it's completely wrong, as I soon found out.

At the end of the seminar this odd man came over to me and started to chew my ear off. He was nice enough, but I didn't really know what he wanted or why he was there. After a pleasant chat, he seemed satisfied and wandered off, to my relief. A little later the event organiser and

I were having a debrief on the night. With a bit of a chuckle I told her about the strange man—whereupon she told me he was the richest man in Alice Springs. A self-made property developer, he was worth tens of millions of dollars.

I should have known better. Looks can be deceiving, so when it comes to selling anything, judging people by their looks can be a sales disaster. I would go one step further and say that often the people we assume are the wealthiest, because of what they are wearing or driving, are the people with the most debt. A smart salesperson will overcome their initial and instinctive desire to judge a person by their appearance and put them in a pigeonhole; that is, they are rich or poor, they are a time waster, they will never buy this. Instead, they will treat everyone exactly the same and this is what makes them different.

I spend a lot of time dressed in suits and travelling. On the weekend or if I am having a day off in a city I like to dress down. I know for a fact that when I walk into most shops wearing an expensive suit, I get served almost immediately and am generally lavished with attention by sales-people. But if I turn up in a pair of jeans and a T-shirt, the level of service is completely different. Most of the time I am ignored, even though the amount of money in my bank account is exactly the same.

Break the habit of judging a person by their appearance and treat everyone as equal. Do this and you will sell more of anything to anyone. As a beautiful by-product, you will get to meet and connect with some truly spectacular people whom you may have previously written off.

Become a listening guru

One of the first sales gurus I looked up to was Dale Carnegie, the man who became a legend for writing classic books including *How to Win Friends and Influence People*. In his simple and unassuming manner he works through many extremely valuable techniques for becoming a better communicator. Ironically, one of his most important observations is that the world's greatest communicators are exceptional listeners, and I agree wholeheartedly.

Today we live in a crazy, fast-paced world. Despite this, we are the centre of our own little universe and, in more ways than one, it is all about 'me'. People tend not to listen as well as they could, simply because they are preoccupied with a million other things.

If you want to improve your sales immediately, learn to listen. Customers desperately want people to listen to them. They want to be able to explain what it is they need and they hope that the salesperson they are talking to can provide it for them.

How many times have you ordered something only to have it arrive and find that it is wrong? And the reason it is wrong is that the salesperson simply wasn't paying attention when you made the purchase.

Becoming a listening guru is the fastest and most effective way to sell more of anything. So how do you do it? First, you have to learn how to ask good questions, those that elicit the information that will enable you to give the customer exactly what they want. For many salespeople, this is the hardest part. They don't know what to ask so they let the customer ramble on, hoping that they are explaining their needs. Second, you have to learn to be a great listener. Combine the two skills and not only will your sales success change but so will your life.

I purchased a new car recently. This happened rather suddenly because a friend of mine borrowed my old car and drove it into a ditch. He was okay but the car was a write-off. This meant that I had to go through the dreaded process of buying a new car, interacting with dealers and getting stalked to make a purchase. I set out on a Saturday morning, dressed like I had just come out of the slums of Calcutta, and started doing the rounds of the car yards. Most salespeople ignored me, which was my plan, giving me time to look at a number of cars I had short-listed. But sadly, once I had looked over the cars and wanted attention, the best I could get was someone pointing towards a brochure rack and telling me to help myself.

My last stop was a high-end dealership. I thought that these cars would be out of my price range, especially the model I liked, but I went in anyway and got ready to be ignored. The first thing that happened was that I was warmly welcomed by several staff members. Then a salesperson introduced himself and invited me into his office. We spent an hour talking—about me and what I needed in a car. He asked intelligent questions regarding my driving habits, the number of people I carried, the length of the trips that I took, and so on.

At the end of the session he recommended two models. Then he suggested we go for a drive in both to get a feel for them. As we drove, he pointed out the features, basing his conversation on my needs and the information I had given him. He was an exceptional salesperson. Both cars were fantastic but I particularly liked the bigger one.

At this stage we hadn't even talked price, but I ended up buying the more expensive car. I spent $30,000 more than my initial budget and I absolutely love my car. I could have been sold an expensive car at six other dealerships before I got to this high-end dealer, but by breaking a number of sales rules they didn't even get to first base.

The point I am making here is that what really sold me on this car was the fact that the salesperson asked me smart, informed and logical questions and then listened to what I had to say. Good business sense? Absolutely. I have recommended at least ten other people to this dealership.

Learn to listen, and I mean really listen, and you will convert more sales than you ever imagined. In fact, by being a listening guru you will become a sales guru.

What is your attitude to money?

I used to have a small travel company that sold day tours to people who were visiting Cairns. I would go to the hotels and meet the customers, mostly tourists from the UK, and show them brochures on the hundreds of things they could see and do while in Cairns.

My sister used to help me and we always competed good-naturedly with each other. My average sale was about $500 per person. My sister's was about $150. Why the difference? Was I that much better at selling? Not really. Wendy was a very open and honest person, she was a great listener and she was very professional in every way. So what was the difference? I believe that it was because we had different attitudes towards money, even though we grew up in the same environment.

At the time, Wendy was a mother of three kids and her husband was in the navy. As in all young families, money was tight. For her, luxuries were thin on the ground and most of their money went into paying the mortgage and putting food on the table. She would never go out and spend $500 on herself.

I was the complete opposite. Married but with no kids, my wife and I loved to spend money on ourselves. We went on holidays, bought nice things and spoiled ourselves often, even if we couldn't afford it. To us, spending $500 on something we wanted was no big deal.

So when Wendy was selling tours, she was applying her values and beliefs around money to the sales process—that is: 'Wow, these tours cost a lot of money. I will recommend the cheaper ones.' Whereas my internal dialogue went along the lines of: 'These are the very best tours money can buy. I know you will love them and, most importantly, they are the ones I would be doing if I were you.'

What are your beliefs about money? What are your staff's beliefs? What does 'expensive' mean to you? What is a lot of money? It is important to understand how our own beliefs will impact upon our ability to sell. Changing these beliefs can be tough, but I tend to find that with awareness about our own views on money, we become more able to detach ourselves from them and sell accordingly.

To succeed at sales you need goals

I am a huge believer in the power of setting goals. It has worked for me in so many aspects of my life. In recent years I have learned some new techniques for setting goals from people like Anthony Robbins and Jack Canfield, two of the most dynamic and successful people in the world. I have also spoken to many people, from all walks of life, about their views on goal setting. What I have concluded is that there are lots of different ways to set goals, but that what is important is to do what works for you.

Without a doubt, no goal-setting technique will work without one key ingredient—motivation. For example, if you want a really nice sports car, and you put a picture of it up on the wall (a very effective goal-setting tool for me), this won't achieve much unless you really, really, really embrace the concept of wanting the car. This should extend to the point of visualising driving along your favourite stretch of road in your fantasy car, imagining what it will smell like, what it will handle like, how you will feel at the wheel of your new beast. Simply saying 'I want a Maserati' is unlikely to achieve much, except a hollow feeling when it doesn't materialise.

When it comes to setting and achieving goals, from little ones to humongous ones, I adopt the following techniques, and they always work for me:

- I am very specific about my goal, as in amounts, dates, colours, etc.
- I regularly spend time thinking about what it will feel like emotionally to achieve this goal.
- I think about my motivation for wanting this goal on a regular basis.
- I put a picture that relates to my goal on the corkboard near my front door, which I walk past several times a day. This is my 'Dream Board'.
- I also cut out articles, quotes or cards that inspire me to achieve and put them on the Dream Board, in my diary or on the visor of my car.
- I never get embarrassed about how big or how personal my goal is. If other people see my 'Dream Board', I don't care.
- I think BIG. I truly believe I can achieve pretty much anything I set my mind to.
- If my goal changes for any reason, I let it go and put up a new goal.
- I read my goals out loud, often.
- I read inspiring stories and autobiographies of people who have done amazing things.

Setting goals is just the start. You have to be prepared to get off your butt and make them happen. I intend to buy a Maserati one day, and I know that putting one on my Dream Board will help me to focus on that goal and will certainly help to motivate me, but I will have to do the work necessary to pay for this magnificent car.

To succeed in sales, you need to set specific goals and targets. They need to be realistic but challenging. Time and time again it has been proven that when sales goals are set, people achieve them.

Product knowledge—a salesperson's most powerful tool

Product knowledge refers to what you know about the thing you are selling. From my observations, most salespeople simply don't take the time to learn about the products they are selling and this is really frustrating for customers. In fairness, some industries have so many new products coming onto the market that it would be impossible to be completely informed about them all. But generally, many people are simply too lazy to take the time to perfect their product knowledge.

On holidays in Thailand a while back, we needed to buy a new suitcase to accommodate our excessive purchases. At a large department store in Bangkok, a young salesperson using very broken English greeted us and ascertained what we wanted. We pointed to the suitcases we liked, and he lined them up and started taking us through them all. It was an amazing experience. It took several minutes for him to show us the specific features of each suitcase and he was extremely thorough. He jumped up and down on one to show us how strong it was, he opened every single compartment, he showed us how to use the locks, the differences between each type of case, the colours available and so on. We chose a suitcase, basing our decision on the recommendations of a salesperson who spoke very little English and didn't once mention price. I was blown away.

All too often we ask salespeople for advice or technical answers about a product or service and their answer is 'I don't know'. And, what's worse, there is no attempt to even offer a solution. As a result, consumers are left to their own devices so they go elsewhere or they go online to research and possibly buy items, knowing they will get better answers than they got at the store. The only reason to go back to the first business would be price.

A business that has really knowledgeable sales staff will always stand out from the crowd. And if they promote the fact that they have knowledgeable staff, people will come from far and wide simply because they are desperate for some advice on what to buy.

To succeed at sales we really need to know as much as possible about whatever it is we are selling. Take the time to learn and you will develop a reputation as a leading sales professional and have people clamouring to buy from you.

Know everything about your competitors

Every salesperson needs to know what makes their products different from the competition. To achieve this you need to do your homework. Some people see this as snooping—maybe so, but rest assured that your competitors are more than likely checking up on you too.

So what do you need to find out about your competitors? As much as you can! Find out how their business compares to yours in terms of facilities, the look and feel of their premises, the level of service they offer, what they sell, the prices they charge, their promotional material, their types of customers, their sales skills and so on.

How do you go about finding all of this out? You need to become a detective. First of all, check them out online. Then phone them and ask about a specific product. Go by and make a purchase. Talk to family and friends who may have purchased from them. Talk to suppliers—they often give out far more information than they really should and I find they are way too loose-lipped when it comes to talking about the competition—thank goodness.

Once you have collected the information, do a comparison with your own business. What do you do better than them? What do they do better than you? Look for ways to improve what you do but, most importantly, find out what your competitive advantage is. If you don't know this then you are selling blind.

Rehearse your sales presentation

I give many keynote addresses at conferences and special events. It's something I love to do and my goal is to become one of the most sought-after keynote speakers in the world. As part of my quest, I have committed to constantly improving and developing my presenting skills.

In the early days, I tended to fly by the seat of my pants. While I was organised about what I wanted to say, I never rehearsed, preferring to figure it out as I went along. This strategy was fine at first when I was talking to audiences of 30 or 40 people, but it wasn't quite as effective when the rooms started to contain 400 or 500 people. The pressure of the bigger audiences made it harder for me to think on my feet as there was so much riding on the success of these presentations.

Other professional speakers recommended that I rehearse my presentations, but I felt stupid standing in a room talking to an imaginary group of people. So I didn't do it. Then one day I was booked to present a keynote talk at a conference for leaders in the publishing industry and I felt that this event could be really pivotal to the success of my long-term career. So I planned my presentation, roped in my long-suffering partner as my audience and started rehearsing. And something strange happened—I discovered all of the holes in the presentation, the parts that didn't really flow and the areas that needed more work. I fixed up the bits that needed fixing, called in my 'audience' and did it again. We went through this four or five times before I was completely satisfied.

I went on to give the best presentation of my career in front of approximately 400 people. It was an amazing experience, one that has had a profound effect on my life. I realised that every presentation is important and that if I truly wanted to be a great speaker, I would need to rehearse each and every presentation.

I believe that if you rehearse your sales presentations they will improve dramatically. Rope in a few friends, loved ones or peers (this is a tough audience, and that's what makes it so useful) and rehearse your presentation, complete with whatever visual aids you would normally use. I suggest even dressing as you would for your presentation. Give some members of your 'audience' specific questions to ask.

Rehearse, modify and rehearse again, regardless of whether you are selling to a large group or one on one. It will pay off time and time again and you will develop a reputation as a smart and professional salesperson who does impressive sales presentations that achieve results.

Look the part or go home

Some time ago I was a commercial diver. One day I got decompression sickness, a malady that can hit divers for various reasons. My particular case was quite bad and as a result I couldn't dive anymore. I was devastated. At the time I was working for a very large Japanese shipping company, and my immediate manager was really committed to ensuring that I retrained and learned new skills. I was offered a job in sales and marketing for the company. Even though I didn't really want to pursue this option I took up the offer, mainly because I wasn't sure what else to do. Through a twist of fate, I ended up at a big trade show in Sydney where travel wholesalers came from around the world to buy various Australian-based tour products. I was selling Great Barrier Reef cruises.

Now, I had literally come from working on boats. I was long-haired, scruffy and relatively unkempt (as was the norm when spending weeks at sea). I was determined not to change because I didn't want to become 'just another suit'. I decided that people would have to accept me for who I was. On the first day of the trade show, I turned up in a pair of jeans and a T-shirt looking like I had just fallen out of bed. I set up my booth, sat behind the desk, and waited for people to come and start buying from me. No one did. Streams of professional 'suits' walked by, took one look and kept on walking, some of them noticeably faster.

Well, I sat there for the entire day and I sold nothing. Not a single cruise. I felt distraught and confronted what I thought was the truth—

that I wasn't cut out for this job. Then I had an epiphany. If I wanted to sell to these people I had to look the part. What signal was I sending them, dressed to retain my 'individuality'? Not a good one. This led to what I call my *Pretty Woman* experience.

The minute the show closed I raced down to the town's biggest department store and searched till I found a rather elderly, impeccably dressed, friendly looking salesman. I told him my story and I told him I wanted to become a really successful sales professional. That was all he needed to know. A flurry of activity followed that had me trying on suits, submitting to the ministrations of a tailor who was called in to make adjustments on the spot, buying shirts, shoes, a briefcase and a host of ties, having my hair cut, even getting a manicure. It cost me thousands but I surrendered to the experience and I put my future in the hands of this old man.

The transformation was mind-blowing for me. From the minute I arrived at the trade show the following day, I started selling and people were receptive. I felt fantastic, I was confident, I was funny, and I looked and acted like a complete pro. And I sold millions of dollars worth of cruises that day.

Two things had changed monumentally—my attitude and my appearance. Both were equally important. Since then, I have always advocated the importance of looking the part in whatever sales role you are in. Be proud of your appearance, dress for the market you are selling to (for example, don't wear a suit if you are selling to farmers) and invest in your appearance. Look the part and reap the rewards.

Be prepared and have everything at your fingertips

There is nothing worse than the sales fumbler. This is the person who seems to be perpetually looking for some vital piece of information or promotional material in the midst of a sales presentation. They never have what they need; they promise to send you the missing information but rarely do. They are disorganised time-wasters and I have little patience for them.

Show your customers respect by being organised before any meeting. This means having all of the appropriate material, information and details—as well as a pen—at your fingertips. The number of times I get asked if I have a pen to sign my credit card slip when making a purchase really surprises me.

Always be prepared for random sales encounters and opportunities as well. This means having on hand your business card, brochures or other promotional material, or samples of your products (if appropriate). Now that you are armed, be prepared to give this material out whenever the situation arises. If the situation doesn't arise, give it out anyway.

Always be ready to make a recommendation

Most businesses are lousy at making recommendations—and it costs them a fortune. Anyone can take money from a customer, in fact some stores are even replacing people with automated machines for this task, but very few businesses are good at making a specific recommendation to a customer. We used to be good at this but somewhere along the way most businesses have simply become passive places to collect money. Any business that has quality staff who can make recommendations will generally be a very successful business.

Many years ago I used to own a dive shop where I sold scuba and snorkelling equipment. I was eighteen when I purchased the business and I had no idea what I was doing. All of the equipment I stocked and the way I sold it was a reflection of the methods of the crazy Canadian I bought the business from. His philosophy, and therefore mine, was to have as much stock as possible and sell it as cheaply as possible.

When customers came into the shop I would go to great lengths to show them the hundred plus face masks, twenty sets of fins, fifty wetsuits, piles of regulators and associated gear. They generally left about an hour later with a dazed look on their face. I figured I wasn't giving them enough information so I would virtually hold customers hostage to make sure I gave them every piece of information about every mask, snorkel, wetsuit or set of fins ever made. Still nothing worked and my business ended up in big trouble.

Luckily I had a good friend who was a very experienced salesperson. He would walk into my shop at any time and sell four out of five people a full set of gear in a matter of minutes and he only ever sold the top-of-the-line equipment. Observing my frustration, he let me in on a few of his secrets. First, he told me I had way too much stock and by association too much stuff to choose from. Second, I was too focused on price, but my customers were not. Last but not least, I didn't make any recommendations, I simply gave them all of the options and left them trying to figure out what was best for them.

So we emptied the shop and only put three full sets of equipment on display: a cheap and basic set, a middle-of-the-road set and then a top-of-the-line set. Interestingly, my friend asked me what gear I used—and of course I only ever used the top-of-the-line gear, because it was the best. When a potential customer came into the shop, we started our five-minute presentation with the cheaper equipment and worked up to the most expensive equipment and finished by saying, 'This is the equipment I use because it is the best.' You guessed it, from that day on I never sold a cheap or middle-of-the-road set of equipment ever again, and the amount of gear I sold was phenomenal.

One of the greatest sales faults is not making a recommendation. Customers are bombarded with choice and it is totally overwhelming. Most of us simply want someone to say, 'This is the best product for you.' We all need to be able to make a recommendation that is based on the needs of the customer, regardless of what business we are in. I am not saying you need to be a slick salesperson; you have to make a recommendation that suits your customer, but the better you meet these needs, the happier the customer will be and the more you will sell. Now that has to be good for business.

Become a business that makes recommendations and you will never look back.

Tell me in 30 seconds or less why I should buy from you

By now we have covered a number of ways you can prepare yourself to sell, including looking the part, being organised, knowing your product, comparing yourself to your competitors and much more. Somehow, we need to be able to put all of this into a simple, short spiel that will convince someone to buy something from you.

In 30 seconds or less you need to be able to answer this question: 'Why should I buy this from you?' Some people call this the 'elevator pitch'. Very few people can master it, but if you do you will open many doors that would otherwise be firmly closed.

Wishy-washy answers don't work. In fact, they have the opposite effect—they make customers get cold feet. An elevator pitch needs to be passionate, emotive, factual and convincing. You need to rehearse it, you need to have variations (or you will start to sound like a parrot) and you need to believe it.

I was recently invited to be a keynote speaker at a conference for the courier company Pack & Send. During a briefing meeting, one of the senior executives mentioned that they were having some trouble clarifying their elevator pitch. To me it was as clear as day and boldly written next to their logo: 'Pack & Send: We send anything, anywhere.' Said loudly and boldly enough it is most certainly a big statement.

I recently met a very interesting man at a presentation I was doing. When I asked him what he did, he looked me in the eye and said, 'I make people like you become multi-millionaires.' Wow, that got my attention! After getting to know more about him, I discovered that he was a financial planner. As to whether he can live up to his promise, we will see.

If you can't convincingly answer the question 'Why should I buy from you?' in 30 seconds or less, you really need to learn how. An elevator pitch is like a new suit—it takes a few goes at wearing it before we are totally comfortable. Try on a few different suits and get some feedback from those around you. Make it fun but, crucially, make sure you can live up to the pitch you are making!

How do you monitor your sales?

All businesses monitor the money coming in—it is the lifeblood of the operation—and cash flow is one of those areas that always needs attention. But when it comes to monitoring sales, businesses generally pay less attention to detail.

If you sell only one product for a fixed amount it is pretty easy to figure out how many you sold at the end of the trading day. Few businesses, however, operate at such a simple level. You need to pay particular attention to what you are selling or, more importantly, what isn't selling and why.

Sales reports can consist of a single sheet kept beside the cash register to be filled in whenever a sale is made. Better than this though is a clever cash register that breaks the sales down according to predetermined categories. As long as your staff press the right keys, the information you receive at the end of the day should be pretty accurate.

Regardless of how you monitor your sales, the data collected needs to be reviewed and ideally compared to figures for last week, last month and even last year. This way you start to develop a greater feel for any sales trends that happen within your business. This is very valuable information as it allows you to develop a much more strategic approach to selling. Larger organisations (and also a lot of smaller ones) have very detailed sales reports. They know the value of understanding what is and isn't selling.

The bottom line is that the more control and understanding you have of the products and services you sell, the more likely you are to develop a sustainable business. It takes the hit-and-miss factor out of the equation.

How can you improve your sales monitoring process within your business? Is it time to upgrade your cash register or buy some new software to give you answers? If you don't have a system, put one in place today—start with a simple form beside your cash register.

What is the customer's main concern in the sales process?

As customers, our biggest concerns when it comes to buying are whether the product will work as it should, whether we are paying too much for it, and what happens if it breaks. It all involves a brief psychological risk-assessment process that often happens without us even knowing it. If you can dispel these unspoken concerns you will be well and truly on the way to increasing sales.

So, how do we do that? Let's look at the first one—the product not working as it should. Clearly you need to tell the customer that if for any reason they are not satisfied with the way the product works, they can bring it back and either exchange it or get a refund (depending on your policy). If there are conditions, let them know in advance, don't make it a surprise.

If they're concerned about paying too much, explain your pricing policy, and if you are more expensive than other places, explain why. Perhaps you have better after-sales service, or the products are slightly different. Or maybe your business is smaller than the competitor's and while you may not have the same buying power, you make up for it with more person-alised service. Give the customer the facts and let them make their own decision. For long-term repeat business, it is much better to be upfront than to let the customer find out for themselves and feel ripped off.

Finally, explain how your guarantee system works. Be specific and make sure the customer is clear on the life of the guarantee and what it covers. If the product doesn't have a guarantee, explain why. Some products don't and there is a legitimate reason for this; if you buy a goldfish and it dies you are unlikely to be able to get a refund.

If you can address the above in a few short sentences, the customer's concerns are alleviated and they should be happy to buy the product.

What are you doing to remove concerns that your customers may have regarding buying your products? Think about how you will answer those concerns and make sure your staff can answer the customers' concerns with conviction as well. Try it—you will be amazed at the results.

Always ask for the sale

The most fatal sales mistake is quite simple: not asking for the sale. You need to be prepared to ask the customer for their business, and this is often described as the point when most sales are lost. The salesperson can go through the whole process, but they simply don't ask for the business at the end.

What does 'ask for the sale' actually mean? It means asking the customer if they would like to buy the item you are selling, and it really is that simple. This is that awkward moment when the customer is deciding if they want to make the purchase or not. If the salesperson is standing there waiting expectantly, often the customer will walk away from the sale simply because they feel under pressure to make a decision.

I have a lot of sales reps coming to my business to sell various products. I sit through presentation after presentation and then most of them just pack up and leave without even asking me if we can do business together. By asking the customer if they would like to buy the product you are not being pushy—you are simply trying to help them to make a decision. Clearly it would be better for your business if they did buy the product, but they can still say no at this stage.

Always be prepared to ask for the sale.

Be detached from the outcome—customers smell desperation

I've had salespeople come into my office and literally beg me for a sale, saying if they didn't get this sale they would lose their job. This is an extreme example, but I will let you in on a secret: no matter how good you think you are at hiding desperation, our human sixth sense can sense it a mile away—and most of us run from it. Regardless of just how desperate you actually may be, it is imperative to clear your head and be detached from the outcome of any sales interaction. Let me explain with a personal example.

Through a strange set of circumstances, when I was in my early twenties I found myself selling encyclopaedias door to door around Australia. My first port of call was Tasmania, in the middle of winter. As the last stop before Antarctica, it's a cold place to be at that time of the year. My job was to go around specific neighbourhoods at 5 p.m., knocking on doors and trying to sell my wares. I had no money at all, and this job was totally commission-based. The first few weeks were really tough. I was freezing, I needed to make money to eat and I had a host of other crazy things going on in my life. I was desperate and I am sure it showed. The result—zero sales.

I soon realised that I needed to change my attitude. I was too needy and desperate and the one thing that the people of Tasmania were not going to do is let some strange, forlorn-looking man with desperation in his eyes into their homes, after dark and in the middle of winter.

So I spent half an hour each day getting mentally prepared before hitting the road. I visualised a full belly, my troubles all gone and introducing myself to some of the nice folks in the area and giving them the opportunity to help their kids get the very best education they could. I changed from being a deranged desperado to a bright, positive and cheery young man, offering help to young families. As you can imagine, I started to sell my encyclopaedias, and lots of them.

The key here is to really believe in what you are doing and thinking. Yes, I was broke, but I would get by somehow. Yes, I had problems to deal with but they could be a heck of a lot worse. And yes, I did believe that the books I was selling really would help these people. The results spoke for themselves.

Do what others won't do

There is real power to be had by standing out from the crowd, being different and going the extra mile. I have always tried to live by this philosophy and I have encountered many successful people who do the same. How you are different is up to you, but actions speak louder than words.

I remember reading about an amazing car salesman who used to send cards to his customers at a time when this was an unusual thing to do. He sent birthday cards, anniversary cards, Christmas cards, Easter cards and so on. Over a period of some 30 years in the industry he built up quite a list of customers. In fact, he was sending out thousands of cards every year. He made a point of always writing them himself and he always personalised each message. This guy sold more cars than any other salesperson *ever*. He received a huge number of word-of-mouth referrals; in some cases he sold new cars to three generations of families.

Standing out is important, but being prepared to go the extra mile is even more so. Do a review of the people in your industry who sell the same things that you do. After a while, most salespeople within an industry start to look and act the same. The things they believe they can and can't do are the same. They have the same blinkers on.

Look for ways to do things that your competitors can't or won't do. This will make you memorable and will win you customers, plenty of them.

It isn't often that we are really impressed by salespeople. In fact we generally expect to be underwhelmed, and I usually am. What a wonderful opportunity every single salesperson has to be different. An example of this surprised me recently from a very unexpected quarter. I have always used a particular credit card to pay all my business and travel expenses as it's generally accepted all over the world and the statements make it easy for my accounts people to allocate costs in the appropriate places. Then one month, due to some mix-up, I was late paying a big credit card bill and I was charged a penalty of $700. It really bugged me but I knew the rules and I copped it on the chin.

A few weeks later I received a call from a salesperson at the credit card company. She wanted to sell me something related to the card, but I wasn't interested. She accepted that and ended the conversation by asking me if there was anything else she could help me with. I used the opportunity to express my disappointment at being charged a penalty after paying my bills on time for the last fifteen years. To my surprise, the woman agreed. She put me on hold for a few minutes, then came back and told me they would waive the charge and were very sorry for putting it on in the first place. I was stunned.

Look for ways to do what others don't and you will become a sales legend!

Do a public speaking course

I did my first public speaking course when I was about fifteen and I am still doing them at the age of forty-three. My first public speaking course was a great confidence boost. I don't really remember why I did it, but I ended up on the school debating team, doing my best to outperform competing teams and learning to think fast on my feet.

These skills served me well in my working life. I learned to be organised and well prepared before any meeting or presentation. I learned to make strong and compelling arguments. I gained confidence and felt more comfortable talking in front of a group of strangers. And I learned how to deal with hecklers.

So, if you haven't already, sign up for a public speaking course: there are plenty of them around. Toastmasters is an international group that is very well known (www.toastmasters.org). It will be a great investment of time and energy and I don't think it is ever too late to learn. I run a Professional Presenters Bootcamp—check out my website (www.andrew griffiths.com.au) for more information.

What to do when you hit a hurdle

The greatest danger for a salesperson is loss of confidence. Anyone who has spent any time selling anything will tell you that from time to time you will hit a hurdle. It might be a really difficult customer, it might be the loss of a big account, or it might be a period where you just can't seem to get a sale. The longer this period goes on, the more your confidence can be shaken.

I have experienced many hurdles in the sales world. I know what it feels like to look at the list of people you have to go see that day and feel nothing but dread at the prospect of not making any sales. What can you do?

- First, accept that you are just experiencing a sales slump, not the end of the world. You haven't lost the ability to sell, your career isn't over, your business isn't about to go bust. You are in a rut and it will end.
- If what you are doing isn't working, change what you are doing. Start at the beginning. Review every stage of your sales system and look for ways to do things differently and perhaps better.
- Talk to some of your current customers. Try to find out what is going on. Is it you, or your business, or is it simply that your customers have stopped spending? In other words, find out the facts.
- Find a mentor, someone who has been in sales for a long time. Ask for their opinion and advice.
- Do a training course. Even if you only cover the basics of selling again, it will fire you up and reinvigorate you.
- Have a holiday. If you need a good long break, take one.
- Do plenty of follow-up calls on your existing customers if this is appropriate and ask them for referrals.
- Have brainstorming sessions with the other salespeople in your business.
- Get organised. Take the time to rid yourself of all of those niggling little jobs and projects that are 'incomplete'. With these sorted your life will feel much more organised and uncluttered and so will your head.
- Buy some new clothes. Whenever I hit a sales slump I went and bought a new suit. It made me feel like a million dollars and this seemed to get my sales going again.

Remember that all salespeople have the occasional slump. If your confidence is at a low level, don't keep beating yourself up. Take some time to refocus, get back to the basics, have a holiday, have some fun, do a course or talk to some positive friends. Before you know it you will be well and truly back on track.

Beware of sales burnout

Sales can be very demanding. It doesn't matter whether you are standing behind a cash register all day at the local hardware store or selling planes for Boeing, it is challenging on many levels. Salespeople can easily 'burn out' if they are not careful. If you don't have a way to recharge your batteries, look after your brain and your body, your effectiveness as a salesperson will be diminished and that will be reflected in your sales.

What are the key indicators of 'sales burnout'?

- You start getting grumpy with your customers.
- You struggle to motivate yourself.
- Your attention to detail starts to drop.
- Your sales results are in a downward spiral.
- You find it hard to source new leads.
- Your creativity dries up.
- Your fellow staff members start to bug you.
- You no longer enjoy selling.

It is important to have a life outside work. If you're not careful, your job can become all-consuming. You can end up spending all your time talking about work, about selling and customers. It is an easy trap to fall into and it is really boring for anyone who doesn't work in the same job.

I speak from experience. I was a total and absolute workaholic for years. Seven days a week, at least twelve to sixteen hours a day, all I did was work, work, work. I eventually had a bit of a meltdown; I had some health issues, and a great relationship ended because of my obsession and I realised that I had to make some considerable changes in my life. As a result, I wrote one of my most successful books, *101 Ways to Have a Business and a Life*, which really addressed the topic of work–life balance. I talk more about this later in this book.

Make a list of the things you really love doing, things that excite you and fill you with anticipation. Let's call them hobbies. If it has been more than twelve months since you did any of them they are no longer hobbies, they are memories.

Salespeople are attracted to other salespeople. In fact, there is an old saying that the easiest person to sell to is a salesperson, hence they often spend lots of time socialising with each other. I have friends who sell everything from radio advertising to new cars and who often spend their 'down' time socialising with other members of their sales team. While it is great to spend time with the people you work with, once again it is vital you have a life outside of your work arena to help prevent burnout.

Do fun things that rock your boat and you will be a far more effective salesperson than if you just work all the time and socialise with the same people that you work with.

Often the most difficult customers become your biggest fans

I have encountered some real doozies over the years, customers who were so tough and demanding that I wondered why they even bothered to come and see me in the first place. While selling everything from encyclo-paedias to commercial diving services, I often came across people who always seemed to have a problem, and when it came to talking money— mamma mia, they were the toughest negotiators imaginable. What I discovered was that everyone who deals with these difficult people finds them challenging, but that most salespeople give up and walk away.

Now, I too believe there is a time to walk away but, as I have said before, patience and persistence do pay off. Some of my toughest customers have become my best ones, though in the beginning I would never have imagined that was possible. I have spoken to salespeople from all kinds of industries who agree that some of the most irritating, demanding and downright unpleasant people can grow into the most loyal and committed customers, and many even become friends. You simply have to be persistent and let the relationship work. If you keep persisting where others walked away early, these customers will sit up and take notice.

Have an extraordinary amount of fun

This seems the perfect note to finish the chapter on. I think many of us take business and life far too seriously, particularly business. Why shouldn't we have fun doing what we do? In fact, I think it should be mandatory. Business is simply not that important.

I know that statement is heresy to some of you and, as a reforming workaholic, I know just how important we think our businesses are. But in reality, it is just another part of our lives. Yes, it helps put food on the table, but surely it needs to be so much more. It should be a way to learn, to grow, to develop deep and connected relationships with other people, to make a difference to the planet and those around us and to give us joy.

When did it become so serious?

This may sound kind of clichéd, but people who absolutely love what they do, regardless of what it is, have a radiance that rubs off on those they come into contact with. They are quick to smile and laugh and this is infectious. Who can have a lousy day when you have lots of fun all the time?

For those of you running your own business or in a selling role, if it doesn't bring you joy, then get out and find something that does. My very best piece of advice is to have as much fun selling as you possibly can. Don't get stressed about it. Lighten up, laugh a lot, make other people laugh. Enjoy what you do and look for ways to have more fun every single day of your life.

14

The changing face of advertising

At some stage in the evolution of any business, the owners will need to address the issue of advertising. When they do, they will be confronted with a myriad of options that can be confusing and complicated. Where should you advertise and why? How do you advertise? How much money should you spend? How do you make an advertisement? What about online advertising? And so on.

Recently I was discussing the option of advertising on television with a client of mine who runs a restaurant. I was busily explaining what we would do, how it would work and how wonderful it would be when he stopped me and asked, 'How do you make a television commercial?' I immediately launched into the usual 'don't worry about that, we'll look after it' response when he stopped me again and said, 'That's not what I mean. I want to know how you physically make a television commercial from start to finish because I have absolutely no idea where to even begin.'

This made me stop and think: his question was the most relevant one for most people in business. Making an advertisement is second nature for people in the advertising industry, but for the average business owner it is like learning a foreign language.

The aim of this chapter is to take some of the mystery out of advertising. I provide a simple way to look at how you advertise your business by following a set of simple small business advertising guidelines.

- The constantly changing face of advertising
- Does advertising really work?
- Where does advertising go wrong?
- Put some seriously good thinking into your advertisement, because most people don't
- The five most important things you need to know about successful advertising
- How do you know if your advertising works?
- How much should you spend on advertising?
- If the words aren't right, the advertising won't work
- Every advertisement or commercial needs a call to action
- Don't scrimp on the graphic design of your advertisement
- Always look for editorial opportunities
- Make it easy for the customer to act on your message immediately
- Use great quality pictures to sell your business

The constantly changing face of advertising

The advertising business is a chameleon. Every day there are new places to advertise and lots of people and companies trying to convince you to spend your advertising dollar with them. There was a time when there was one newspaper, a couple of television and radio stations and perhaps the odd roadside billboard to choose from. Now where do you start?

This is the new nature of the advertising industry. It is dynamic and constantly evolving, with new ways to advertise being invented daily. This can be a little overwhelming for the average business owner, so I suggest you take some time to listen to new advertising sales pitches and be prepared to try unfamiliar advertising mediums, but always adhere to the general guidelines provided in this book.

Remember also, every advertising sales representative walking through the door will tell you they have the very best product available. They can't all be the best, but hopefully you will come across one that is perfect for your business and is affordable. If you want independent advice, consult a marketing or advertising consultant to offer impartial advice on where to spend your advertising dollar so it works hardest.

The main point to be gained from this chapter is to keep an open mind. In coming years there will be even more avenues for advertising and smart business owners will take the time to look at all of their options before making any commitments.

Does advertising really work?

A question I get asked all the time, usually by people who are sceptical about the benefits of advertising, is: 'Does it work?' I have to say unequivocally that yes, advertising does work, but it is not an exact science and, more often than not, it is a matter of trial and error. This answer may not inspire a lot of confidence in the advertising process but, like all forms of business promotion, the more information you have and the more time and energy you put into your advertising, the better the results will be.

I see a lot of businesses that simply dabble in the field of advertising. After running one newspaper advertisement that didn't produce the expected results, they make sweeping statements like 'newspaper advertising doesn't work'. Of course newspaper advertising *does* work, but it depends on a number of factors: for example, the design of the advertisement, where it is placed in the newspaper, what the product or service being promoted is and a myriad of other outside influences that could affect the results. More often than not, businesses don't have good monitoring systems in place to determine where new customers are coming from, making it virtually impossible to determine if an advertisement has worked or not.

Another common problem with advertising is that many business owners have unrealistic expectations about the returns from their advertising. For a couple of hundred dollars they expect the advertising to return tens of thousands of dollars. This just doesn't happen. If it was that easy, every small business owner would be a multi-millionaire.

I have worked with many businesses that have started their advertising with some trepidation, but slowly built their businesses with smart and effective advertising to the point where they have grown into large corporations that spend hundreds of thousands of dollars a year on advertising.

So in response to the question 'Does advertising really work?', the answer is yes, it most certainly does, but the key is how and where you advertise.

Where does advertising go wrong?

By understanding the most common advertising mistakes, hopefully you can avoid them and save yourself a lot of money. Advertisements and commercials go wrong mostly because they:

- are done on impulse, without enough time spent planning the advertising
- are aimed at the wrong people
- are cluttered and confusing
- feature in the wrong medium
- feature in only one advertising medium
- are seen at the wrong time
- don't stand out from the crowd
- don't give the customer a reason to act immediately
- don't make the product or service appealing enough to interest the consumer
- are stopped before the advertising can work; in other words, a lack of repeat advertising.

Put some seriously good thinking into your advertisement, because most people don't

Many businesses spend most of their time and energy deciding whether or not to actually advertise, but then put little or no thought into the actual advertisement itself. I find this amazing, but people get busy, they often have limited knowledge about advertising and they put their faith in the company that sold them the advertising (a brave move!).

While I am not saying you need to plan for months before launching a single advertisement, you should spend time thinking about the following:

- What do you want to achieve from your advertisement?
- How will you get the customer to pick up the phone (a call to action)?
- Have you got a good photograph that can be used in the print advertisement?
- Have you sat down and looked at your competitors' advertising?
- Have you included all of the relevant details (telephone number, address, website, etc.)?
- Have you got enough stock to supply the increased demand?

There are bound to be other important questions—I suggest that you make up your own checklist and then, when you do advertise, take the time to really think through your advertising and what you are hoping to achieve.

The five most important things you need to know about successful advertising

So what is it that makes an advertisement effective? There are five key areas that I believe are the very essence of successful advertising. They are:

- establishing the exact message you are trying to put forward
- being clear about your target audience

- making your advertisement stand out from thousands of others
- ensuring people see your advertising often
- giving your advertising time to work.

Let's look at each of these areas in more detail.

Establishing your message

A lot of advertising sends a very confusing message to potential customers. Advertising needs to be planned and it needs to be simple. Sit down and allow yourself some time to think about the exact message you are trying to pass on to potential customers. Give them a reason to pick up the telephone or to drop into your business.

Often advertising becomes cluttered and confusing because there is simply too much information in the advertisement or commercial. If you can't summarise what you want your message to say in one short sentence, go back to the drawing board until you can. Once this magic sentence has been determined, build your advertisement to portray this message clearly. Your advertising will have far better results if you repeat this message rather than trying to introduce a number of other messages.

Take a few minutes to flick through today's newspaper and pay close attention to the advertisements that really stand out. They are often the least cluttered and will have a clear message. They may promote a lot of products but there is no doubt about what they are selling and what message they are trying to get across.

For advertising to work for any business, deciding on the specific message you want to pass on to potential customers is critical.

Who's your target?

If you are advertising parachuting courses, it is unlikely you will get the best results from a commercial on television during daytime soap operas (apart from some adventurous retirees, perhaps). Likewise, if you are selling a new product to relieve the pain of arthritis, advertising during the coverage of an extreme sport challenge is unlikely to produce the results you desire (although many participants will definitely need the product in a few years!).

Knowing exactly the type of person you want to see your advertisement is an essential component for planning your campaign. This is a question most advertising sales representatives will normally ask you (and if they don't, they should). The advertising lingo for it is the 'demographic' you are trying to reach. This can include such details as the age and gender of potential customers, their wealth status and their geographical location, to mention only a few of the elements of a demographic breakdown.

Advertising should be planned to reach particular kinds of consumers in a specific manner. The clearer you are about your targeted customers, the more effectively you can plan your advertising. Placing advertisements randomly in any medium is not an effective way to advertise. Different people watch television at different times (and of course they watch different shows). Different people read various sections of the paper, listen to particular radio stations and so on.

Whenever you are planning an advertising campaign, take a few moments to stop and consider the exact type of person you want to see your advertisements.

Stand out from the crowd

The main reason advertising doesn't work for a lot of businesses is because the advertisement or commercial fails to catch the attention of the targeted customers. It is very important to remember that consumers are bombarded with advertising almost from the minute they wake up until the minute they go to bed. Some statistics have shown that on average we can be exposed to over 30,000 advertising messages a day. This may sound ridiculous, but start paying attention to what you see and hear during a typical day and you may be surprised.

If you are woken by a radio alarm, the station you are listening to is the start of the day's selling process. As you shower and get ready for work a multitude of products continue to fight for your attention. Then you might sit down to watch the morning news while having some breakfast and you are bombarded by advertisements on the television as well as on the products you have for breakfast, such as the cereal box. If you read the paper in the morning you are also going to be exposed to hundreds if not thousands of advertising messages. Then it's time to go to work. During a 30-minute drive it is likely you will see hundreds of signs along the roadside or on other vehicles advertising businesses, while you listen to more ads on the radio. If you travel by public transport there are signs inside the trains and buses. When you get to work and check your mail you will see even more advertising. Check your email and there is more again. By now it is about 9 a.m., you have been up for only a couple of hours and you have already seen thousands of advertisements.

It is easy to see why it is important your advertising stands out from the crowd.

Advertise often

'Frequency' is the advertising lingo used to describe how often an advertisement will appear and, as a result, how often people will see it. This is really the most simple aspect of advertising—get as many people as possible to see your advertisement as often as possible and your advertising will bring much better results.

The downside to this is that the more frequency you want for your advertising the more it will cost. A simple example of this is that of television advertising. To air a commercial at 3 a.m., a time when few people are watching television, will cost a fraction of a commercial aired during the nightly news (generally the most viewed program).

The aim is to look at your whole campaign and make certain you are going to reach as many people as often as possible. Advertising in more than one area is a key to this, so it is wise to consider this strategy. We always recommend to our clients that they consider at least two mediums, such as television and radio or radio and newspaper, for their campaigns.

Give it time to work

An interesting phenomenon of advertising is that you have to give your advertising time to take effect. It is very rare for a potential customer to see your advertisement once, then race off to pick up the phone or jump in the car. It takes seeing an advertisement a number of times (often in a number of different places) before consumers are convinced they need your product or service. One example of this is selling through internet sites.

Often a person will visit a website up to seven times before they make a specific purchase. Each of these visits will have a different but equally important reason behind it, most being subconsciously to do with establishing the credibility of the company the customer is looking to make the purchase from. So placing one advertisement and expecting to be inundated with responses is generally not realistic.

On the upside, though, the response to an advertisement will generally increase the longer it is out there because more people will see the advertising more often. I have monitored many advertising campaigns where we have done the same amount of advertising for a specific product over a six-month period. Each month the response increased, with the last month being the most successful, illustrating the long-term benefits of advertising. Likewise it takes a while for advertising to stop working once the momentum is gained. For those campaigns we ran for six months and then stopped, new customers continued to flow for up to two months before finally slowing to a trickle or stopping.

Hence I often hear business owners say that when they stopped advertising there was no impact on the number of new customers for the business. A few months later, however, they usually come back saying that new customers have dried up and they need to start advertising again (and quickly).

I like to use the analogy that advertising is similar to pushing a broken-down car (something most of us have had the joy of experiencing). Getting the car moving is tough, but once it is moving it takes less energy to keep it going. If you stop pushing the car it will take a while to stop as it moves under its own momentum.

How do you know if your advertising works?

There is an old saying in the advertising industry: 50 per cent of advertising works and 50 per cent doesn't—the real key is to identify which is which. Most advertising is assessed by general feelings such as 'I don't think it really worked', or 'It worked a bit', or 'I'm not really sure if it worked or not'. Surely anyone who spends one dollar on advertising would want to know whether or not it works and, most importantly, how well it worked? All advertising needs to be monitored and assessed on a regular basis to see how well it is working, and there are a number of ways to do this.

The simplest method is to monitor sales of the particular product or service you are promoting. If sales go up when you advertise, it is reasonable to assume your advertising works. If sales don't go up (assuming you have given the advertising time to work) then your advertising probably isn't working and you may need to revisit your campaign.

Another method I strongly recommend is a simple questionnaire for customers. This can be placed at the front of any business (for instance, at the reception), allowing staff to ask customers how they heard about the business. The form can be a flick-and-tick format, where the staff member ticks the appropriate box. Alternatively, most modern-day cash registers can be programmed to collect this information and reports can be prepared accordingly. Asking this question over the telephone is also an option.

I encourage all of my clients to make certain they ask new customers where they heard about the business. Customers are usually more than happy to answer this question, regardless of how you choose to collect the information. The key is to make sure you do collect the information so you can use it to plan future advertising. The information can be reviewed, say once a week or month, and it gives a good indication of what advertisements are being seen.

How much should you spend on advertising?

This is probably the most common question I am asked and it is a good one. Over the years I have read many facts, figures and opinions on what businesses should spend on marketing (which includes advertising and promotional material), but personally I don't think there is a black and white figure that should be quoted. It really depends on a number of issues.

The easiest way to summarise what your advertising expenditure needs to be relates to how much new business you want. If your business is in a growth stage, then advertise more. If your business can handle a lot more customers with minimal operational changes, advertise more. If you are trying to consolidate your business after a particular growth spurt, advertise less. My own ballpark figure recommendations are: for businesses in growth stages, spend 10 per cent of your turnover; for those in a consolidation stage, spend about 5 per cent.

Regardless of how much you spend, make certain you budget for this activity to be an ongoing expense, not just something done when there is a little extra cash in the bank account. If you feel you can't afford to advertise, perhaps it is worth looking at the prices you charge. Advertising is a normal business expense and it should be included when you are planning your yearly budgets.

Sadly, a lot of businesses only advertise when they are desperate for new customers and that puts them under a lot of pressure to get results. Businesses that advertise regularly tend to get the best and most consistent results. A problem that can arise from spasmodic advertising is a sudden, large influx of new customers, which the business then struggles to accommodate. This can actually lead to losing customers because the level of customer service drops, delays are encountered and staff become stressed.

If the words aren't right, the advertising won't work

Sitting down to a blank page that you have to put some words on is a daunting task for many people. Even more daunting is the fact that you are paying money to advertise so you need it to work, but you aren't really sure how to write exactly what you want to say. How do you go about it?

I do a lot of training for people in this area and the first thing I say is that most people cannot write advertising 'copy' (as it is known) naturally. It is a learned skill, so don't feel bad if you can't do it straight off. By following the simple steps outlined below you will be well on the way to writing good copy for any advertisement or commercial.

One point to note: just as many people talk too much when they are nervous, a lot of people write too much when they are nervous about drafting copy. With confidence comes the ability to be happy with white space. Cluttered advertisements are often less effective (but not always), so as you develop your copywriting skills try a few variations of your advertisement. Take an interest in what other people write in their advertisements and listen closely to radio and television commercials to gauge how they are written. At the end of the day, all advertising needs someone to write something.

Step 1: Be very clear about what you are trying to achieve

Expressing the desired objective of what you want to say is a very good starting point for writing copy. Whether you want to get people to pick up the phone to make a purchase or make an enquiry, or you want to let people know you have moved premises, or you are having a one-day sale, be very clear about your message to achieve your desired end result.

Step 2: Make a list of the important information

This means making a simple list of the information and messages you want to get across to the potential customer. Look at the list—is it too long? Remember, it's better to send one strong message than five weaker messages.

Step 3: Write a big, bold heading

I am a strong believer in the use of big, bold, attention-grabbing headlines. I particularly like headings that are questions. This is a view shared by many leading advertising professionals, yet few businesses actually follow this path. Try asking a big question in your advertising and see the difference in results.

Step 4: Write down all the other information that needs to be included

Much of the information to be included depends on where the advertisement or commercial is being placed. You will obviously need contact details—an address, telephone and possibly fax number, email and website. You may need advice for overseas or interstate buyers. Plus, there may be legal requirements you might have to state, such as terms and conditions of sale. List all these before starting on your copy to ensure they are included.

Step 5: Answer the question in the heading

If you ask a question in the heading, answer it in the first sentence of the copy and then lead into the what, when, why and how.

Step 6: The what, when, why and how

This covers the details of your copy—what you want the customer to know in order to entice them. If you are having a giant sale, tell them what is happening, when it is happening, why it is happening and how the customer can get a piece of it. A big question that needs to be answered here is the benefits for the customer. Why should they buy your product?

Step 7: Decide on a writing style

Decide whether you want your advertisement to be written in the first person ('I am Dirty Harry and I own Dirty Harry's Chinese Restaurant'), the second person ('You have heard about the team at Dirty Harry's Chinese Restaurant') or the third person ('People visiting Dirty Harry's often compliment the chef'). You also need to decide if you want the copy to be funny, serious, conversational or educational.

Step 8: Keep sentences short and sharp, and the words simple

Advertising copy really does need to be kept brief. Sentences need to be short and the language straightforward. Use descriptions, but don't try to be too flowery or else people will start to get bored and lose interest.

Step 9: Put it all together

By now you should just about have the basis of your advertisement worked out. It's time to put it all together, check the spelling, and see that it flows and makes sense. If you have asked a question in the heading, ensure it has been answered in the following copy. All of the details should be filled in, the style should be consistent and the spelling correct. Now is the time to move things around or change words that don't seem to work.

Step 10: Close with a call to action

The customer needs to be given a reason to act now. They need to know what to do next and they need to be convinced.

By following the ten steps above you will be a long way towards having a well-written advertisement or commercial for any advertising medium.

Every advertisement or commercial needs a call to action

I touched on this point in the last tip about copywriting but it's worth examining further, because the reality is that a lot of advertising works really well—until the end. The advertising stands out from the crowd, the information is passed to the potential customer, they are motivated and interested . . . and then nothing. The advertisement or commercial simply ends and the next one comes on to compete for the customer's attention. So, just as important as getting attention is a call to action.

What does this mean? You simply tell the potential customer what to do next. It may be to pick up the phone, come down to the business, log on to the internet, stop hesitating and buy today, tell your friends, cut this coupon out or join today. There are hundreds of possible calls to action.

The call to action is the clincher. Most advertising seems to end in a mumble when it really needs to be powerful and convincing. Use strong words that will inspire the reader or listener to say, 'Yes, I will do something about this right now.'

One of the best calls to action I've seen being used is on home shopping–style commercials, where the viewer is constantly encouraged to call right now and they will save money and get a free gift. Another is used by takeaway food shops who advertise around dinnertime, with bright, visual commercials showing steaming hot food straight out of the oven and a clear directive: 'Call now and you can have this pizza in front of you within 30 minutes.'

Take some time to make your call to action impressive and inspirational. Spend as much time working on this as you would on the parts of your advertising designed to catch attention and you will reap the benefits.

Don't scrimp on the graphic design of your advertisement

If you are going to spend considerable money on placing an advertisement in a magazine or anywhere, don't let yourself down by scrimping on the graphic design.

Having the one graphic designer working on all of your advertising and promotional material has many benefits. They get to know what you like and what you don't like, they have all of your images and logos on file, and the longer you work together the greater their understanding and feel for your business will be.

Graphic design really is the cheapest part of advertising and I am constantly amazed at how many businesses try to save money on this area. Why bother? If the advertisement doesn't work you have wasted a lot more money than the cost of getting the artwork done. This is false economy.

Find a graphic designer you like, develop a relationship with them and be open to their suggestions and creative input. Your advertising will ultimately be more effective and you will attract more customers.

Always look for editorial opportunities

Whenever you are negotiating advertising in magazines, newspapers or online, always ask questions about free editorial. Many advertising media will offer free editorial and you can use it as a bargaining tool. Don't sign up for advertising and then ask for some editorial, because at that stage you are already committed.

Its availability is normally dependent on the size of the advertisement you book or how much you plan to spend on advertising over a certain period of time with the company, so you may find you are upsold to spend more to get some editorial. However you get it, I think there is a lot of value in free editorial.

Receiving editorial coverage in a specialist magazine is an excellent way to build credibility with the readers. If you appear as a contributor you are regarded as something of an expert. The same applies in newspapers and on websites.

To increase your chances of getting editorial coverage it is always prudent to have an article and some photos ready to supply at short notice. I suggest paying someone to actually write an article about your business so it is always ready when needed. Ideally have a 500-, 1000- and 1500-word article on stand-by, and make sure any accompanying images are high resolution. Individual magazines or newspapers may prefer to rewrite the article or modify it to their style but at least they have something to work with and your business gets the benefit of the editorial.

Make it easy for the customer to act on your message immediately

Recently I received a flyer in the mail (a direct mail piece) promoting a pretty amazing fishing lure that I was certain would finally give me a competitive advantage over the fish of the world. I wanted to buy it but as I searched through the brochure to find out how to, I became aware that this was going to be tough.

The business didn't take credit cards (and they pointed this out in large print, which was a big dent in their credibility for me), so I had to send a cheque or go to the post office and get a money order—straight-away I lost enthusiasm. A money order? I also had to photocopy the order form before sending it to them (for reasons too complicated to explain), which once again made ordering nearly impossible.

They had got me interested in buying the fishing lure but then every way I tried to buy it there was an obstacle. In frustration I rang the company only to receive the answering machine which referred me back to the order form. Arggggghhh!

Look at your advertising and make absolutely certain every barrier to making a purchase is removed. Accept all credit cards, make the order form detachable if there is one, leave enough space on the form for people to write their details, have a contact telephone number that is manned, and preferably make it a toll-free number.

The easier it is to buy the product, the greater the chance customers will actually buy.

Use great quality pictures to sell your business

When it comes to print and online advertising, always use excellent images, ones that evoke the right emotion and enhance your advertisement. The use of poor quality images really takes away from an advertisement and does little to enhance the credibility of a business.

I think professional images are a smart investment in your business, but if you are worried about the cost you can always buy high-resolution images from numerous royalty-free stock photography websites.

A picture really does say a thousand words. Flick through any glossy magazine and this fact is clearly reinforced. Use the best images you can and your advertising will be far more effective.

15

Get things right online and profit follows

The internet is a huge area and one that is in many ways fluid, constantly changing, evolving and improving. This makes it difficult to provide specific recommendations that don't quickly become outdated, but there are a number of underlying strategies or tips that will always be important, regardless of changes in technology. These are what I cover here.

I have tried to avoid jargon as much as possible, so I am sure there will be the odd technical person who may be mortified by some of the things I have to say or how I say them. However, this section is not written for IT professionals but for the layperson trying to get their head around the online world.

The following advice deals with developing the right strategy for your website. The technical folk can look after the building and functionality of your site, but none of this matters if you are starting on anything less than the solid foundations of a good strategy.

- Do I really need a website?
- Don't just 'throw a website together'—think about it

- Homemade websites are like homemade logos—plain wrong
- Register the right domain name (and make sure you are covered legally)
- The number-one reason that business fail on the internet
- It's not about how much information you have on your site but how easy it is to find it
- Digital footage is becoming much more relevant (but avoid gimmicks)
- A website is never finished—it will always be a work in progress
- Before launching, ask some customers to take your website for a test drive
- Social media is here to stay, so figure out how to use it
- If no one can find your website, there isn't much point having one

Do I really need a website?

For online aficionados this will seem like a bizarre question, but small business's uptake of the internet as a promotional tool has been surprisingly slow. Quite a few still don't even have a website and these days, that spells trouble. Regardless of the type of business you are in, having a website is as essential as having a product or a service to sell.

The world has changed: the new way to find information is via the internet. Words such as 'Google' have become ingrained in our language and for younger generations a web search is the only way to find out about any topic (or purchase) that they are interested in. Hard-copy telephone directories are being discarded in favour of online searches, meaning that if your business can't be found online, and your competitors can, you are in trouble.

If a lack of money is preventing you from putting up a full site, at least get a one-page site up with simply your logo, what you do, your contact details and anything else that is relevant.

But you then need to plan to have a full website up as soon as possible. A bad website is exactly the same as a bad brochure: it makes the business look amateurish and cheap and it does very little to give potential customers the confidence they need to do business with you.

Earlier we examined the biggest challenge facing most businesses today: the ability to evolve in a world that is changing at an incredible rate. The online world is an integral part of this new world and if you are not part of it, you will be left behind.

Don't just 'throw a website together'—think about it

The internet is like any other marketing tool—it's bound by financial and creative limitations. If used wisely, the internet can help your business to grow and become more profitable, but we also need to be realistic about what you can achieve financially from your online activity.

All too often websites are literally thrown together with not a lot of thought. The brief to the web developer is to take a hard copy brochure and make that into a website, which is a very limited way of thinking about a resource like the internet. I strongly recommend that you develop a simple internet strategy with five key components:

1. Have a clear understanding of what you are trying to achieve online. Do you want to sell products, pass on information, promote your business, attract new customers, or offer additional services to existing customers? Spend quality time thinking about this. If you have staff, get them involved, ask some customers for their ideas and take the time to be really clear about what you want your website to achieve.

2. Develop a realistic budget. There are two stages to developing an online budget: the cost to develop the initial site and the cost to update it on an annual basis (and don't forget the ongoing cost of hosting the site). It will be hard for a web developer to give you a firm quote to cover the cost of developing a site without some specific information from you. How do you want it to look and

feel? Do you have a corporate image for them to base the look on or do they have to start from scratch? How many pages will the site be? Will you need a shopping cart? Will you have video footage? Will you also want to spend money on SEO (search engine optimisation), which helps your business to be found more readily by punters doing a web search? Generally a good web developer will give you a list of questions that are worth thinking through before you sit down to do stage one of your website plan.

3. Do your research. Look at other sites and note what different businesses are doing: could you adapt and use these on your site to make it more innovative and professional? Think outside your own industry and look at a multitude of sites to find out what catches your attention, improves navigation, and so on. Giving your web developer a list of the sites that you like can speed up the web development process.

4. Check out your competitors' websites to identify the good, the bad and the ugly. Look for ways to build a much better site than theirs, ideally with more features and a better navigation system to make your website easier to use.

5. Ask your customers to give you feedback about your site, and listen to their suggestions and comments.

Developing an internet strategy needn't be a highly involved process, but having one will really increase your chances of developing a better, more effective site, which means more value for money and greater potential for revenue if you have an e-commerce site.

Homemade websites are like homemade logos—plain wrong

I admire those people who are keen to try to develop their own websites, but just like homemade logos, they very rarely work. Instead they look amateurish and less than impressive, and technically they are usually just plain wrong.

To understand the psychology of people checking out a business online we have to realise that often it is an easy way to do a risk assessment before making a purchase. Customers are scoping your business out to see if they want to go one step further, which may mean emailing you, calling you, visiting your business or placing an order. Because of this, it is imperative that you do everything possible to make your site look credible, impressive and inviting and, most importantly, you need to pass their mental risk assessment.

Register the right domain name (and make sure you are covered legally)

Registering your domain name is an important part of the web development process. Personally I always like to try to register both the .com and the .com.au domain name for any business that I register. This makes it tough to find the right name as both need to be available, but if you want to operate globally, .com domains carry more credibility.

To register a .com.au domain name (an Australian domain name) you must also have the same business name registered. This makes it a little more complex but it also gives you greater protection. There are many Australian businesses out there using a .com.au domain name that they have registered but they don't own the actual registered business name locally. At some stage they run the risk of losing the Australian domain name if someone else registers the exact same business name as their .com domain name. I know this may sound a little confusing but your web developer can help you with this.

The real bottom line is that you should have a domain name that reflects your business name. So if your company is called ABC Plumbing, you would want to register www.abcplumbing.com.au. For a localised service it probably isn't worth registering the .com domain name. If you want to be a bit more zippy and register something like www.needa plumberinahurry.com.au, which is a great idea, you can either register that as a .com domain name (if it is available) or alternatively register a business name—Need a Plumber in a Hurry—in Australia, which means you can then register the .com.au domain name.

It sounds a little complex but any web developer can explain this to you in more detail. Whichever way you decide to go, you must have a domain name to create a website.

The number-one reason that businesses fail on the internet

Everyone is trying to sell something on the internet but unfortunately very few businesses are successful online. The main reason why internet selling fails is because of slow response rates by website owners (if there is any response at all).

The internet is the ultimate instantaneous marketing medium. The closest old-school marketing medium would probably be the infomercial, where viewers ring up about a product that they see on television right that minute.

With the internet, at any time of the day or night you can find out about virtually anything in the world. While many businesses can offer online and real-time sales of products or services, many still require more detailed email correspondence first, for example, to gather additional information from a potential customer before a price can be submitted.

Businesses that succeed online are quick to respond. Even allowing for time differences, response time to an enquiry should definitely be within 24 hours and I personally think it should be much less than this.

Those companies that answer their email enquiries very quickly will sell more products than those that take a long time to respond. I am constantly surprised by how slow many businesses are in processing emails and responding to requests for prices or other information. For example, wanting to do a diving trip with great white sharks in South Australia recently, I emailed five companies that offered this service—not one responded to my request. I emailed six companies in South Africa that also offer the same service and all six responded—admittedly several took over a week to get back to me, but by that stage any response was a good one.

Once again, the whole idea of having a website is to encourage people to do business with you. If you are lucky enough to get them interested in buying something, respond to their emails as soon as possible. This shows not just that you value their business but that you are also organised and efficient and therefore credible. It's easy enough these days to have an automatic response, which at least acknowledges that you have received their email and will be in touch shortly.

This same principle applies to any form of contact from prospective customers—respond quickly and you will have a far greater chance of getting their business. I once read a fascinating article which claimed that the number-one reason for lost sales and lost customers was poor communication. More specifically, it was a lack of follow-up. We have all heard the old 'I'll call you straight back' and 'you'll have the price on your desk in the morning' lines that ultimately go nowhere. To really drive your business, follow up quickly and efficiently—not just on the internet, but with all communications—and your chances of thriving will increase significantly.

It's not about how much information you have on your site but how easy it is to find it

When it comes to how much content to have on your website, I suggest that you have as much as you possibly can. But—and this is a big but—the vast majority of people will only want some brief snippets or specific information initially, then they will be prepared to look a little deeper to find more detailed information.

So based on this, the real issue is not really how much information to have on your site but how it is structured. My advice is to keep the initial pages short and sweet, but the 'deeper' pages can be more information-rich.

Remember also that it can be harder to read information on a computer screen than in hard copy. Page after page of information in small font is a recipe for getting people to switch off and find another site that is easier to use, particularly as more and more people use mobile phones as portable internet browsers.

It all comes back to the importance of a well-thought-through navigation system, one that is not only logical for the customer but also relevant in the amount of information that is delivered on each page.

A great website is easy on the eye, simple to navigate, logical, interesting and appealing.

Digital footage is becoming much more relevant (but avoid gimmicks)

With ever-increasing internet speeds, there is no doubt that digital footage (or video, for those of us not up to speed on terminology) is playing a bigger role in the online environment. Just take a moment to look at YouTube; if you want to try to take an idea viral, YouTube is the place to do it.

Generally I am against tacky gimmicks like music, corny animations and movement on a website. Simple, well-designed and clear websites work more effectively across a range of browsers. But in saying that, digital footage is a great way to make your website more interactive and appealing. It makes it multidimensional and, for most of us, it is much easier to watch a short video as opposed to reading long pages of text, hence the popularity of YouTube.

Making your own short films has become much easier with cost-effective video cameras and digital editing equipment, which means that with a little creative direction you can have a reasonable quality film online in a short amount of time and for very little money.

A website is never finished—it will always be a work in progress

This is often hard for people to come to terms with, but once you launch a website you have to be prepared for the fact that it is only the beginning of the process, not the end.

Nothing looks worse than an out-of-date website, with old or incorrect information, dated pictures and a general feeling of neglect. Websites are dynamic marketing tools that need to be given regular attention, updated often and redesigned periodically.

Because of this, we have to allow funds for updating our websites regularly. I budget for monthly updates to my site.

Before launching, ask some customers to take your website for a test drive

Often the process of developing a website becomes so intensive that we can forget to look at it from a customer's point of view. I strongly recommend that before launching any website you get a small group of selected customers to take it for a 'test drive'.

I have done this many times with impressive results. It is both amazing and embarrassing what we can forget when we are totally absorbed in the process of building a website.

Social media is here to stay, so figure out how to use it

The seemingly never-ending supply of new social media sites can be quite daunting: these are millions of blogs, plus Facebook, YouTube and Twitter, to mention but a few. It is estimated that close to one billion people per day are using some form of social media.

In the USA, social networking accounts for 22 per cent of all time spent online. Twitter averages about 40 million tweets per day. Facebook has become the third-largest 'population' in the world. Australia has some of the highest global social media usage stats and Australians are the biggest users of Facebook in the world, with some nine million users spending nine hours per month interacting. Surprisingly, the age demographic who use Facebook the most in Australia are the over 50s.

The world has changed. Social media communities are now as relevant as geographical communities—I bet most of us know more about people in our Facebook family than we do about our next-door neighbours.

For many people it is hard to see this social media phenomenon as anything more than a giant waste of time, but this is a mistake. Sure, lots of social media seems to revolve around swapping mindless thoughts about fairly insignificant things, but beneath this superficial surface there are a lot of very smart businesses using social media as a key element in their marketing arsenal. It is foolhardy to dismiss social media.

Social media unites a group of people with some kind of common interest. They really are giant clubs, in most instances giant fan clubs. People interact, recommend, buy from, support, argue with and generally engage with others in their online communities, just as we do in the 'real' world.

When it comes to business, rather than wasting time getting your head around the value of social media—that argument is already proven, in my view—get your head around how to use social media to build your business.

Do a Google search on this topic. Spend some time researching other websites and businesses with Facebook sites or Twitter accounts and see what they are doing in these spaces. How are they embracing the social communities to grow their business? Once again, I guarantee that when you start to look into it, you will see some very smart ideas being utilised. I am sure you will find ideas that you can adapt and use.

Social media is being used to get people talking about products and services; it is the new 'word of mouth'. Today consumers are more likely to make a buying decision based on a recommendation from someone they trust in the social media world than based on advertising alone.

One of the big challenges for most business owners is the time it can take to update information on social media sites. Yes, it can be time consuming, just like writing a monthly newsletter is. But by planning it out and allocating a small amount of time each day, it becomes less onerous. None of this will matter though if you don't believe in the power and potential of social media and what it can do for your business.

Invest some time, do some research and find out more about the world of social media. Do a course, buy a book or ask other people how they use social media as part of their business. This is an area where we need to keep an open mind and become students of the social media world. I believe that it will pay off down the line.

If no one can find your website, there isn't much point having one

Having the best website in the world will mean little if no one can find it. So actively promote your website by including the domain name (or URL) on all your promotional material, on vehicles, on letterheads and business cards, on packaging and in advertising. In other words, display it everywhere.

Secondly, I strongly suggest that you engage a professional to help drive traffic to your website. This is a complex topic and certainly one that changes quickly, hence the suggestion to find an expert. There are many small and large businesses that specialise in building traffic. They do this through a range of processes that include search engine optimisation, advertising (Google Adwords, for example) and other techniques that I don't know a lot about—but I do know that they are important.

Once again, your web developer should be able to point you in the right direction of a business that can help drive traffic to your site. I do suggest that you use a specialist in this field—a lot of businesses that develop websites offer this service, but I am not convinced that knowledge in one area makes you a specialist in both. I am sure some companies are, but check out their testimonials and ask for some hard facts and case studies to verify how much they have been able to improve traffic numbers for a business (and also the quality of the traffic, remembering that an increase in visitors is useless if they are not the ones you need).

16

Set the pace for your competitors to follow

We all have to deal with competition and I believe this is a good thing, not a bad thing. Competition keeps us trying to be better, it stops us from becoming complacent and it fuels innovation and creativity. Customers like the concept of competition. Apart from the obvious reason that it tends to make things more affordable, it also gives people much more choice, and we all like to have a choice.

There are two ways to look at a highly competitive market: it can be stressful and difficult to make a business successful or it can be an amazing opportunity to drive your business forward and stand out from the pack. In some ways it can be the motivator to keep you constantly striving to do what you do a little bit better each day.

Knowing what we mean by being the best is the place to start. It will mean something different to different people, but without this understanding, how will we ever know when we have reached our goal?

The following tips and recommendations are designed to show you how to use competition to make your business a winning one.

- Have a genuine desire to be the best at what you do
- Enter your business in awards whenever possible
- Get your name in print
- Be prepared to get up in front of a crowd—challenge yourself and become the expert
- Being green is good for business
- Be supportive of competitors, even if it is one-sided
- Spend time researching your industry online
- Learn from your mistakes
- Even better, learn from your competitors' mistakes
- Don't become obsessed with your competitors

Have a genuine desire to be the best at what you do

Being the best at what you do has to start with a very firm and genuine belief you *can* be the best. Beginning with the aim of being as good as your competitors is noble, but far too limiting.

A long time ago I had a business that was really struggling. A friend sat me down and explained in very simple terms that to be the best you have to do everything better than the competition. It's a fairly logical concept, but one that is often not really understood.

Being the best may mean shaking up old traditions and beliefs and stepping outside of your comfort zone, perhaps redefining what is considered the norm in your chosen industry. Believing you are the best is the starting point: from here you need to implement the right actions to make sure you actually are the best at what you do and that you can deliver on your promise.

With my business at the time, this change in thinking was really the starting point I needed to untangle the mess I had created, and to put a very clear goal in place. This desire to be the best needs to be shared with your staff, your suppliers and your customers.

Get a big sheet of paper and write your commitment statement on it: 'I am going to make this the BEST [whatever your business is]', then sign your name to this commitment. Put your statement on the wall in your office or place it in a prominent position where you'll see it constantly.

Enter your business in awards whenever possible

Winning an award is great for business. It gives you recognition, it gives your customers faith in what you do and it motivates the entire team. Everyone loves a winner. There are lots of different awards being run all the time. Some are industry specific, some are geographically specific—it doesn't really matter, an award is an award.

Many businesses don't bother entering awards because filling in the submissions can take quite a bit of time. But entering awards should be considered a marketing activity and allocated time and thought on that basis.

If you are looking for a competitive advantage, being an award-winner is certainly one very good boost. If you are fortunate enough to win an award, make sure you let everyone know. Put the certificate on your office wall in a prominent place, and make mention of the award on your website and on all of your promotional material. Keeping the certificate in the bottom drawer really is a waste of time and a missed opportunity.

Get your name in print

There are many benefits from having your name in print (and these days that means both in print publications and online). It gives you and your business a lot of credibility, it reinforces to your customers that you know what you are talking about and it generates new business from people who like what you say. The more your name appears in print, the more it will continue to appear as your reputation grows.

There are more opportunities to get your name in print today than ever before, with thousands of newspapers and magazines all needing content. If the editors and journalists can find industry leaders who are prepared to comment on relevant stories or submit articles, there is a good chance those leaders will be published in some format.

The best way to get your name into print is to supply a brief profile to the various publications outlining who you are, what you do, and which specific areas you're able to offer informed comment on. It is also a good idea to supply a high-resolution electronic photograph of yourself (taken professionally) so the publication can publish it with any associated stories.

There are also lots of freelance journalists looking for subjects to write articles about. Check local newspapers and magazines for the names of specific journalists and send them your profile and associated information.

This kind of exposure is relevant at any level—nationally, internationally or on a smaller local stage. All it takes is a little bit of courage to actually submit your information and accept the fact that you are good at what you do. You are just as qualified as anyone in your industry to offer an opinion.

Be prepared to get up in front of a crowd— challenge yourself and become the expert

For many people, a slow and painful death would be preferable to the thought of standing in front of a crowd and giving a talk. As an experienced public speaker I can really relate to this. But if you are prepared to step up and talk to a crowd, or perhaps be interviewed as an 'expert' by the media, you automatically give yourself a strong competitive advantage.

My business development for many years has been based around this concept. Whenever I am asked by the media to comment or am invited to speak at an event, the end result is that I get more work. People come to me because I have credibility as either a presenter or an 'expert'.

I did my first public-speaking course when I was at high school and I am very glad I did. I also like to do refreshers every once in a while as I am firmly committed to improving my skills as a public speaker. The opportunities that public speaking presents are considerable, including the chance to share your expertise in your chosen field.

There are many situations where people are called on to present in a group situation and if you let others know you are prepared to do it, more opportunities will come your way. So take the challenge, face the fear, become an expert in your industry and go for it.

Being green is good for business

Running a successful business certainly covers a lot of ground. But what is often overlooked is that being committed to running an environmentally responsible business is not only good for the environment, it is good for the bank balance.

I have quite a lot of experience marketing environmentally focused businesses and this is a topic I am passionate about. Green consumers (those who make many of their buying decisions based on environmental/ social responsibility) are growing in numbers rapidly; they are prepared to pay more for green products and services and they are informed and intelligent about those products. Best of all, they are easy to market to because they are actively looking for environmentally responsible products and services.

If your business is more environmentally aware and responsible than your competitors, you will attract customers on this point of difference alone. Of course, if you are an environmentally responsible business you need to tell your customers what your commitment is.

One excellent example of this is The Body Shop. This impressive organisation has grown to be a leader in beauty products with the main sales point being that the business will not sell any products that don't fit into its stringent corporate philosophy on environmental and social responsibility and respect for animals. Consumers know that if they purchase a Body Shop product they can rest assured that it has not been tested on animals, a rainforest has not been cut down to produce it, and a five-year-old child has not been involved in the manufacturing process.

There are lots of ways to be green, far too many to list here. Look at your business from every possible angle and start with small changes, building up to much larger and more significant ones. When your business is environmentally aware you will reap both the moral and financial rewards.

One important note here is that if you are running an environmentally responsible business, take the time to explain to your customers what you do to adhere to this code. This can be explained in your promotional material, on your website or on a sign in your place of business. Make sure your staff are well versed in your philosophy and commitment.

When it comes to finding a competitive advantage, if your business is green and your competition is not, you are way out in front for most consumers.

Be supportive of competitors, even if it is one-sided

Taking a mature approach to your competitors is a very positive business attribute, even when it isn't reciprocated. In my home town there are quite a few marketing companies, all competing for the same clients, but we have developed a very positive network of referrals and support. My business isn't suited to all clients and if I recognise that a competitor will be better matched to a potential client's needs I have no hesitation in recommending them for the job. In fact, I have offered marketing advice on a professional basis to a number of my competitors; likewise I have used their services when I needed them for my own business.

True success comes from rising above petty points of difference and working towards providing the best products and services as a whole industry. The more you work with your competitors, the more you will benefit.

I have experienced this firsthand in the tourism industry. The regional city where I live, Cairns, is the main stepping-off point for the Great Barrier Reef. Every year we have about two million tourists coming to our city to enjoy the natural attractions. As you can imagine, the tourism industry is well established, mature and sophisticated. There are hundreds of different tours, hotels, attractions and specialised tourism-related retailers. There is also a strong underlying foundation that spurs most of these businesses to work together to promote tourism in the region, even if their particular business doesn't always directly benefit. The aim is to attract more tourists—full stop.

It can be very reassuring to sit down with your competitors and talk about business in general. It is nice to know that the trials and tribulations you face are also faced by your competitors. But it takes one person to extend the olive branch or to open communication channels. If you already have good relationships with your competitors, what can you do to make them even better?

Spend time researching your industry online

A very fruitful exercise often overlooked by business owners is to spend some time seeing how your industry operates in other countries. Checking out websites from around the world can give you a wealth of information in a short time.

Not only will you pick up good ideas for building your business but you will more than likely find valuable information about industry trends that could have an impact on your business. If you find out about these trends before your competitors do, your business will be well out in front of the field.

Spending time seeing how other people do the same thing as you is time well spent. Smart entrepreneurs know the value of research and they never begrudge spending time on it. Winning businesses are always one step ahead of their competitors.

Learn from your mistakes

Business experience is mostly about learning from our mistakes. I know I have made far more than my fair share, but as the years go by I am getting a little smarter and learning the lessons a lot quicker.

There wouldn't be many successful entrepreneurs who could say they have a mistake-free background. In fact, I would be impressed to meet just one and that is what makes entrepreneurs so amazing. When they get it wrong, they pick themselves up, dust themselves off and get on with the next opportunity at hand.

We all make mistakes and we will continue to do so—the trick is to learn your lesson and move on. If you make a business mistake and it costs you money, there is no doubt it will stay in your mind for a long time to come, and that is no bad thing. There is no point crucifying yourself; after all, even the most experienced and high-profile entrepreneurs end up going wrong at some stage. Punishing yourself more than necessary is not only counterproductive but can also shake your confidence and increase your chances of making more mistakes.

Letting go is often easier said than done but it is an art that will be very beneficial in your business life. Accept the fact that we all get it wrong from time to time, learn your lesson and move on. The University of Life is offering PhDs daily to just about every small business I know.

Even better, learn from your competitors' mistakes

In the last tip we discussed the importance of learning from your business mistakes and moving on. An even better option is to be a close observer of your competitors, learning from their mistakes.

Most business owners tend to take a keen interest in what their competitors are doing—and if you don't, you should. Being aware of what is happening within your own market needs to be an ongoing part of your business. As you observe your competitors, note what they do well and what they do poorly. Clearly, both bits of information provide you with an opportunity.

If your competitor makes an obvious mistake—perhaps by changing their pricing structure they have outpriced themselves, or their latest advertising campaign is ineffectual, or their overall level of customer service has dropped—and you find out about it, their mistake can help your business to grow. This is especially so if you take the time to really think about where they went wrong and what was the main cause of their mistake: did they misread their customers, was there a change in staff or owners, or was there some other key contributing factor?

Being a successful entrepreneur involves being a good observer of the many different things that you can learn from or that can have an impact on your business. Learning from your competitors' mistakes is one way to avoid making them yourself.

Don't become obsessed with your competitors

I come across a lot of business owners whose entire life is based on what their competitors are doing. Every decision they make is the direct result of something the competition has done or is planning to do.

Having a healthy awareness of your competitors is essential to be truly successful in business, but don't build your business around what they are doing. Rather, focus on what you can do to lead the way.

Often an obsession with the competition is the result of insecurity and fear, and the reactionary steps taken by the business tend to reflect these negative traits. This is how price wars start (and no one wins a price war except the customer); advertising becomes ad hoc and knee jerk instead of systematic and well planned, and customer service is forgotten as the business owner is too busy looking at what the competition is doing rather than what is happening within their own business.

Be aware of what your competitors are doing and evaluate their actions, but don't make their businesses the centre of your universe.

17

Can you really have a business and a life?

I meet and work with many business owners around the planet and, without doubt, the biggest challenge that most face is trying to find some kind of business–life balance. For many, including myself at times, this is something of a Holy Grail.

The main problem is that running a business is extremely demanding. I think that we often make it harder than it should be and perhaps from time to time we get our priorities misaligned, but when you have your house and your financial future tied up in the business, it's hard not to take it seriously.

This translates into working excessive hours, huge amounts of stress, challenges outside of our normal field of expertise and a whole lot more. I think business owners have a strong sense of responsibility, often driven by the fear of 'what if': 'What if I can't pay my rent?', 'What if I can't pay my staff?' and so on.

The main reason nearly all of us struggle with business–life balance is that the changes which cause us to be out of balance occur slowly over time. They creep up on us until all of a sudden we wake up and realise that we are out of control and don't know what to do about it.

The simple reality is that if we don't figure out how to find some kind of balance, long-term success is very hard to achieve. The victories we will have along the way somehow seem hollow. Even worse, we may end up with success but find that our relationships are in tatters and so is our health.

I am sad to say I see a lot of severely burnt-out business owners who on the surface have finally achieved their financial goals and dreams, but who have no one to share this success with. Often their own health has even suffered to the point where their life expectancy has been shortened significantly.

The following pieces of advice come from my own experience with the business–life battle and I strongly advise you to learn from my mistakes. You can win this battle if you are committed and if there is enough pain associated with not winning to motivate you to take the necessary action. This is a big chapter, simply because it needs serious attention. I know there is a lot to take in, but most stressed-out small business owners will be able to relate to a lot of what I have to say and the advice I have to offer.

- Why do we get out of balance in the first place?
- What are the long-term effects of being out of balance?
- Decide right here, right now, if you are ready to change
- Be clear about how you want your life to look and feel
- Understand the enemy—what specific things throw you out of whack?
- What bad habits have you developed?
- What do you need to do right now to change the way things are?
- Start every day on the right path
- Reward yourself for staying on track
- What are the things you have always wanted to do?
- Be prepared to invest in the process
- Visit your doctor, healer or naturopath
- When you start to lose control—stop, breathe and regain focus
- Do you remember when you used to laugh a lot?
- Master the art of saying no

- Don't be afraid to sack some customers
- The torture of perfection
- Do the work you love—give the rest to others
- Enlist outside help—why not use a personal trainer?
- Make movement a part of your life
- Guilt-free pampering
- Respect yourself enough to take the time to look your best
- Develop your own style of meditation
- Keep a diary of what you eat and when
- Alcohol, coffee, nicotine, sugar . . . what's your drug of choice?
- What exactly does eating well mean?
- Learn to enjoy food again
- Water water everywhere
- Eating out doesn't need to be unhealthy
- Encourage healthy eating in your workplace
- When it comes to food, always be prepared

Why do we get out of balance in the first place?

Ironically, we get out of balance by trying to do what we think is right. We work hard, we commit completely to our businesses, we argue that to succeed we need to be devoted to growing the business, especially in the early stages, and, most significantly, we are energised and excited about the future.

Over time we get busier, our responsibilities grow and our needs and expectations are overtaken by the needs and expectations that others have of us. Then the feeling of being overwhelmed starts to move in.

The better you are at what you do, the more likely you are to start feeling overwhelmed—because more people want what it is you are selling. As your business grows there are more staff, more customers, more suppliers, bigger sums of money to manage and generally more paperwork to contend with. So in some ways, feeling out of balance with your business and your life is a reflection of the fact that you are great at what you do—take it as a compliment.

But before you get too carried away with patting yourself on the back and being proud that your life is completely out of control, remember that as your business has grown, you have had to learn a host of new skills to deal with this growth. Learning how to have a business and a life is just another set of skills that need to be learned along the way.

The following list identifies the ten most common reasons for getting out of balance. While there are many more, these are the biggest culprits:

1. Overwork—simply putting in too many hours and being a slave to the business.
2. Financial problems—struggling to make ends meet in the business and worrying about how you will pay your bills.
3. Over-commitment—agreeing to do too much for too many people and not leaving enough time or energy for yourself.
4. Poor stress management—not knowing how to manage your own stress or not being able to admit that it is a problem.
5. Relationship issues—with partners, family and friends, co-workers and customers.
6. Poor lifestyle—eating badly, lack of exercise, and alcohol and drug abuse.
7. Lack of direction—feeling trapped and isolated in the business and uncertain about your future direction.
8. Lack of boundaries—being too accessible to too many people.
9. No space to rejuvenate—no holidays, time out, hobbies or distractions to remind you why you do what you do.
10. Having a negative environment or negative people around you every day.

There are two ways to deal with being out of balance. The first is to change yourself and your perceptions. The second is to change your circumstances. Most likely both will be necessary. However you look at it, there must be a constant and ongoing commitment to do what is best for you, and the courage to create the necessary changes, so that you are honouring yourself, the people in your life, and the planet.

What are the long-term effects of being out of balance?

I can attest to the long-term effects of having a life out of balance—and they aren't pretty. The effects on health are the most noticeable, generally starting with headaches, skin conditions and an upset stomach, often accompanied by a general feeling of being unwell. Some people have a permanent cold or flu, get bags under their eyes or start to hear the comment 'Gee, you look tired' a lot more often.

Along with the physical symptoms come the emotional ones. We start to get more irritable, we don't sleep as well as we used to, perhaps we start to get anxiety and even panic attacks, and we are irritable and generally highly strung. Under these conditions we can find ourselves leaning on crutches in the form of drugs and alcohol: after work we start to have three or four drinks to wind down; maybe we have three or four cups of coffee to get going in the morning. We eat chocolate to perk us up, which we need often because we have no energy, but which causes us to put on weight. Without making conscious decisions to change, and without knowing how to change, things will only get worse.

Of course, the longer you have bad habits, the harder they are to change and the more damage they can do. Business owners often tend to struggle the most with establishing a fitness and health regime, simply because they don't give themselves enough time or energy to focus on it. Someone who has a regular job generally has a start time and a knock-off time, and can more easily build a fitness program into their life.

Decide right here, right now, if you are ready to change

If you are not 100 per cent ready to wrest control of your life back from your business, you won't achieve it. I attended an interesting motivational seminar recently at which the host asked one man in the crowd of 4000 people what was wrong with his life. The hapless fellow rattled off a list of his woes, from no girlfriend to no money, niggling but not serious health issues, and a losing battle with his weight.

The well-known host, with a big grin, asked what was stopping him from getting his life together. The poor man gave a lengthy list of reasons why he couldn't change any of the things in his life that he was unhappy with. They were all good reasons and they sounded reasonable to me, albeit a little defeatist and whiny. The host then said, 'If I gave you a million dollars right here, right now, could you change your life immediately and rid yourself of the issues that are plaguing you and preventing you from making the most of your life?' In a heartbeat the man said, 'Absolutely—yes.'

Now this is interesting. It's not the problems or the solutions that are the issues. They are simply the mechanics of the situation. Any reasonably intelligent person can sit down and write a list of the issues that are affecting them and what they need to do about it, or find someone to help them do it. The secret ingredient to make change work is motivation. If you have the right amount of motivation, you can change anything in your life. If you haven't, the change will only be token.

As a somewhat strange example, let me tell you about a friend of mine who is a very committed smoker, and has been so for 40 years. Of course he has tried to quit many times but with little success (well, no success). This all changed with a visit to his doctor during a nasty dose of the flu. The doctor did some tests and broke the news to my friend that it looked like he had emphysema. This very sobering diagnosis made him throw away his cigarettes; he didn't have a single craving while he waited three weeks for the results.

In a nervous appointment with his doctor he was advised that he didn't have emphysema—yet. So he walked outside and bought a pack of cigarettes. While his motivation was strong enough—the immediate possibility of emphysema—my friend was effortlessly able to quit. But without this threat hanging over him, the motivation was gone.

Find enough motivation and we can do just about anything.

Be clear about how you want your life to look and feel

Just as important as making the time to sit and reflect on your life as it is today is being clear on what you want your life to be like, or how you want it to look and feel, from here on.

I find that being clear about this makes everything else fall into place. The more specific you can be about how you want your life to be, the more likely you are to achieve it.

Often it is hard to be clear about just what it is we want out of life. Faced with a blank piece of paper, I struggled for a long time with my attempt to list how I wanted my life to look, or how I wanted my business or my body to look. I found it easier to write down the things I didn't want first of all—that made working out the things I did want much simpler.

Before I started my marketing company I had done a number of different things. I had been a commercial diver, run a small travel company, worked around the world as a sales professional, sold encyclopaedias door to door—and much more. I had reached a crossroads in my life where I was trying to decide what I wanted to do. So I wrote down all the things I liked about each of my previous professions, and all the things I didn't like, and from those lists determined what kind of business I wanted now.

The results were very specific. I had spent a lot of time working outdoors and being cold, so today I live in the tropics—but I didn't want an outdoors job. I used to be on call 24 hours a day when I had my travel company—but I didn't want to answer the phone at 3 a.m. anymore. I certainly didn't want to knock on doors to sell anything—but I did want to meet people and to travel.

What came out of the melting pot was a very clear set of criteria to be met by my next business—and that's how I came to be a writer and marketing consultant.

So when we are talking about regaining control of our lives and being able to successfully balance business and life, we need to know exactly what that means to us as individuals.

Writing it down makes it real. The form in which you do it—lists, tables, a flowchart—doesn't matter. Write down exactly how you want your life to look. Be very specific. Don't say you want to spend more time with your children—say how much more time. If you don't want to work as many hours, say how many hours you do want to work. If you want to earn more money, say how much. Specifics become reality. Airy-fairy, non-specific goals rarely get to be achieved.

The more specific your goals are, the greater your chances of making them a reality.

Understand the enemy—what specific things throw you out of whack?

If someone asks me what disrupts the balance between my business and my life I can easily list the culprits:

- Overcommitting my time (I can't say no and I get excited by interesting new projects).
- Aspects of running my company that I am no good at (bookkeeping, operational procedures, etc.).
- Day-to-day distractions that stop me getting my work done (I get hundreds of emails, countless telephone calls, letters, visitors, and so on every day).
- The internet—I love it and get distracted by it, and have to find the time to finish projects that I didn't get done because I was distracted (as you can tell, I have a very short attention span).
- Poor time management.

That is me being perfectly honest about myself. I get lots done, I work long hours and I have very high expectations of myself, but the above issues bring me undone faster than any others. Fortunately for me I have a great team of people to work with; they are very aware of each of these issues and do their utmost to prevent them from impacting on me.

I suggest that you write your own list. What causes you the greatest frustration in your business? Is it worrying about money? Having to manage your staff? Is it caused by your suppliers? Or your customers? Again, try to be specific if you can. Often we haven't actually taken the time to think through the causes of our day-to-day angst. You can then start to do something about it and, even more importantly, you can enlist the help of those around you, who can generally see you slowly destroying yourself as you battle the panicky feeling of being overwhelmed by your business.

What bad habits have you developed?

The underlying cause of being out of balance is generally related to bad habits that have become part of your normal, day-to-day way of doing things.

These habits may relate to your health and wellbeing. Perhaps you eat badly because there isn't enough time in a seriously busy day to go that little bit further and get a healthier lunch. Or exercise consists of wrestling open a bag of chips, your only meal, sometime during the day.

Or perhaps you are drinking a lot of coffee to fight the fatigue of working longer and longer hours. Or maybe you are unable to make even simple decisions anymore simply because your mind is so full.

Whatever your particular bad habits are, rest assured, you are not alone. They come with the territory and I have had them all. I do know, though, that bad habits will trap you if you don't act on them, and from my experience they are particularly hard to shift. Just like smoking, it's easy to start but amazingly difficult to stop.

Not all bad habits are obvious. It can sometimes be a matter of what you are not doing that is significant, like not taking enough time to relax, not recharging your batteries by doing the things you love. These inactions are generally by-products of the bad habits we have developed—but they should be listed as well to help you start the change process.

Make a detailed list of all the bad habits that you have developed and the impact they have on you. Be honest, be specific and be prepared to be a little shocked. If you're not comfortable with this, don't show anyone else, but don't kid yourself either. Write them all down.

What do you need to do right now to change the way things are?

Any change needs commitment. If you are desperate to make an improvement to your situation then you probably have the right amount of motivation. Without the right amount of motivation any change will be minimal and in all likelihood it won't last.

So right here, right now, you need to stop and think about just how important it is that you introduce some real changes to your life that will stop the feeling of being overwhelmed, and help you to start to take control of both your business and your life.

Think about how you want to feel, what it is that you want to do with your time, how you want to look, how you want to act and how you want to live your life. Once you are clear on this, or at least willing to start really looking at each aspect of your life, you can move on.

Remember that this is a journey—but it's not an overnight journey. It's about changing virtually every aspect of your life so that you can really get the most out of the years ahead. So there may be some pain, other people may not like the changes that you need to make, especially in the short term, and some may even try to sabotage the process (people generally don't like change, especially in those closest to them). This is where you need to be strong, dedicated and very clear on where it is you are heading.

229

Start every day on the right path

I am a great believer in the importance of starting your day the right way. If you begin under the hammer, you will spend all day under the hammer. Taking some time each morning to start your day in a gentle, focused and balanced way lays the groundwork for the rest of the day.

I tend to spend a few minutes lying in bed, thinking about the day to come, getting my head ready and right. Or if it is a nice day I will sit on my balcony and watch the sun appear over the hills, and enjoy its warmth on my face. Whatever else happens, there is a definite relationship between the way I feel first thing and the way my day turns out.

I used to jump out of bed while it was still dark, gulp down some coffee, have a quick shower and head to work, where I was full-on from the minute I arrived until the minute I left, normally many hours later, in the dark at the other end of the day. This is a very stressful way to live—there is virtually no room to stop, breathe or enjoy what is happening around you.

Since I changed the way I start my day I definitely feel much better, more in control, more relaxed, and ready to take on the day and all its challenges in a calm manner.

This works for me, although I can't promise it will work for you. What is important is to start to bring a few rituals of relaxation into your life. They will remove the mayhem, ease the sense of being overwhelmed, introduce calm and allow clarity into your daily life, and make you feel so much better.

Reward yourself for staying on track

One observation I have made of small business owners is that they generally struggle with the notion of rewarding themselves, often associating reward with purely financial considerations. Instigating all the changes we are talking about can result in more than a little turmoil in the short term before greater balance kicks in. This is normal, but the turmoil can be disconcerting, and we need to give ourselves some rewards along the way.

I suggest making a list (yes, I know, another list!) of things you consider to be rewards. Some may be material objects, others may be more symbolic. This doesn't matter—what does matter is that they are things you really like and want.

Once you've compiled this list, create a second list detailing the changes you need to make to achieve balance, and at strategic points on your second list, indicate an appropriate reward—so that when you change this habit, you get that reward. For example, your list might say that for one week you are not going to stay at work later than 6 p.m., no matter what. If you achieve this, your pay-off is to buy yourself a new fishing rod. Or, if you commit to going to the gym twice a week and you do it for a month without fail, you get to have a night out at your favourite restaurant. But you must make the change before you claim the reward.

This is part of the reprogramming process that you need to undertake. There are many names for 'reprogramming', and many ways to go about it, but it does work. We need to be rewarded—whatever that means to us individually—to really feel that what we are doing is worthwhile.

What are the things you have always wanted to do?

Make a list of all the things you have always wanted to do but have never found enough time, money or energy for. I find this a very interesting exercise. It's your 'life wish list', and what goes on it is entirely up to you. When we are feeling overwhelmed one of the biggest issues is that there doesn't seem to be any way out, and there isn't a lot to look forward to except more of the same.

Having a list of things that you have always wanted to do makes them more real. My list is long (about 30 items) and ranges from spending a month in India to feeling a polar bear's fur. I am glad to say that I have achieved a few of these things in recent years, and that feels sensational. Quite often I find more things to add—there are no hard and fast rules to this tip. It's your list—make it what you want. Sometimes you might even want to take a few things off, because as time goes by you can change and they may no longer be as important to you.

What you do with this list, like the others you make as you work your way through this section, is of course up to you. I made up a folder that holds all my information, and that works for me. I keep it handy and review it almost every day. Some of the more important parts I have laminated and placed on my wall. I don't care who reads them; in fact I find that seeing my life wish list motivates my friends to get off their backsides and put their own lives into action mode.

Life is short, but we have the opportunity to do so much. By taking control of your life and putting your business back into perspective you will get to enjoy so many more of the amazing things this planet has to offer. Some achievements are huge, some are small, but most are worthwhile. Running your own business is an amazing experience and provides a true sense of accomplishment, but this is magnified one hundred times if you can enjoy your social life at the same time.

Be prepared to invest in the process

We have earlier touched on the need to invest in your business's number-one asset, you, and the same philosophy applies here. To get back the balance that is missing in your life you will have to invest. This investment will be in the form of time, energy and money.

You will need to set aside the time to sit and plan what you want your life to be like. More time will need to be allocated to going to seminars, reading books, talking to other like-minded people, getting fit, learning better techniques for managing people, and for reflection. Time is our most precious commodity and the one most of us complain we don't have enough of. Of course, the old cliché is that we all have the same amount of time available (and I don't really need to talk about the likes of Bill Gates, Rupert Murdoch and Richard Branson all having the same amount of time as the rest of us do). Using your time to bring balance and harmony back into your life will reap great benefits for you and all those close to you.

Your energy will be needed on a number of levels. You need energy to make the changes necessary to bring balance back to your life. You need energy to break out of the 'comfort zone' (the safety of the familiar) that tends to hold us in the state of being overwhelmed, and you need energy to keep going once you have made these breaks. The more successful you become in business the more opportunities and distractions come your way. Each one of them can play a role in throwing balance out the window. Energy is a powerful weapon in the harmony arsenal.

And last but by no means least is cash. You will have to invest in yourself in order to get fit, to reward yourself, to learn new skills and to change the way you do business. The amount you need to spend will depend entirely on you. If you are a self-starter and can get and stay fit on your own you probably won't need a personal trainer, but if you are like me and need to have someone stalking you to get moving, you will have to allocate money to this.

I find it quite strange that we are so focused on having money when we retire yet we devote very little time or money to maintaining our health and wellbeing in the meantime to ensure we get there! From where I sit I don't want to ever retire, and I certainly don't plan to. But I do want to be healthy and full of energy until the day I die. Investing in my health and wellbeing today is far more important to me than my retirement fund. You may disagree, but as always it's up to the individual.

The moral of this tip is that to fuel the changes necessary to have a long, healthy and rewarding life in which business is a major component, it is very likely that you will have to be prepared to invest time, energy and money on a regular basis.

Visit your doctor, healer or naturopath

A big component in achieving balance between business and life is being healthy. Stress encourages poor health and most business owners are under a lot of stress.

I suggest that you visit your chosen medical adviser and have a thorough check-up. Use it as a baseline: where is your body at today?

Whether mainstream or alternative (and best start with the mainstream), they will probably get you to have a number of tests, prod and poke you a bit, and give you advice that you don't want to hear, but the information will help. Tell them that you are planning to make some significant changes in your life and this is one of the first stages. They may be able to recommend some professionals or organisations to help.

I donate blood once a month, and have done so for almost twenty years off and on. I do this for three reasons: first, I get to lie on a bed for an hour and have a little quiet time, followed by a cup of tea, a biscuit and a chat to one of the lovely old ladies who looks after the donors. Second, it makes me feel that I am doing something good for society. Last but not least, I get a free check-up once a month. Before taking my blood they give me a fairly comprehensive physical that covers blood pressure, weight and various other things. If there is anything wrong it gets picked up quickly and lets me keep track of key health indicators. Occasionally I get a letter from the blood bank saying my last donation showed an issue that needs to be followed up; a quick visit to my doctor and all is well.

When you start to lose control—stop, breathe and regain focus

Being overwhelmed and feeling out of control in your business is a terrible feeling. Sometimes you just don't know where to turn. There are hundreds of emails that need answering, a pile of telephone messages to return, correspondence to read, meetings to be had, deadlines of every kind, staff needing direction—and then you get the call saying there is a problem with your biggest customer, and it's a doozy.

If all this sounds like your normal kind of day—and it's only 9 a.m.—no wonder you are feeling a little out of control and in need of some balance and harmony in your life. I can relate completely. When you are in the midst of an overwhelming downer, it's easy to slide even lower. Taking a moment to rethink and regroup is the best thing you can possibly do.

A friend of mine who is a pilot said that this is one of the key training techniques used in flight school. When things are starting to go pear-shaped, simply take a moment to stop everything, take a big, deep breath and think logically about what you are doing. Sounds simple, doesn't it? But we rarely do it.

Another good friend of mine who has had the pleasure of watching me over the years going from periods of Zen monk calmness to sheer madness gave me a sticker that simply said 'JUST BREATHE'. And it is advice I will take to the grave (which thankfully is further away because I have figured out that to 'Just breathe' is far more powerful than it sounds).

Years ago I had problems with anxiety attacks. I was a commercial diver at the time so, as you can imagine, it's not good to experience a panic attack 50 metres below the surface. The psychologist I saw said a similar thing: 'You have to learn to breathe.' At the time I was not very impressed by these words of wisdom, thinking I had clearly just wasted hundreds of dollars seeing an eccentric hippie, but as the years went by and I did learn to breathe, I realised just how right she was.

When we are stressed and freaked out we breathe very shallowly. This makes us feel short of breath and even more stressed, which of course stresses us out even further. It's a nasty cycle.

If you can learn to stop, take a few very deep breaths and then do what you need to do, the results will be far better and your feelings of being out of control will be greatly reduced in intensity. It is simply a matter of reprogramming your normal response mechanism, which is to dive in and try to fix everything at once.

Do you remember when you used to laugh a lot?

Day-to-day pressure builds up over time. One of its most noticeable symptoms is that the amount of laughter in a person's life tends to drop proportionally as pressure and stress increase. Why we stop laughing is unclear, but the weight of the world on our shoulders is a heavy burden regardless of where we are in life. The pressures of day-to-day living are as relevant to the teenager facing high-school exams as they are to the head of a corporation with 100,000 employees.

We all look sympathetic when the 'pressure' of running a large corporation makes the CEO miserable, yet we say that teenagers are being melodramatic when impending exams make them lose their sense of humour. I have to reinforce the fact that all pressure is relevant and important to the person feeling it. There are no universal measures saying that the feelings one person experiences are more important or significant than any other person's.

One thing is certain, though: most of us remember times when we had less pressure and stress in our lives, fewer demands on our time, money and energy, and generally these were times when we were quick to laugh and quick to make others laugh. We rolled with the punches, we took setbacks in our stride and we didn't seem to take life quite so seriously. Well, you can have those times back again, and this chapter is intended to help you find them.

Take a moment to think back to that time in your life when you used to laugh the most. Close your eyes and spend a few minutes with this visualisation. Start to think about that time when you felt so carefree and happy. What year was it? What was happening in your life? Where were you living? Who were you spending time with? Where did you work? What were you wearing? What did you do on weekends? What music were you listening to? What were you reading? What kind of car did you drive? Where did you hang out? What smells remind you of that time?

Now open your eyes and spend a few moments jotting down the words that best describe your emotions and feelings when you think about that time. What was it that made your life feel so good? I am sure that even then there was a lot of pressure—money could have been an issue, relationships might have come and gone, a lack of certainty about the future might have figured highly, among other challenges. Even so, the feelings you remember most are joy and happiness and being carefree. So what is the difference between then and now?

Identifying this difference is a significant point. Try to find the one word that describes what has changed for you. Once you know this word, you know your enemy and you can finally do something about it.

As an example, let's say that the one word affecting you is 'pressure', meaning that you feel so much more pressure to perform, to deliver, to provide—whatever. Now you have a name for what has to change in your life. While it won't be that easy to remove the pressure, it is relatively easy to change the way you perceive it, react to it and think about it.

Doing this exercise on a regular basis, when you're feeling overwhelmed and anxious, will have a very positive effect. It will help you to change your life and the way you deal with the main issues preventing you from achieving balance.

Master the art of saying no

Being responsible for everyone and everything is exhausting. Business owners often assume responsibility way beyond the call of duty, and this can become extremely stressful. A comment that I hear frequently from business owners is that they are tired of being responsible for everything to do with the business.

At the end of the day, however, you *are* responsible for everything to do with your business, but it is up to you how you interpret this responsibility. In fact, you need to share the responsibility around and empower others to take some of it from your shoulders.

This can be a little tricky at first, especially for the business owner who has developed the habit of saying yes to everything. There are many ways to share the load, but the most powerful tool to ease the energy drain associated with responsibility overload is learning to say no. Let me show you how I did it.

I do a lot of public speaking and have a relatively high profile in my home city. The problem with this is that I am frequently asked to do free speaking jobs for charities and other organisations like universities and business groups, and usually by being put on the spot. In the past I didn't feel that I could say no. Then it felt like an extra commitment that really stressed me out and added to my already considerable workload.

I always used to kick myself after I'd agreed to one of these engagements, but I didn't know how to stop this from happening.

Now I have a system that works fantastically for me. Whenever someone asks me to speak to their organisation, whether they ask me face to face, over the phone or by email, I never commit to an engagement on the spot. I always say that I have to check my diary and other commitments first and that it might take me a day or two to get back to them.

This gives me a little breathing space to decide if it is something I can do and, more importantly, something I want to do. If the answer to either of these questions is no, I call the person back and tell them that I can't do the event.

I can't overstate how much pressure this has taken off me. I follow this system with virtually every request for my time in my business life. You can also develop similar habits and buffers that simply give you room to properly consider a request on your time.

Learning to say no will certainly have a major impact on the day-to-day responsibilities and demands that so often cause undue stress and prevent any form of balance in our lives. Master the art of saying no and your life will change.

If you need some extra help, I recommend reading *How to Say No Without Feeling Guilty* by Patti Breitman and Connie Hatch. This book will certainly help you to overcome the impulse to say yes. In addition, work out your own system that will work for you so that you can start to say no more often.

Don't be afraid to sack some customers

One of the main reasons I chose to have my own business is so that I can decide who I do business with (and who I don't). Some people are just too much hard work as customers. Sometimes the old saying, 'the customer is always right' is really wrong.

Chapter 5 looked at the idea that 'if you lie down with dogs you get up with fleas' and how having the wrong kind of customers can be just as toxic as having the wrong kind of friends. The key here as far as getting some balance back into your life is to say *adios* to those customers who are more trouble than they are worth.

Over the years that I've been consulting I have learned to be a good judge of character. When meeting potential clients for the first time I look at it as an interview—for them and for me. I listen to my gut instinct about the client. Are we on the same wavelength? Are they clear on what they want? Do I think we can work together? If I can't answer yes to these questions, then I prefer to be upfront and honest rather than try to make it work, so I suggest that they go elsewhere. This saves me a lot of time, energy and heartache in the long run.

Likewise there are times when a relationship with a client changes and no longer works. If they keep haggling over price, become unreasonably demanding or don't communicate effectively, it is time to move on. I have 'sacked' clients on a number of occasions. It was very satisfying and gave me a healthy sense of self-respect.

My marketing company used to have the advertising account for a large shopping centre. It was the account that everyone in town wanted. It was lots of work and carried enough prestige to make me feel good about it. But the client was extremely demanding, needing everything in very short and generally unrealistic timeframes. They constantly bartered with us to get the work done cheaper and often they were very slow to pay.

So I did a review of the account and came up with some interesting realisations:

- We didn't actually make any profit out of the account.
- It stressed out everyone in the office.
- We couldn't take on more profitable work because all of our resources were tied up with this one account.
- We had no long-term security, as the client would not sign a contract.

Having done that review, I made the decision to resign the account. It was one of the smartest business moves I have ever made. I replaced this account with four new clients, generating four times the revenue for the same energy input. Don't get me wrong—to resign this account I was saying goodbye to over 70 per cent of the business's monthly income. But it was profitless volume, with little or no satisfaction, and ultimately I risked losing my best staff out of frustration with managing the account.

Some customers aren't worth having. If they cost you more in energy, time and satisfaction than they bring in, say goodbye—in the nicest possible way, of course.

The torture of perfection

Being a perfectionist is hard work, and often those of us afflicted with this trait struggle when working with people who don't meet our expectations. I am certainly a perfectionist in many aspects of my work. I have tried to change but it just won't stick. However, it can be very draining (and unrealistic!) to try to make everything 100 per cent right all of the time.

Many small business owners are perfectionists. However, we must learn to compromise in some way, otherwise we'll drive ourselves—and those around us—insane.

As much as I struggle with the idea, sometimes near enough is good enough. It is simply too challenging to make every single aspect of a business perfect, especially when there are other people involved and their perception of what is acceptable is in all likelihood completely different from yours.

So how do we perfectionists overcome this issue? The following tips have worked for me:

- I always communicate very clearly what I expect in terms of the products and services that we deliver.
- I mentally prioritise what is really important and what is not, and I focus my perfectionist tendencies on the really important stuff.
- I have learned to accept that while other people may do things differently, it doesn't mean they are wrong.

- I closely monitor customer feedback regarding quality control. This will tell me if things are slipping.
- Sometimes I just walk away—let the individuals do what they do and don't get involved.

It is great to be good at what you do. It is even better to be really committed to producing the very best quality products and services you can. But at some stage, you have to learn to let go and accept that perfection is nice, but excellence is okay.

Do the work you love—give the rest to others

One of the most draining aspects of running a business can be doing the jobs you hate. We all have these dreaded tasks. Some may relate to the type of work you do, while others may be day-to-day tasks required to run the business.

I loathe bookwork, always have, always will. I have no desire to get all touchy-feely with it and overcome my arch nemesis. Instead, I outsource it with very clear instructions on what I want and when I want it. I can't describe the relief I felt when I first outsourced my bookkeeping. Sure, there have been a few hiccups over the years, but far fewer than if I were doing it.

I believe that, as a business owner, you need to be able to do a bit of the picking and choosing in your life, even if the business is just you. Outsource what you don't like (and probably don't do very well anyway).

Often your role in the business changes as the business grows. You may have started out doing what you love, but now find yourself stuck in the office looking at spreadsheets instead of being on the floor and doing the work or dealing with the customers directly.

You may need to rethink the way you run your business to get back to doing the things you really enjoy and are good at. In order to get energised I need to work on challenging projects. For me, being pushed and challenged is really important for job satisfaction. Luckily I can pick and choose my projects, or sometimes they pick me.

I think more small business owners should give away the day-to-day tasks that drive them crazy, and instead spend their time making money and doing what they love. Now, how energising does that sound?

Enlist outside help—why not use a personal trainer?

So you've adjusted your priorities and decided to take baby steps towards a healthier, more energetic you. I did this, but I needed one more weapon to ensure that I really got moving—a personal trainer. In this age of outsourcing, why not enlist the sheer energy, enthusiasm and motivation a good personal trainer can offer to assist you in your own balance battle?

I am a firm believer in personal trainers, having experienced exceptional results firsthand. But not all personal trainers are the same and finding the right one for you might take a few attempts. A few years back I did one session with a male personal trainer who spent 40 minutes telling me how fat and unfit I was, all the while trying to chat up the girl on the machine next to us. I was humiliated and really angry.

I'm surprised that I ever went near a gym or a personal trainer again. But luckily I did and now have two trainers (one just wasn't enough), and we have been working together for almost four years. The experience of working with my trainers, Sam and Kelly, was completely different to my earlier experience with the jerk.

First they sat me down and gave me a complete and thorough evaluation. They really got to know me and what I wanted to achieve. They asked about my lifestyle, my business and the demands on my time, what type of exercise I liked and what I didn't like, how I ate, when I ate, my emotional state, my motivational buttons, and so on. Then we set about working together on fixing what they considered were my main issues. The first issue was when I was eating—no more mornings fuelled only by coffee! They insisted I must eat a healthy breakfast every day. I started doing gentle yoga and light gym work with weights, working up to more active cardiovascular work.

I couldn't imagine life without them. Forget any stereotypical images you may have of a drill sergeant yelling and screaming at some poor sod (in this instance, you) to do another 30 push-ups. A good personal trainer will motivate you, encourage you, challenge you, make allowances for when you feel down, and share your passion to reach your goals.

Every few months I sit down with my trainers and we review where I am at and how I am feeling. It really is all about me. There are times when I am on the road for weeks at a time and they ring to check that I am okay and getting in some exercise. They have taught me to only ever stay in hotels that have well-equipped gyms, how to do yoga in confined spaces such as hotel rooms or on a plane, how to eat out and not blow the diet, and so much more.

While I train we laugh, we joke, we share good times and sad times. Along the way we have become very close friends. They have seen me at my lowest point physically, and they have been there for some of my greatest tribulations. They have also shared in my sense of accomplishment at each milestone, and I acknowledge that without them I wouldn't have achieved what I have.

If you need a little help to get your mind, body and soul on track, a personal trainer who is a real professional, to whom you can relate and who communicates well with you, is an amazing asset. Take the time to find the right one (or two) for you.

Make movement a part of your life

In an age when so much effort goes into making us do less physically, no wonder we find it hard to get moving. We spend hours sitting in front of large television screens and home theatres, surfing the net and playing electronic games, as well as long hours at work, often with little or no physical movement involved. Yet our bodies are made for movement, not to sit still.

Back when humans lived in caves, the only time they weren't moving was when they were asleep. The rest of the time there would be this little thing called the battle for survival to keep them on their toes.

I have spoken about change, about treating your body with respect and the benefits of a healthier lifestyle. Making movement—even the smallest and simplest of movements—a part of your life will really help.

Every day, think about what you are doing to see if there is a way that you could increase your level of activity. For most of us the obvious place to start is with our cars. Perhaps you tend to get a little lazy and drive to the shop, even though it's only a ten-minute walk away. Maybe you tell yourself that you don't have the time to walk. Why not? Let's make more time and slow things down a little, just to get you moving again.

Using the stairs instead of a lift or escalator is another really easy way to move and it only takes a bit of extra effort for a short amount of time. Arrange to meet a friend to go for a walk instead of a meal. It is surprising how many people are more than happy to do this.

There are many ways to get more active. A little effort here and a little there will make a bigger difference than you realise. Most of the difference occurs in your head when you change the habit of thoughtlessly reaching for the car keys. Once you begin to get more movement in your life your body will start to respond and like it a lot. From there the level of movement can be increased. The more you move, the more relaxed you will feel and the closer you will be to finding balance in your life.

Guilt-free pampering

Pampering means different things to everyone, but at its simplest it's something that makes us feel good. That alone is good reason to be pampered every once in a while.

First of all, figure out how you like to be pampered. For example, is a day in a health spa your ideal pampering experience? Being worked on from head to toe, rubbed, scrubbed and oiled up, every muscle massaged and washed off? If it is, why not do it regularly?

You'll probably come up with excuses straightaway as to why you shouldn't. Your first thought is probably that you can't afford to do it all the time. Fair enough, it is not a cheap exercise, but is it really *that* expensive? How much are your own wellbeing, sense of calm and overall sanity worth? We need to see pampering ourselves as a form of investment and, in my opinion, one that has exceptional returns.

Your second argument is probably that you don't have the time—don't you think that's all the more reason to make time? Generally there is never enough time, or a good time to do the things we need to help us feel more peaceful and calm. Our own needs end up on the bottom of the very long to-do list, and this needs to change.

Finally, you will likely say that you feel guilty spending a day away from the business getting pampered. Now that is a shocking excuse. If your business can't survive for a day without you being there, then you haven't got a business—you've got a jail sentence.

If taking a whole day off is too much to contemplate, try breaking it into baby steps and organise to come in late one morning. Spend that time before work doing something that really nurtures you and makes you feel wonderful. For example, I often get up early and go for a drive to a beautiful creek about 40 minutes from my place. I go for a swim, sit and watch the birds and the rainforest wake up, then head home for a shower and to get ready for work. On days when I do this I generally get to work about 10 a.m., but I feel incredible.

Overcome the guilt of pampering yourself by breaking it into stages that you are comfortable with. Then figure out how you really like to be pampered. Be selfish, be honest, be decadent—it doesn't matter. It is all about you. Take a few hours off in the middle of the day to see a movie, have a golf day once every few weeks, do a course in something not related to your work, donate some time at the local animal shelter, go to the gym—whatever does it for you.

Be prepared to pamper yourself often. You deserve it.

Respect yourself enough to take the time to look your best

I am a big believer in the importance of personal grooming and appearance. Investing time, money and energy in how you look shows a sense of self-respect.

Often, as people get really overworked, exhausted and run-down, personal grooming and appearances start to slide. Men stop shaving as often, they wear creased shirts and scuffed, dirty shoes. The same lowering of standards applies to women, but I am not a brave enough man to go into specifics! We all simply run out of energy and something has to give.

Many years ago I did a series of courses to become a scuba-diving instructor. I was fortunate enough to have a great mentor at the time, a huge man by the name of Bob Baldwin. I remember him looking me in the eye and saying, 'If you want people to respect you, dress like you respect yourself.' I have found this to be very true. If you take the time to dress well and groom yourself, people are more likely to extend you courtesy and respect. They also listen to what you have to say—which is why police and military personnel have to comply with such exacting standards in terms of uniform and personal grooming.

As part of your battle to regain control of your life, can you spare some time to ensure you look the part? Is your suit old, out of date and moth-eaten? Is it time to let the comb-over go and be proudly bald? If you aren't sure, find some friends who you can trust to be really, really honest and ask for their opinion. We all need a bit of a makeover from time to time. This rule can be extended to other parts of your life and business as well. Is your car dusty all the time? Is your office in need of a good spring clean?

This tip is simple—give yourself enough time to spend on grooming and appearance. The better you look, the better you will feel, and the more in control and confident you will be. If it means new clothes, so be it. If it means a new hairdo, go for it. Invest in yourself; there's never a good time or enough money, so today is as good a day as any.

Develop your own style of meditation

Meditation is one of those things that some people think is really 'out there'; others have tried it and haven't really been able to do it properly; some think it is a bunch of baloney; and others swear by it as an amazingly recuperative practice. I have held each of those views at different stages in my life.

Today I think meditation is an exceptional tool for helping to calm a full, or in many cases overfull, brain. It is a way of slowing down, gaining focus, putting issues into perspective and restoring and revitalising.

So what is meditation? The dictionary defines it as 'quiet contemplation', and that is really what it is all about. It is a process of slowing down the mind, getting all of the distractions and racing thoughts out, and simply focusing on one main thought, idea or problem.

We very rarely get to contemplate one thing at a time in today's frantic world. As discussed throughout this book, stress is the result of huge demands on individuals, the never-ending push and pull of daily life. Meditation is a mini vacation away from this.

So how do you meditate? A good question and a tough one to answer. Like virtually every activity related to wellbeing, there are vastly different definitions and descriptions. For me, meditation involves simply finding a quiet place, making yourself comfortable, then taking deep breaths in and out, thinking about one thing and one thing only. It is hard to do and the mind wants to race all over the place like crazy. The battle is to keep it focused; it will take time to learn and develop this skill. You might do it for just five minutes to get started. You might fall asleep. I call this a 'mini meditation'. I am sure there are die-hard meditation Nazis who would be aghast at this description, but really, even the simplest of meditations has to be better than nothing.

There are also many places where you can go and learn to meditate with a group. I have tried a number—some good, some not. What beginners need are lessons; someone talking you through the process really does help. To sit in a group, chanting and 'ohmming' for an hour while sitting with your legs crossed is very hard for a beginner.

Meditate to suit you. If you like it and you want to learn more, you will certainly find places and organisations to assist you. If you are content to do your own 'mini meditations' they will definitely help, and you will grow to really enjoy these times of quiet contemplation and reflection.

Keep a diary of what you eat and when

We are often unconscious of the relationship between stress and food. Some people stop eating when they are stressed; others eat more when they are under the hammer. As a general rule, and from my own experience, when people's lives get out of balance, so do their eating habits. They start to eat poorly, favouring junk food and quick energy fixes or 'pick-me-ups' instead of more wholesome and nutritious fare.

I know because I lived like this for many years. It is a vicious cycle as the worse you eat, the worse you tend to feel and the more you crave the foods that are not good for you. The human brain does a great job of softening this blow for us by justifying what we eat, and we simply go into the world of denial.

A few years back I was wondering why I couldn't lose weight. On the suggestion of a good friend I started a food diary to see exactly what I was eating and drinking every day. I soon noticed that I was drinking quite a lot of tea and coffee, about ten cups a day. In each cup I would have two teaspoons of sugar—that adds up to 140 teaspoons of sugar a week, which is about the same as drinking four litres of soft drink. Now that was a scary realisation, enough to make me cut back my coffee and tea intake dramatically.

Try this exercise yourself. Write down everything that goes into your mouth—the good, the bad and the ugly. Be honest; after all, no one needs to look at your diary except you. In addition to this, you might find it helpful to also write down what was going on during the day. This may provide some insights into when you eat, what you eat and why.

On particularly stressful days do you tend to go for chocolate? Or do you stop eating altogether? Do you drink more coffee on a Monday morning to get you going for the week? Try to find a relationship between your stress levels and the types of food you eat when you are stressed.

Once you know your eating habits it becomes much easier to start changing them. But until then most observations are only 'guesstimates', often with a conveniently distorted view.

Alcohol, coffee, nicotine, sugar . . . what's your drug of choice?

If you're anything like me, when you are run-down, under pressure or out of control you reach for your own particular poison, or combination of poisons. For most people these are alcohol, caffeine, nicotine and sugar. Personally I have used all four with dazzling effect at various stages in my life.

It's easy to justify that takeaway coffee to get the brain going, a few drinks after work to relax, a sugar fix for that afternoon energy boost or a quiet cigarette break to get out of the office. But the more stressed and overwhelmed you get, the more you rely on these chemicals to get you through your day.

I'm not going to demand you go cold turkey—after all, that is up to you—but I do suggest that you get to know your 'poison'. Mine is coffee—I used to drink about twenty cups a day (and sleep like a baby). That was a long time ago, at a stage in my life when I was utterly overwhelmed by my business. I didn't realise what a crutch coffee had become; also, for some reason it liked to hang out with its brothers, alcohol, nicotine and sugar, so before long I was using them all just to get through the day. Coffee and nicotine in the morning, sugar in the afternoon and alcohol at night—and I was only eighteen at the time.

Today my only vice is coffee, but I now limit myself to three cups per day (to some people that would still be a lot). It is a battle and I have to be vigilant, because the more stressed and under pressure I am the more I crave caffeine and the rest. I also know how terrible I feel if I relapse and dose up on coffee and sugar. My brain goes all foggy, I get nervy and jittery and I usually get a headache. Just the way you want to feel when a hundred people are clamouring for your attention.

I have a number of friends who drink a bottle of wine every night, 'to help them relax'. When does it become a crutch or an addiction? It is a thin line, one that I know many of us have walked along. Be honest with yourself and be clear on the benefits of being healthier; the lifestyle changes will soon follow.

What exactly does eating well mean?

Today, most of us think we have a pretty good idea about which foods are good for us and which aren't. There are literally thousands of books and websites on this topic; however, much of the information is conflicting, which certainly makes deciding what is good for you more than a little confusing.

To illustrate this point, at certain times in my life I have been advised, either by teachers, doctors or through the media, to avoid the following: eggs, potatoes, red meat, oils, dairy products, nuts, bread, breakfast cereal, tea and red wine. At other times I have been advised to make sure I eat the following: eggs, potatoes, red meat, oils, dairy products, nuts, bread, breakfast cereal, tea and red wine.

When it comes to food, I think people have to make up their own mind which 'food philosophy' they are going to follow. I came up with my own food philosophy simply because I got sick and tired of all the conflicting information.

My food philosophy is:

- Try to eat organic food wherever possible.
- Shop around the 'outside' of the grocery store (i.e. in the fruit and vegetable section, meat, grain and fresh food sections) away from the processed foods.
- Avoid processed foods as much as possible.
- Avoid sugar (especially hidden sugars).
- Read the labels.
- Everything in moderation.

There is a powerful link between eating well and performing well. If your body is functioning as it should, you will be better able to deal with stress and the pressures of running a business and having a life. To some people this tip will seem so blatantly obvious as to be absurd. Yet unfortunately, for many people, health falls low on the totem pole in a world full of pressure and demands.

I have a good friend, Paul Hockey, who is a one-armed mountain climber. He recently became the first disabled person to climb the face of Mount Everest, and I asked him what he ate when it came to training for major climbs. His advice was simple—eat lots of fresh fruit, vegetables and meat, and avoid processed foods and chemicals.

There are so many sources of information when it comes to deciding what to put into your body. The best tool you can use to decide what is good for you is education. Learn about the different foods, but read widely and don't just accept the first thing you read in a book or on the internet. Check the source—is it credible and knowledgeable? Talk to other people who are healthy and informed. Ask your doctor and other health professionals for their opinions. But most importantly, collect as much information as you can and make informed decisions on your own health and wellbeing.

One of the best ways to restore balance and harmony to your life is to eat well and have a healthy, well-fuelled body.

Learn to enjoy food again

One of the biggest challenges I face in relation to food is finding the time to eat it. This sounds silly, but in the heat of the work day, with phones ringing, meeting after meeting and people lining up outside my door with various issues to be dealt with, it really is easy to simply bypass eating until later in the day.

That is exactly what I did for many years. I would eat very little during the day, and then I would go home and gulp down a huge, rich meal at around 8 p.m., convincing myself that it was okay because I hadn't eaten much during the day. The rest of the day I lived on coffee and sugary treats to keep my energy up.

Now I know how unhealthy that was and what a strain it was on my body. During a six-year period of eating like this I put on about 40 kilograms.

Through a very necessary and heartfelt desire to lose weight I started to learn more about healthy eating and realised that I was doing it all wrong. The three main areas where I was getting it wrong were:

1. I never ate breakfast.
2. I ate big meals at night.
3. I ate really fast.

All of the above made me realise that for me eating was a chore, not a joy. I didn't see meals as an opportunity for social interaction or to stop and take a breath; rather, eating was something I was doing just to stay alive.

So I had to reassess the way I ate and retrain myself. Yes, I started eating breakfast, but the biggest thing I did was to start to enjoy eating again, to look forward to it and to take the time to savour it rather than gulp it down.

Today, eating is a joy rather than a chore. I eat out for lunch just about every day, and I look at this as an opportunity to eat a good meal and spend time with friends, clients or work colleagues. It is a break in the day, it is fun and I eat in restaurants where I know I can get a healthy meal.

However, in really busy times I find myself sliding back into the old habit of missing meals, and I have to stop and read myself the riot act. No matter how busy my day is, I know that I need to take a break and enjoy the food in front of me. Then I can get back into it with all the more energy and enthusiasm for having had a good meal.

If this tip strikes a chord with you, don't worry, you are not alone. It surprises me how many business owners put themselves last in all that they do. They pay themselves last, they feed themselves last, they leave the office last. It is time to start putting yourself first!

Water water everywhere

When we get stressed, overtired and overwhelmed we often turn to stimulants to get us through. Unfortunately this can become habit-forming, and it is easy to develop a dependence on things like sugar and caffeine for that little 'pick-me-up' during the day.

What you really need, though, is more water in your system. Drinking water is calming and relaxing. Some experts suggest that we should drink up to two litres of water every day. The most important consideration is having plenty of water available so that it is easier to grab a glass of water than a sugary or caffeine-rich alternative.

Today I have two water coolers in my business (for about ten people), and I am thinking about getting another one in my own office. Having access to high-quality filtered water should, in my opinion, be a basic requirement in every workplace.

When water is readily available there's a greater likelihood you'll drink more of it. Here are some ways to incorporate more water into your life:

- Start your day with two glasses of water, ideally with a couple of squirts of fresh lemon juice. This is a great way to start the day and cleanse your system.
- Get into the habit of always ordering water with your meal, your coffee or your alcoholic drink.
- Keep a jug of water on your desk. Fill it up every morning with fresh water and aim to drink around two litres a day.
- Carry a bottle of water with you wherever you go. This becomes habit-forming after a while. Keep some bottles ready to go in the refrigerator so that you can grab them and run.

The more water you drink the better. A water cooler is a cheap item and one that every business should invest in.

Eating out doesn't need to be unhealthy

Eating out can cause the best laid plans to come undone. This can be a real problem for people who have to entertain clients a lot. Many of us eat out more often now than ever before, and I recommend it as a great way to reduce stress and get you out of your workplace to clear your head. So we could all use a few ideas to make the experience a healthier one.

Try the following tips—they work for me:

- Some restaurants are simply better than others when it comes to healthy food choices. Try to select a restaurant that you know has healthy options. Be open with the people you are dining with and let them know why you want to eat in a particular restaurant.
- Think about the type of food you want to eat before you get to the restaurant. Visualise it and set your mind on it rather than arriving there not really knowing what you want.
- Take your time reading the menu. Don't just pick something because it's easy and you're feeling pressured.
- Avoid menu items that have rich or creamy sauces, or are deep-fried.
- Don't be afraid to ask questions about the menu; there are always alternatives. For example, ask for salad dressing on the side or steamed vegetables instead of chips.
- Ask the waiting staff for healthy recommendations. Get to know the staff at the restaurants where you go regularly. They are more likely to go the extra mile if you remember their names and are polite and friendly. Tell them that you are on a health kick and ask for their help. You will be surprised at how supportive they will be.
- Most restaurants are happy to make you a healthy meal if you ask them. If you are worried about ordering something that is healthy but might take a long time to prepare, ask the staff to rush the order through.
- Avoid incidentals such as soft drinks, alcohol, desserts, breads and rich foods. Take these five things off the menu and you can dine out just about anywhere and still leave feeling healthy.

Encourage healthy eating in your workplace

In an attempt to do a good deed I once let a local charity put a chocolate box in my reception. I am sure you know the ones: you pay a couple of dollars and in return you get a handful of chocolates. A nice concept until everyone in the office starts putting on weight, getting pimples and falling prey to mood swings.

I had to ask the charity to remove the box; I would gladly give them a weekly donation if I could do it without getting the sugar in return. This exercise made me realise the duty of care we have as small business owners when it comes to encouraging healthy eating habits in our workplace. Of course, you can't dictate what people eat, but you can ensure healthy options are available.

A few years ago I tried to put this into practice by purchasing a box of organic fruit once a week for everyone in the office. Unfortunately, after about two months I stopped doing this because most of the time I threw the fruit away, which was a real waste. Having said that, I think we have all become much more health conscious recently and it is probably a good time to try this exercise again.

There are lots of ways to encourage healthy eating in your workplace. A really good one that I have seen work in a number of businesses is a healthy-eating noticeboard, with takeaway menus and phone numbers of healthy options located close by the business. Members of staff who have an interest in healthy eating update the board and ensure that the information is current and accurate.

In the office, providing caffeine alternatives and low-fat milk all help to encourage healthy lifestyles. If there are only sugary and caffeinated options around, that's what people will drink. As mentioned previously, ensuring that there is an abundance of filtered water available provides an easy, healthy alternative to soft drinks.

Encouraging without dictating is key here. I recently visited one business where coffee wasn't 'allowed' on the premises, and neither were soft drinks, chocolate or any other junk foods. I don't think that being a dictator on what people can and can't eat is the right way to go about it.

It is just like the old adage: you can lead a horse to water but you can't make it drink. If someone told me what I could or couldn't eat or drink at work, I would tell them a thing or two in return.

So let people make their own decisions about what they want to eat or drink. The best way to encourage healthy eating is to lead by example. From my experience, the more healthy the boss is the more healthy the rest of the staff tend to be.

While it is really important to be aware of what you are eating, it is also very important to think about when and where you eat. Whenever I go into a workplace where everyone is eating at their desk as they work, gulping down whatever they can get their hands on, I get a real sense of things being out of balance.

As business owners we should provide a calm, clean and relaxed environment where people can eat, and we should ensure that staff take the time to stop and enjoy their meal. If you are trying to be more balanced, focused and peaceful, yet everyone around you is freaking out because they are overworked, tired and unhealthy, you are fighting a big battle and one that I don't think you can win.

To be cool, calm and collected you need all those around you to be the same. Be proactive and create a healthy work environment; you will be amazed at what a difference this will make. As a delightful by-product, your business will also run more smoothly and be more successful.

When it comes to food, always be prepared

One of my excuses for not eating well was that I never had any healthy food in the cupboard. I dreaded going to the supermarket and dealing with the crowds, the hassle and the decisions that had to be made (pathetic really, I know). Once again, with the help of my long-suffering personal trainers, I retrained my underdeveloped shopping skills and turned what was once a chore into something I now really enjoy.

They helped me to realise that if I didn't have food at home, I was likely to buy takeaways on the way home, and that generally this would be something hot and fast and not that healthy. So I learned to plan ahead and drop in to the supermarket most days on the way home from work. In addition, I started to visit the local fresh produce market, where all of the really good foods can be found—the freshest of fruits and vegetables, the best cuts of meat, seafood straight from the ocean, and so on. After a short time, both of these activities actually became quite enjoyable. I got to know the store owners and stallholders and other customers, and slowly but surely my shopping trips became social outings and a nice way to while away an hour or two on a Saturday morning.

Changing my shopping patterns has meant that I now usually have a good range of fresh fruit and vegetables in my apartment. This forms a solid basis to make plenty of healthy meals and to avoid snacking on junk.

I learned that the key for me was planning ahead, something I am sure that many of you would simply take for granted. Now, in the morning I think about what my day has in store—if I know I am going out for lunch I will plan to have a light meal in the evening, and make a mental note of what I have available and what I need to buy.

To make it even easier to plan healthy meals I started a recipe book that I keep in the car. Now I can flick through my favourite meals and decide what to buy before I head into the supermarket. I go in with a mission and I can be in and out as fast or as slow as I like. Beats standing in the aisles, ravenous but without a clue what to buy.

I know that the few minutes I spend each day actually planning what to eat and when has really helped me to be more aware of what I put into my mouth, in turn making me a much healthier and more relaxed person. Sure, I don't get it right all the time and I have a few more kilograms to budge, but every year I feel healthier than the year before, and that means I am winning the battle.

18

How is your corporate karma account balance?

So what is the Karma Bank? Well, I think it is the collective sense of goodwill that the broader community has towards a business. Do they feel that it is a 'good business', one that plays a proactive role in the community? Is it a business that is committed to doing the right thing—environmentally, socially, financially? Is the business honest? Are the people running the business trustworthy? Is the business concerned with the long-term good of all, or the short-term benefit of a few?

The Karma Bank certainly influences the media. Those companies with big Karma Bank accounts—let's pick Virgin as an example—can in many ways do no wrong. They are the 'sweethearts' of the corporate world and it is reflected in the media. They don't receive this status randomly—it is their actions over many years that build their Karma Bank balance. They can get away with making a blunder or two as long as their balance stays in the black, so they generally get through challenges in much better shape than other companies (and with the cheeky grin of Sir Richard Branson not far from a camera).

So how do you build your Karma Bank balance? There is no one single activity that will build your karma balance but rather an all-inclusive attitude or culture. Your organisation needs to be 100 per cent committed to the community or communities where it operates. This means being genuinely and actively involved in supporting the people, the businesses and the environment. The key word here is 'genuine'.

Second, the business needs to have a strong and clear leader who is vocal and who personally lives the culture of making a difference. A good leader steps up when the company makes a mistake and apologises sincerely and quickly. They don't get caught up in whose fault it is, they focus on fixing the problem as the main priority.

Third, the culture of making a positive difference is encouraged throughout the company. The staff get involved, buying decisions revolve around making a difference or supporting others as opposed to saving a few cents and, as the business grows, there is a constant and never-ending desire to find more ways to make a difference.

Last but by no means least, the business needs to be very good at communicating, and I am not talking about putting 'spin' on things but genuine communication with all people who have some form of interaction with the business. This means sharing their challenges as much as their victories, being open about their values and vision for the future, and making clear where they stand in the community and how they intend to make a difference.

The concept of the Karma Bank is equally applicable for small businesses as it is for large corporations. All businesses need to be aware that they have a Karma Bank account open, and that the balance of their account is entirely up to them. When everything is going well you can get away with a negative balance, but when things get tough or your business faces some challenges, a negative balance is enough to close the doors when the business does not get the support of the greater community.

One of the biggest struggles that many business owners seem to have is the awkwardness of telling others, specifically their customers, about their corporate citizenship. As always, I go back to what the 'big boys' are doing. Every publicly listed entity in the Western world has a space on their website explaining what they are doing to make the world a better place for all involved. Many will promote their philanthropy in the media with television commercials explaining the programs they run and the not-for-profit organisations they support. Small business should do the same—maybe not at quite the same scale, but still communicating the message.

The time to be coy about your company's community involvement is long gone. In fact, if you don't promote the fact that your business makes a difference you will lose customers. Given the choice between supporting a business that makes a difference and one that doesn't, the vast majority of customers will always choose the more responsible business, even if they are a little more expensive.

Clearly we need to let our customers know what we are doing. This can be done via a website, certificates displayed on the wall in the office, a newsletter, by adding our logo to a not-for-profit's promotional material, in the local media, on company vehicles and just about anywhere else where we can communicate the fact that we care and we are trying to make a difference.

My advice is simple: take the right actions to keep topping up that karma account. Make it a daily activity and be genuine and sincere about it—it may just save your business one day. Remember the wise words of Henry Ford: 'A business that makes nothing but money is a poor business.'

Here are some more specific 'how-to' tips that can help you to become an exceptional corporate citizen. They could best be summarised as 'step up, play a role, make a difference'.

- Look for opportunities outside of the normal
- Stand up and be counted
- Share your knowledge and experience with others
- Encourage your staff to be good corporate citizens
- Some things can't be measured in dollars and cents
- Invest in the future of your industry
- Offer praise wherever possible to other members of the community
- Hatch a plan to make you the ultimate corporate citizen

Look for opportunities outside of the normal

Trying to decide how to get involved in your community can be quite challenging as there are so many opportunities; however, there are always some opportunities that are a little less obvious but equally worthy.

A while back I used to work for a bus company operating specialised tours. One day I read in the paper that the local blood bank was having trouble getting office workers to donate blood. A little research showed that the main cause was the time it took for the workers to leave the office, have some lunch, get to the blood bank, donate and then get back to work. It just took too long. So we offered to put on a special bus service where the workers could eat their lunch on the way to the blood bank. We guaranteed to have them back at work within an hour and in a short amount of time we had built up a regular following of donors. The bus service was free and the blood bank had a noticeable increase in donations when the service was running.

Look for problems in the community and see if you can offer a solution. It may not be as big and bold as some community-based projects, but to the people involved it is equally as important. Plus it is a rewarding experience to be able to solve a problem yourself. Read the newspapers, listen to the news and look for problems where your business could help provide a solution.

Stand up and be counted

When you get caught up in your own business, it is easy to start to break your life into two very distinct halves: the business half and the non-business half. The business half can easily become the biggest part—after all, you have a lot riding on it and you are enthused and passionate about what you do. While this is happening, you need to keep playing a role in the other areas of your life.

Business owners are generally respected in the community. People understand they give a lot back to the community, they provide jobs and they make the economy go round. For this reason their opinions are valued. This makes it very important for business owners to play an active role in the running of their community.

When there are important issues being debated in your community, have your say. Voice your opinion and don't be afraid to be a little controversial. It is easy to say nothing in case you offend a customer who has a different opinion, but it is more important to stand up for injustice or the things within your community worth fighting for.

When you have your own business, don't stop being a part of the community where you live. Write a letter, voice an opinion, call the local radio station—whatever it takes, just play a role.

Have you become an observer of your community or do you play an active role? If it's been a while since you were able to get passionate about things you disagree with in your community, maybe today is the day to redirect some of your business passion back into the place you call home.

Share your knowledge and experience with others

Helping other businesses to grow and succeed is a worthy community activity. You can offer to share your experiences at a business gathering or even a presentation at a school. It is surprising how many of these organisations struggle to find interesting people to share their knowledge.

Take on a work experience student in your office. Give them the opportunity to see if they like the industry you are in. Think back to when you did something similar and how it benefited you. But don't wait for the schools to contact you—give them a call yourself and let them know you are interested in taking on work experience students.

Coach a sporting team. There are never enough parents to get behind local sporting organisations. Introduce what you have learned about leadership and team spirit to a group of kids wanting to play sport.

Run a free seminar on something you know about—maybe running your own business. If you have managed to survive for a while you are suitably qualified to share your views with others.

Whatever grabs you, being prepared to share your knowledge and experience is a good way to become a better corporate citizen.

Make up a list of ways you can share your knowledge and experience with other people in your local community. Then get on the telephone and turn the list into reality.

Encourage your staff to be good corporate citizens

If you are prepared to be a good corporate citizen, your staff will be more likely to want to get involved as well. Make it easy for them to do this and encourage them to participate. Some people may not want to get involved and that is fine. They should not feel like their job is at risk if they don't.

What you are trying to do is to provide the right environment for your staff to feel they would *like* to get involved. This may mean making a few allowances for them giving up their time, it may even mean some financial support; for example, if a group of your staff want to enter a fun run, offer to sponsor them.

Community involvement is a great team-building exercise and it is rewarding in a lot of ways—not the least of which is the realisation that as an individual you can really make a difference. Provide the right working environment and most workplaces will automatically produce some community-minded individuals who will drive the process from within. Encourage and support them as much as you feel able and recognise their efforts.

Are there ways you could be more encouraging of your staff to help them become better corporate citizens? Why not get your team in and ask them? If you already have a proactive team who are heavily involved in the community, can you acknowledge their efforts more?

Some things can't be measured in dollars and cents

In every marketing plan I write I always make a point of encouraging the business to become more involved in their community. I outline the importance of being a good corporate citizen and the fact that consumers these days want to deal with businesses actively involved in their community.

Some business owners just don't get it. They ask questions like 'How much free publicity will I get?' or 'How many new customers will it get me?' or 'How much will this add to my bottom line?' Some things simply can't be measured in dollars and cents, and community involvement is certainly one of those things.

I can't tell you how much more money it will make you, but I can tell you there are a lot of consumers out there making conscious decisions about where they will spend their money. Given the choice between spending it on a business that plays an active role in the community and one that doesn't, what choice do you think they will make?

Apart from that concept alone, what about doing the right thing and having integrity? You need to think much deeper than just returns on investment. Even the largest organisations in the world have realised this and they are going to great lengths to show the world both corporate compassion and corporate responsibility.

This is why I have no problem with businesses that promote themselves as being actively involved in their community; in fact, I recommend they do. If it means the community wins, that is all that matters. We are all charged with the responsibility of making the world a better place.

If you find yourself asking questions about returns on investment when it comes to helping to build a better community, you need to develop a measuring system other than money. Call it karma or whatever you like and accept this is as relevant a currency as money, and in many ways it is a much better one.

Invest in the future of your industry

Investing your time, energy and even possibly some money into the future of your industry is another part of being a good corporate citizen. Clearly it is different to helping a charity or another community-based organisation but it is just as important.

One example I can talk about is a relationship I have with my local university. They have a good business faculty with a strong bent towards marketing. I regularly give guest lectures, appraise projects or assignments and invite students to work in my office to get experience. I gladly give my time as I believe very strongly in putting back into my industry and also providing assistance to the next generation coming through.

Too many people have a 'what's in it for me?' approach to business. Truly successful people are always prepared to give of themselves as they understand the big picture.

Look for ways you can support the future of your own industry. Ask other people in your industry what they do and how you can help or get involved.

Offer praise wherever possible to other members of the community

I recently helped plan a large outdoor concert where all of the funds raised went to the organisation Lifeline. Lifeline does an amazing job in the community, mainly through its 24-hour telephone crisis line for people who need someone to talk to in a dark period of their lives. The concert was great and the event was considered a success on many different levels.

A few days later I received a letter in the mail from an elderly lady thanking me for getting involved in this concert. She explained how Lifeline had helped her when she had lost her husband to cancer, was feeling very alone and had seriously contemplated committing suicide. I couldn't prevent the tears rolling down my face as the human side of getting behind my community was made clear to me.

Since that day I have made an effort to drop a short letter or email to people who I see playing an active role in making my community a better place to be. Sometimes it's just to say thank you, sometimes it is more personal where I tell them of an experience I had, just like the lady who wrote to me.

Taking the time to say thank you to people who give tirelessly of themselves is a good thing to do. It will mean a lot to them. They certainly don't expect it but I am sure they appreciate it—I certainly do.

The very next time you read about someone who has gone out of their way to help make your community a better place, do some detective work and track down their address, then send them a card or a thank-you letter.

Hatch a plan to make you the ultimate corporate citizen

Like any component of a successful business, the better you plan, the greater your chances of succeeding. The same principle applies to the goal of becoming the ultimate corporate citizen. Making up a plan for how you and your business will play an active role in your community is a wise choice of action.

This plan should address:

- which types of organisations you would like to get involved with
- how much time each week you can spare
- how much financial support you can afford to give
- what products and services you can offer (remembering they still have a cost so don't send yourself broke helping others)
- ways to encourage your staff to get involved
- specific details about how you will tell your customers you are community-spirited
- how you will recognise other people in the community who get involved
- how you can share your own knowledge and experience.

This doesn't need to be a long or in-depth plan, just a few pages addressing all of the questions above. Start a file called 'Becoming the Ultimate Corporate Citizen' and you are well and truly on your way to achieving this goal. Once you have your plan in place, take the time to share it with your staff. They will, after all, be playing an important role.

19

Networking is not a dirty word

Okay, let's be honest: for most of us, networking really has become a dirty word. We know we need to do it, but we are so sick and tired of standing around in a room full of strangers, eating cocktail sausages, making small talk, feeling awkward and dreading someone coming over to us and starting a conversation that we will never be able to escape from.

But—and this is another very big but—networking events are a fantastic way to get new business. Rather than dreading them, we should be leaping in the air every time we get an invitation because it really means we will have access to a room full of potential clients for not very much money.

I do quite a lot of networking training for my clients and I find that once they have some clear instructions that will help them out, they never look back.

So what are some of the strategies that will remove these feelings of dread and have you running to networking events fully prepared to do business? Here are the top ideas that have helped me to build my business over many years:

- Do your homework
- Don't judge a book by its cover
- Learn to ask open-ended questions
- Read today's newspaper
- Don't get there too early
- You are not going to the gallows, so remember to smile
- Don't just stick with people you know
- Drinking does not make you more networkable
- Take plenty of business cards and promotional material
- Keep a pen handy and write notes on the back of cards
- Wear something distinctive
- Hang out near the food
- Look for groups of people rather than individuals
- Enlist the aid of others to introduce you
- Offer a compliment (and be sincere)
- Focus on the person in front of you
- Go with a target in mind
- Use the other person's name in the conversation
- When asked about your business, make sure you are enthusiastic in your response
- Follow up quickly to get results

Do your homework

I am a firm believer in doing my networking homework. I like to know who will be attending a networking event and I find that this helps me to get mentally prepared and ready to understand the types of conversations that could be had, the mood of the room, the reason for the meeting, and so on. Turning up blind tends to lead to wandering aimlessly and spending the whole session figuring out who is there and why. If you have been invited as a guest by someone, ask them to give you some background so you know what you are attending. It really will pay off in the long run.

Don't judge a book by its cover

My biggest peeve at networking events is being dismissed by someone who acts bored the minute they meet you—and they don't even have the decency to hide it. Instead they look everywhere but at you, like they are looking for someone more interesting (okay, in my case they may be, but it really is rude!). It is a cliché but never judge a book by its cover in the world of networking. Take the time to communicate with the people you meet, find out as much as you can about them and then, if you can't see a way to do business (I actually ask this question—how can we do business together?), it is fine to excuse yourself and move on to your next prospect.

Learn to ask open-ended questions

This is a great skill for anyone who really can't stand the awkwardness of small talk and meeting people for the first time. The golden rule here is to ask the other person questions about themselves or their business. So rather than asking simple questions that can be answered with a yes or no, go for the questions that need a real answer: 'So, can you tell me about the services your business offers?', 'What is your competitive advantage?', 'How has your industry changed in the past ten years?', 'Where do you think your industry is heading in the next ten years?' and so on. This gets people actually communicating.

Read today's newspaper

For many people, the hardest part of networking is running out of things to say. So I make a point of reading that day's newspaper and taking note of five or six stories that are general enough to be conversation-starters in any situation. There are always a few current 'hot topics' which will get people talking, especially if you get good at asking open-ended questions: 'So what do you think about . . . ?'

Don't get there too early

I always try to avoid arriving early at a networking event. There is nothing worse than standing in a room with one other person, feeling a sense of awkwardness and praying desperately for more people to arrive. Of course, I guess you could see this as an opportunity and a captive audience, but it rarely feels that way at the time.

You are not going to the gallows, so remember to smile

It is amazing how many people network with a grimace on their face as opposed to a warm, friendly smile. If you look like you are in pain it is unlikely that people will get trampled in the stampede to come and meet you. Make eye contact and show a few teeth (ideally in a smile, not a snarl) and you will be amazed how many people welcome you into their conversations simply because you look friendly.

Don't just stick with people you know

Many of us look around a room full of strange people trying to find a friendly and familiar face so that we have someone to clutch onto. Once we have found that friendly face it becomes way too easy to spend the entire networking event chatting to someone who already knows you and what you do, instead of seeking new business contacts. The key here is to be brave enough to walk up to strangers and be prepared to stick your hand out and introduce yourself. The more you do it, the easier it gets.

Remember, networking is marketing and marketing is all about building your business. By all means say hello and connect with friends and current clients, but use networking as a tool to get new customers.

Drinking does not make you more networkable

Sorry to break this bad news to those folk who think that a few stiff drinks will help them to relax and make it easier to mingle. It might, but what message does it send? Seeing someone guzzling beer does not make them more appealing as a person to do business with. I suggest that you avoid alcohol at these events. The concept that you need to drink to be social went the way of that 'driving yourself home from the pub because you were too drunk to walk' dinosaur. The idea of a networking event is to portray the fact that you are a professional, someone that other people will want to work with, not drink with.

Take plenty of business cards and promotional material

It is amazing how often people turn up at networking events without business cards. I have a mental checklist: business cards, two pens, some brochures and possibly a couple of my books, depending on the event. The key here is to be prepared before you head to a networking event. How many promises to catch up and follow up never happen because you can't find their card, then you can't remember the business name, so you simply put it in the too-hard basket?

Keep a pen handy and write notes on the back of cards

I always write memory joggers on the back of business cards—these might be something the person said, something they were wearing, a distinctive characteristic or some follow-up that is required. These notes have jogged my memory when I have stumbled across a business card from people I met years earlier. One word of advice though: don't write these notes down when the person is standing in front of you as this can be seen as rude, especially in certain cultures like that of Japan. Find a quiet space to do your note writing, but don't put it off too long.

Wear something distinctive

This is an oldie but a goodie. Some people make a point of wearing something distinctive so they stand out and can be remembered at networking functions. It might sound corny, but in a room with 300 people it can be hard to stand out. And as much as we might really want to blend in, standing out will get us noticed and that leads to new contacts, being memorable and new business.

Hang out near the food

When people are eating they are far more likely to strike up a conversation. They are relaxed, often feel a bit guilty because they are eating something they think they shouldn't, and there is of course a common topic for discussion—the food. So if you hang out near the buffet you may find it easier to meet people and have some good conversations.

Look for groups of people rather than individuals

It is always wise to find a group of people where you can kind of muscle your way in, stand and observe quietly and then slowly become a part of the conversation. When we are in a group we behave a bit like penguins— we will shuffle to let other penguins in and then huddle back together. My advice here though is to be quiet when you first enter a group, wait a while and someone will talk to you. If you enter a group and start taking over the conversation, the group will often disband and you will be left on your own.

Enlist the aid of others to introduce you

If I am going to a networking event where I know one or two people who are very well connected, I will often ring and ask them if they would mind introducing me to others at the event. In fact, I have done this many times and it works really well. The person then has a mission and a job, that is, to drag me around and introduce me to as many quality contacts as possible—so it is an express form of networking. Best of all, if we get stuck in a scenario where we don't want to be, the colleague can easily excuse us with the statement, 'Sorry we can't chat, I am trying to introduce Andrew to as many people as possible tonight.' Perfect.

Offer a compliment (and be sincere)

If you struggle with an opening line when meeting new people, the oldest tried and tested method is to offer a compliment. You may choose to go up to someone and compliment them about something they are wearing, or perhaps comment on something they have done (if you know a bit about them). The biggest key to making this work is to make sure your compliment is sincere. If it's not, people will often dismiss you, and deservedly so.

Focus on the person in front of you

At networking events, it is important to give 100 per cent of your attention to whoever is in front of you, even if they may not be a potential contact or business lead. Rather than acting bored (and looking rude), excuse yourself and move on.

Go with a target in mind

Heading to a networking event with a specific 'target' in mind will often give you a sense of purpose and an outcome from the event. Do your homework, know who you want to meet and why you want to meet them and then go for it. Setting goals always gets results.

Use the other person's name in the conversation

As Dale Carnegie stated, 'The sweetest sound to any person is their own name.' When you are introduced to a person, respond using their name and use it repeatedly in the conversation. If you are one of those people who forgets a name as soon as someone says it, you may find that this technique will help (and see the other tips in Chapter 12).

When asked about your business, make sure you are enthusiastic in your response

When you meet a person at a networking event, the one question they are bound to ask is: 'So, what do you do?' Now, how you answer this is vitally important—remembering that the words don't mean as much as your body language and the emotion in your voice (non-verbal communication accounts for up to 90 per cent of the meaning we take from any encounter). So it is important to have a positive, energetic and memorable response to the question 'what do you do?' Easier said than done, but be playful, try new ideas, have a laugh at yourself and people will remember you.

Follow up quickly to get results

Many people are great at networking but lousy at following up. So why bother to network in the first place? Great networkers will follow up the next day. If you say you will do something, do it. This will impress people and show that you are not only professional but also keen.

There may be a lot here to take on board before your next networking event, but if you slowly try to introduce a few of these points at each event you attend, I promise it won't take you long to become a networking machine who gets a lot of business from every event you attend.

A final idea: I gave a client of mine a copy of these points and he has printed them onto little business card–sized cheat sheets so he can subtly check them if he finds himself in a hole. He never used to attend networking events because he felt so awkward; now he looks forward to them.

20

Instead of changing staff, try changing yourself

I get a little brassed off when people complain about their staff, though I have been guilty of the same crime myself on a number of occasions. Most of the time the problem isn't with the staff, it's with us. Perhaps we have simply employed the wrong person for the job, or put a person in a job and given them no training to enable them to do their work properly.

One typical example I would like to use to illustrate my point here is generation Y. Most business owners have at some stage moaned mercilessly about staff in this age group (generally people born during the 1980s and early to mid 1990s), saying that they can't communicate, it's all about 'them', they don't stay put in a job, they only do the tasks they want to do, and the list goes on.

Well, I tend to think that while generation Y may be 'guilty' of all of these things, the perspective is not quite right. They are in fact excellent communicators among themselves. They dislike wasting time with non-essential and slow communication or, the ultimate sin, in endless meetings that take forever to decide something that could have been resolved in a few seconds via email.

Generation Y tend not to stay put in a job, and that is because they are ambitious and goal-driven. But they know that they have to earn any climb up the corporate ladder by improving their skills and knowledge, so they look at every job along the way as a place to do exactly that. Accept that you will only keep generation Y staff with you for a maximum of a few years, but they will be very keen to learn, they will want responsibility and they will want to share with you what they know. They may also have ideas for doing things better, if you take the time to ask them and then listen to their answers.

Generation Y have a strong entrepreneurial spirit, and they know other generation Yers well enough to sell to them. If you want to grow this market in your business, employ generation Yers to do it.

The key here is to know what you are getting. If you want someone compliant, who will do as you say and put this widget in this widget hole, then don't expect a generation Yer to be the person for the job.

The following recommendations look at ways to avoid the most common recruiting issues, managing your staff and keeping your staff. It is a complex topic and one that is hard to get right. This advice should help to avoid the most common mistakes.

- Put the job description in writing
- Always check references
- Agreeing on a trial period protects both you and the new employee
- Train your staff (and yourself) properly
- Lead by example and your team will follow
- Communicate effectively with your staff
- Conduct performance reviews
- Be conscious of security issues—protect your business
- Dismiss staff who don't work out
- Don't send yourself broke by hiring too many staff

Put the job description in writing

Very few businesses take the time to write a position description for each member of staff. This is typically a brief document that outlines the employer's expectations of their new recruit. The hard work is normally in writing the first position description; after that, it can be adapted to suit other positions as required. The type of information that can be included varies from business to business, but the following would be typical:

- The company's general philosophy and mission statement to ensure that the employee understands where you are coming from.
- What the employee is expected to do and when they should have it done by. This ensures that everyone is clear about the job and all that it entails.
- Exactly what the employee receives for doing the job. This should include how much they will be paid, the number of days allowed for annual holidays and sick days, the company's contribution to superannuation, and other items such as medical insurance, maternity/paternity leave and any performance-based incentives. This section should also include any other form of remuneration for the employee, including such things as the supply of uniforms, free parking, length of breaks, and so on.
- Company policies detailing issues that may be relevant to the new employee. These can cover everything from staff discounts to dealing with complaints by other staff, security, insurance, and so on.
- General housekeeping issues such as what time they are expected to start and finish work, how they should dress, how they should interact with other members of staff, the notice period required for resigning, when they will be paid and how, and so on.

The position description should be read and signed by the new employee and they should be given a copy for their own records. It protects both you and them. If you are uncertain about any aspect of the document, get your legal representative to have a look at it. Many business advisory boards will have standard forms that enable you just to fill in the blanks.

Use the position description to start the relationship off on a professional footing. Disputes that arise between staff and management simply because there is nothing in writing can be very costly in terms of time and lost productivity, and often lead to resentment.

It's also a very good idea to periodically review the position description with your staff. This ensures that everyone is up to date and that any potential problems are addressed.

Always check references

There are a number of ways you can go about finding people to work for you. Some organisations like to use an employment agency to make the process less cumbersome. It's then up to the agency to find suitable applicants that they feel will meet your requirements. Of course, you pay for this service, but it can save you a lot of time.

If you employ people by placing your own advertisements, you will probably be used to receiving lots of résumés. I have yet to see a résumé that doesn't make the person look impressive; after all, that's the whole idea of sending them out. The problem is that just because someone says they are great, it doesn't mean they are.

I always check references. While the majority of people are honest, some are not. Often past employers are surprised to find that they have been included as a referee, and they may tell a very different story about the applicant and their abilities.

I have agreed to be a referee for about twenty people during my working career. I have only ever been contacted twice to verify the abilities of the people I have recommended. It's surprising to me that more employers don't check references. They often employ people based only on what is written in the résumé and a brief interview.

When checking references, ask detailed questions and make sure that the facts add up. Don't just ring the referee and ask if the person worked for them. Ask them if there were any problems. Tell them about your business and what you do. Do they think that the applicant will work well and produce results for your business?

Another point worth noting here is that if you agree to act as a referee for a former employee, be honest if someone contacts you to check on them. This honesty should extend to both the person's good points and bad points.

These days there are issues with privacy and what you can and can't say of course, so check this out with your lawyer if you are not sure, but the key is to ask the right questions and you will get the right answers. There are numerous online resources to guide you through this process.

Agreeing on a trial period protects both you and the new employee

It is an excellent idea to put new staff on a trial period when they start working for you. This may be a few weeks or a few months, depending on the complexity of the job. The duration of the trial period should be made very clear to all applicants and should be included in the position description.

The whole idea of a trial period is to protect both you and the new employee. It is becoming harder and harder to terminate staff if they are not working out. If you have a clearly defined cooling-off period, you know that you have an out if you need one.

Likewise, an employee may find themselves in the job from hell, with a psychotic boss they cannot work with. A trial period removes any awkwardness and provides the employee with a simple explanation when they apply for future jobs: 'I worked for The Widget Company for a trial period of one month, but I felt that the work wasn't really challenging enough for me so I left at the end of the trial period to enable my employer to find someone better suited to the job.' This is a mature and responsible way to handle short-term periods of employment that haven't worked out.

I have to admit that I have hired people and not instigated a trial period, and I have really regretted it. Finding the right person for the job is difficult at the best of times, and it's a simple fact of life that sometimes the first person you employ just doesn't work out. Provide yourself with a backdoor exit clause by having a trial period.

Train your staff (and yourself) properly

This is a bit of a bugbear for me. I often see inadequately trained staff being blamed for poor performance simply because their boss is too cheap to pay for training. If you expect someone to do a job properly, you need to give them the necessary skills.

I believe that many businesses look at new staff as an inconvenience rather than a promising opportunity to boost the business. This is often true in larger organisations, where lots of people come and go on a regular basis.

If you are going to pay your staff every week, surely you want them to do the best job possible for you? After all, the better the job they do, the happier your customers will be and the more profit your business will make.

Training takes many shapes and forms. It's essential to train your new staff in how your business operates. They need to be made aware of your expectations and those of your customers. Every business is slightly different—even two virtually identical hamburger restaurants will have different operational procedures that staff need to be taught. Take the time to orientate new staff and train them fully so that they know how to do their job for you.

Another type of training covers general skills. This may include telephone manner, customer service, selling skills, and even things like time management. These general skills are used by most businesses, but for many people they don't come instinctively. Enrol your staff in a training course, or contract a trainer to come to your workplace to conduct in-house training. The cost will be covered by improved efficiency and a higher degree of customer satisfaction.

A third type of training covers specific skills that are relevant to your type of business or industry. People often choose to work for a particular company because it will give them the opportunity to learn new skills. Give your staff the skills to keep them at the forefront of your industry and you, and they, will reap the benefits.

Just as it is important for your staff to be well trained, don't forget to put your hand up from time to time to undergo training yourself. I haven't met anyone who couldn't benefit from some form of training. We all need to expand our skills and expertise. Often, when we find ourselves running a business, we know how to do our job very well, but we may not know how to do bookkeeping work, how to manage our time or how to be a better negotiator.

Another common problem that I see with training is that organisations tackle it in bursts—they may have five training courses in one month and then nothing for the rest of the year. Try to plan your training so that it's conducted at frequent intervals throughout the year. I like to do training during non-productive times, when business tends to be quiet. Rather than having people sitting around doing crosswords, have them learning new skills or improving existing skills.

There are many organisations that offer training. Some training is very expensive, while some is not. I recommend consulting your local business groups to find out what kind of training is available in your area. You may even be entitled to financial assistance for certain types of training. Spend a little time researching your training options before implementing a course of action.

Another smart business move that I have observed is to ask your staff what areas they feel they need training in. This can, of course, open a can of worms (you might not have the room to run synchronised swimming classes), but you might be surprised by the types of things they want to learn.

We have done a number of surveys for organisations asking this exact question, and I have always found the responses enlightening. Two of the main areas that people appear to want help with are stress management and dealing with change in the workplace. Both are clearly reflections of the modern-day working environment.

Lead by example and your team will follow

If you turn up for work in a pair of shorts and a T-shirt yet you expect your staff to wear Armani suits, you are asking for trouble. If you take long lunches every day and complain when your staff are a couple of minutes late after a break, you are sending conflicting messages.

Your words and actions will determine the words and actions of your staff. If you work hard, they will work hard. If you are polite and friendly, they will be polite and friendly. If you are less than honest, they will be less than honest. It is important to understand that, in your business, you set the ground rules that everyone plays by. Make them good rules and stick to them yourself, and you will reap the rewards.

Communicate effectively with your staff

Some people are good at communicating, while others are not. Having clear communication with your staff ensures that your business will run efficiently and effectively.

From my experience, there are two main types of managers: those who don't communicate at all, and those that bombard staff with memos, meetings and hundreds of other forms of communication. Somewhere in the middle is clearly the best approach.

Often poor communicators simply don't know how to pass on information. There are several easy ways to do this:

- *Staff meetings.* These should be held regularly, preferably at the same time each day, week or month, depending on your needs.

They provide an open forum for information to be shared in both directions.

- *A noticeboard.* This enables information to be passed on without disrupting normal work practices. Putting the noticeboard in an area where all staff have to go at some time during the day makes it easy for them to read the notices. I read about a company recently that put its noticeboards in the toilets, because it was the only place that all the staff visited during the course of the day.
- *Memos.* These are normally one-page documents that are distributed to all staff with a specific point being the subject of the memo. The problem with memos is that often people don't read them. I suggest that memos should be signed when read and then passed on. This can, of course, be time consuming and not necessarily the best way to get a message across, but it's a tool that can be used.
- *Email.* Intracompany email has become the quickest and most cost-effective way of passing on information within larger organisations. Unfortunately, because email is easy to send, it can be over-used. A friend of mine receives up to 100 intra-office emails every day, many of which aren't relevant to his work. I suspect that this is a common problem and one to watch out for.

I am a verbal communicator, so I prefer to sit down and talk face to face with my team. You need to determine what works for you and what works for your business. The important point to take from this tip is that having an effective mechanism for sharing information in your business will improve your chances of thriving.

Conduct performance reviews

In reality, jobs change and so do an individual's responsibilities during their period of employment. For this reason, position descriptions should be reviewed periodically. This process also enables both parties to air any grievances or concerns they may have.

By conducting performance reviews, you are sending a clear message to your staff that they are expected to perform. Regular reviews can help to prevent non-performing staff from hiding among the crowd.

Depending on the size of your organisation, the performance review can be a formal process or a simple chat over a cup of coffee. However it's done, it should be documented, with one copy kept on file and another copy given to the employee.

As with many workplace issues, you may need to ask your legal adviser about the best way to conduct these meetings. I would recommend that you do this to ensure that you are covered legally. Often performance reviews require a third person to be present to act as a witness.

Have a simple agenda when doing a performance review. This can include:

- The employee's thoughts on how they are performing.
- Your thoughts on how the employee is performing.
- Identification of areas where the employee is doing well.
- Identification of areas that the employee needs to work on.
- The employee's goals and plans for their future involvement with your organisation.
- Your plans for the future of the employee.
- Review of the employee's responsibilities and pay structure, if applicable.
- An open session to air any problems or grievances.

This review period is also an excellent time to offer rewards for a job well done.

It may appear that all I am doing with this suggestion is creating more work for you. In reality, I am suggesting a way to increase the productivity of your staff. A harmonious workplace is much more likely to produce profits than a tense, aggressive environment where staff are constantly embroiled in internal politics. By being open and honest, you are sending a very clear message that you expect the same from them.

Be conscious of security issues—protect your business

I used to be a cynic when it came to security. After all, who would want any key information about a little marketing company like mine? I have since witnessed so many security breaches, not only of my business but also many of my clients', that I am no longer a cynic.

I can guarantee that your competitors would love to know your most intimate business secrets, even simple details like who your main customers are, who your key suppliers are, how much you charge, and so on. Of course, with a little investigative work it isn't hard to find this information, but there are people who will often give it out, sometimes innocently, without your knowledge.

Unfortunately, the internet isn't only one of the greatest promotional tools, it's also one of the easiest ways to breach a company's security. While writing this book, I watched a documentary on television about internet hackers and what they could achieve, and it was very, very frightening. If your computer is connected to the internet, you are at risk.

Of course, the big question is: what do you do about internet security and security in general? If you have information that you absolutely don't want other people to know about, then don't put it on your computer. Produce a number of hard copies and then delete the file or store it on an external disk that you take with you. Computer security software and protective barriers such as firewalls are improving all the time, and for most of our businesses they are more than sufficient. However, if you have any doubts, the only way to ensure that someone doesn't steal information from your computer is not to have it stored on the computer, or to use a computer that isn't connected to a network (other computers) or a telephone line. I know a number of businesspeople who use a separate computer for their financial records that is completely password-protected and separate from all other computers and phone lines.

When it comes to other information that could be either stolen or passed on by staff, let them know what information can and cannot be freely given out. Once again, you are setting the ground rules by letting them know what is acceptable and what is not.

Staff theft is always an issue, and unfortunately it's becoming a greater problem for businesses. Staff often don't consider taking products home as theft; some see it as a benefit of the job. You need to set very clear boundaries and parameters for what staff can and cannot take or use, and you should make your views on, and the ramifications of, staff theft very clear. Grey areas invite theft and can cost your business a lot of money. Likewise, poor stock control invites theft, simply because you can't tell when things go missing.

Shoplifting is also a growing problem and one that any retail business needs to address. Store layout has a lot to do with shoplifting, and there are many things that can be done to minimise losses as a result of stealing. Shoplifters are organised, brash and very confident, and they often work in teams.

Many organisations use cameras. I don't like the idea of this myself, and in some instances it can be a real invasion of privacy; however, in other instances, such as late-night petrol stations and convenience stores, camera surveillance is essential.

If security is a real issue for you, get some advice from a specialist. There are plenty of companies that can help you develop your security to the level that you require.

It's often a good idea to talk to your insurance company about security as well. The cost of a specialist security consultant can often be recouped by reduced insurance policies for having a more secure premises.

Dismiss staff who don't work out

This is a tough one. No one likes to tell a member of staff that they are no longer required, and no one likes to hear those dreaded words.

I once had a publishing business that employed several sales representatives who sold advertising. One rep just wasn't working out. My partner and I tried everything, including sales training, motivation, money, begging—the lot. It was clear from day one that she was wrong for the position. On several occasions I started my 'I don't think this is working out' line, but I could never follow through. We made the decision that she had to go. The date was set and the appointment was made. In she came, a tiny girl in a big boardroom chair. My partner and I had steeled ourselves. This was the day; nothing was going to stop the inevitable. I started my 'I don't think this is working out' speech. Her bottom lip quivered, as did my nerve, but I kept going and just as I was about to say 'Today is your last day', my partner rushed over and gave her a big hug and said, 'But don't worry, we're willing to keep trying.' Well, my jaw hit the ground. She stayed with us for several more months before finally leaving.

Let's be honest: sacking someone is the ultimate in rejection and people don't like it. There are times in any business when, for one reason or another, you will have to dismiss staff and I believe that people generally know when they are about to be laid off. It's important to have a clear process or procedure that you can use in this situation.

Check with your legal adviser to find out what your obligations are when it comes to terminating a member of staff. If you don't follow the appropriate steps, you may open yourself up for legal action in the future. I also feel that it's better to talk to someone face to face, rather than just drop them a DCM (don't come Monday) via their email.

I once met someone who had worked in a government organisation for 25 years. He found out that he was getting the sack from the pay department when he went to change his account details. The accounts clerk showed him a memo from management saying that he was being terminated. He was devastated and later successfully sued his former employer. I have also heard horror stories of staff being advised of their termination over the loudspeaker for all to hear.

How you go about terminating an employee is up to you, but do it legally, with dignity and with sensitivity.

Don't send yourself broke by hiring too many staff

Without doubt, staffing costs are one of the major overheads that businesses face. As soon as you start employing people, your weekly overheads go through the roof and many a failed entrepreneur will lament that they let their costs get out of hand by employing too many staff. Consider also that the salary is just the beginning. There are all of the added expenses of space, computers, other equipment that may be needed, a car perhaps, uniforms, holiday pay and sick pay, telecommunication costs and so on.

The real art is learning to balance your staffing levels against the amount of work that needs to be done or the number of customers that need to be served. This skill normally evolves over time, but it's an area that needs to be constantly addressed and monitored.

The use of casual or part-time staff is a great way to build up your workforce in a manner that works with your cash flow. We employ a lot of part-time telemarketers who work on various projects. Most of them have other jobs and work for our company to earn extra income. This isn't a new idea, of course, but it's often a better way to go than employing full-time staff.

I have seen many businesses get themselves into trouble through having far too many staff for the amount of income they generate. Most businesses have busy periods and quiet periods, reinforcing the need for careful planning. Be cautious when employing new staff, and focus on making your staff as productive as possible.

In Australia I think we have a huge opportunity to employ older people, perhaps retirees. They have a wealth of knowledge and a depth of skills, yet they are often put out to pasture because of company policy. These people are mature, intelligent workers who bring much more to the business than just filling a space. Think differently about employing people and look for creative solutions to staffing, and you will have a winning formula.

21

Working with family, friends and lovers

If you own your own business, it is generally only a matter of time until you find yourself working with either family members, friends or a lover or two. In many ways business has always been that way. Family members in particular were enlisted to work in the 'family business', simply because they were there, could be trusted (generally) and would work for very long hours for little money.

There are some wonderful upsides to working with family, friends or lovers. I worked with my former wife in our marketing company and it really was great. We were both totally committed to the business, we had lots of fun every single day, and we had each other's best interests at heart. Unfortunately, we were better at working together than we were at being married. In saying that, no one had ever taught us *how* to work together, we were just figuring it out as we went and, like most couples who work together, we made plenty of mistakes.

Today I work with many family-based businesses. It might be a husband and wife team, a father and son combo, or a mother and daughter enterprise. There are certainly great upsides, but there are some pretty big pitfalls along the way. Likewise, most small businesses in particular need extra help from time to time and business owners are more likely to employ someone they know, a friend generally, to lend a hand. Once again, there are many upsides to doing this, but be warned that dangers are also lurking close by.

The following advice comes from my own experiences as well as the experience of many people I have met and worked with who have family, friends or lovers working in their business.

- Set the ground rules and make them clear
- Good pillow talk versus bad pillow talk
- Establish clear roles and responsibilities within the business
- Have time apart and outside interests
- Solve disagreements (ideally before they happen)
- Have a clear vision of where the business is heading and make sure everyone knows about it
- Accept that we all work, think and act differently—and that is okay
- Know your strengths, know your weaknesses and be big enough to admit to both
- Never stop having fun, playing and, most importantly, celebrating your victories
- If you leave the business, leave the business

Set the ground rules and make them clear

Regardless of your relationship with whoever is going to be working in your business, it is really important that the ground rules are established and that they are clear to all involved.

Ground rules are the fundamentals of the business that apply to every single person employed, and they really should not be different for family members or friends, otherwise resentment will build up with 'regular' workers.

I would go one step further and make certain the ground rules are written down. Everyone involved needs to read them, agree to them and sign a copy. They can cover important topics like behaviour, commitment to customers, ethical considerations, operational issues, expectations and anything else where there could be some ambiguity.

You choose what the ground rules are, or develop them together with your employees if you are new to the business world. Review them when you need to and discuss them openly if there are issues. Things that are left unsaid and blurred boundaries are the enemies of any business that involves family, friends and lovers.

Good pillow talk versus bad pillow talk

I think we know what good pillow talk is so I won't go into detail, but here are a few examples of 'bad pillow talk':

- 'Honey, can you pass me the calculator and the profit and loss report from 2004?'
- 'Oh baby, why didn't you get that package to the freight forwarders this afternoon? This was your only responsibility today and you let us down again.'
- 'You dirty boy—why don't you take better care of your overalls? If I have to tell you one more time that you look like a slob . . .'
- 'Hey, let's get naked and go through all our bills!'
- 'In tomorrow's staff meeting, how about we . . .'

Hopefully my lame examples illustrate the point. Some of you may laugh, but I have certainly been in the situation where my partner and I have climbed into bed, the candles are lit, Barry White is playing, there is an abundance of atmosphere, then one of us asks a (dumb) question that starts a business conversation and ends with us fighting about something. Bedrooms are for sleeping and other very specific activities—not for work talk.

The moral of this point is very simple: we need to have razor-sharp boundaries between work and home. This doesn't mean we can't talk about work-related things at home—in fact, I think it's essential to talk about worky stuff when you are away from the business—but we need to set boundaries. Limit the amount of time you talk about work, say what needs to be said, and then move on. It can take a bit of discipline because most of us 'think and spurt'—we get a thought and then spit it out.

Something I learned to do was to keep a notepad in the kitchen, and if I had a work thought I would write it down, build a list and, at a scheduled 'business meeting time' at home, we could run through my list and my partner's.

Do whatever works for you, but please make certain that you have a system of some sort. Acknowledge your relationship, honour it and treat it as a priority. If the foundation is good, most other things will work well. And next time you find yourself having inappropriate pillow talk, make a mental note, laugh out loud, talk to your spouse and discuss how to avoid it.

Establish clear roles and responsibilities within the business

Of all the pieces of advice I can offer, this is probably the most important for husband and wife teams: we need to have very clear roles and responsibilities within the business. Now this doesn't mean that we don't step in and lend a hand when needed, or that we don't have the capability to do every part of the business, but we really need our own specific part of the business to be in charge of. Whenever I work with a family business that is having trouble, it is generally because there are no clear boundaries. Instead everyone does a bit of everything and it leads to all kinds of problems. The most successful family-based businesses are the ones where roles are divided in some way: for example, the husband takes care of the books and paying the bills and the wife is the doer, the person who deals with the customers or makes the product.

If you are planning on starting a business with your partner or a family member, take the time to sit down and work out who will be responsible for what. Even if you have been running your business for a while and you feel that the boundaries are blurred, sit down and do it now. The same applies if you employ a friend to come and work in your business. It is all about managing expectations.

Sometimes you may need to change these roles and responsibilities. I know that over the years I have ended up in charge of parts of my business that I am really not very good at, but I had to give it a go to find that out. The point here is to be prepared to speak up if something isn't working and come up with an alternative.

Finally, don't micromanage. Don't give someone responsibility and then watch every single thing they do like a hawk, adding comments all the way about how you would do it or, even worse, how they should do it. If they come to you for advice, by all means offer it. But unless you enjoy frosty responses, let family or friends do what they have been empowered to do, even if they do it differently to you.

Have time apart and outside interests

When I worked with my wife, the only real time we had apart was when we got into our separate cars and drove to work. As we only lived about ten minutes from the business, that is not a long time to have your own thoughts.

When we work with our partners we tend to become the one organism and, as I would continually emphasise, there are wonderful upsides with this, but it can be tough.

I know many couples who work in a business together and actually take their holidays separately each year, just so they can get a break from each other. To me this is tragic, but I understand it and certainly empathise with them.

I believe that it is vitally important to have time apart and to have your own life outside of your business. All too often our businesses take over our lives and we stop doing the things we love to do, like hobbies and even socialising with people who aren't involved in the business. This 'cutting off' is not good in the long run. One day we stop, look around and ask ourselves, 'Is this all there is?' In other words, if your life is all about your business it may initially be good, even great, but at some point there will be a sense of all work and no play, which leads to the question: 'why are we doing this?'

Breaking old habits can be tough. Sometimes we have to remember how to have outside interests and hobbies, or even that we *do* love to do other things. The best way to approach this is in baby steps. Maybe take a morning off by yourself once a week where you can do anything you like, and then get your partner to do the same.

However you approach this, you need to do it. For husband and wife teams it is essential, but I see it as being a necessity for parents and their adult kids working together as well. If you don't, it will almost certainly lead to problems either in the business or in the relationships over time.

Solve disagreements (ideally before they happen)

A very big issue, particularly in businesses with two family members as partners, is resolving disagreements. If you both have equal say and you both disagree about some aspect of the business, how do you resolve this?

Typically what happens is the dominant person gets their way and the more submissive person gets resentful. Give it time and this relationship will end in tears. A person can only give in so many times, and just because you are louder or more assertive doesn't mean you are right.

One idea that I have found very handy is to have a third party adjudicator to resolve issues. Both partners need to agree on who that person is and they have to agree to accept the outcome. You also need to find the right person to be the adjudicator. They need to know you both, be fair and ethical, smart, business savvy and trustworthy—a big ask.

When an issue arises that you both feel strongly about, you get to pitch your case to the adjudicator and they decide. And you must abide by the end result. You may be surprised how much better you become at resolving issues when there is the 'threat' of calling in the adjudicator.

This might not work for you, but whatever you do, remember that a dominant/submissive decision-making process leads to disconnection and power struggles within a relationship that ultimately play out in non-productive ways. Come up with a way to vote, resolve issues or make big decisions within your business. Everyone has to agree on the process, and they have to do this willingly. Then get on with getting on.

Have a clear vision of where the business is heading and make sure everyone knows about it

When working with a family-based business and talking to the individuals about where the business is heading and their big picture for the future, I am often surprised to find that there is no one clear vision but rather a range of quite different visions.

This 'big picture' view of the business is really important. It gives a reason for doing what we do, and most importantly a clear direction. Visions change over time and that is okay, but when there are numerous people involved the vision needs to be known by all. Ideally everyone in the business should share in creating the vision—it is really the only way to get 'buy in' from your staff. Putting a piece of paper on the table and saying, 'Here is our vision, make it happen,' rarely creates the desired outcome, unless it is done in a smarter way than that.

The key here is to first figure out where you are right now. Do you have a vision for the future? If you do, is it a combined vision or just yours, and the others are along for the ride? If you don't have a vision, now is the time to create one, with everyone involved.

Accept that we all work, think and act differently— and that is okay

Earlier in this chapter I briefly mentioned the need to appreciate the differences our family, friends and lovers bring when we are working with them, but I think that it warrants more discussion. I encounter many families that drive each other crazy because they can't accept that we all work differently. The fact is that it is not just okay to be different, it is highly desirable.

Businesses rarely grow if they don't evolve. The way they evolve is by trying new things, being receptive to new ideas and appreciating the unique qualities that we all bring to the table. This is imperative when it comes to working with family, friends and lovers.

Earlier I also mentioned the habit of people moaning about the new generations coming through, particularly generation Y, who always seem to bear the brunt of criticism (mostly from people with grey hair). The reality is that we will never change generation Y and nor should we. I find them amazing—they are exceptional entrepreneurs who are very good at communicating among themselves, they don't like wasting their time and they have high expectations of those they work for. I don't actually see any problem with these characteristics. The real key here is to work to their strengths, not to their weaknesses.

Any business that has lots of long-winded, waste-of-time meetings will not appeal to generation Y. Any business owner who is a control freak will struggle with generation Y. Any business that doesn't have a well-structured career path, with constantly increasing expectations and matching rewards, will struggle with generation Y.

You might decide that this is all too hard and of course that is your choice, but businesses that embrace this generation and learn to work with their strengths, instead of moaning about their perceived short-comings, are getting incredible results.

Embrace 'different'. Give people the space they need to do what they do best. Be patient and provide guidance rather than control. This will create a culture that leads to a very successful and rock-solid business.

Know your strengths, know your weaknesses and be big enough to admit to both

To work with family, friends or lovers we need a degree of humility, and that manifests most clearly when it comes to knowing what we are good at, what we are not so good at and what this means to the business.

Leading on from the last tip, as much as we need to accept others, we really do need to know ourselves. You might love doing one particular job within the business, but are you really that good at it and—logically extending the question—are you the best person to be doing it?

Having an honest internal discussion with yourself about your own strengths and weaknesses is important. A really well-run business that is bound to be successful is one which combines the right people with the right tasks or responsibilities within it. All too often I see people who are not working to their individual strengths, in fact the exact opposite: the entire business seems hell-bent on working to everyone's weaknesses.

Once you think that you are pretty clear on your own strengths and weaknesses, have an open and honest conversation with your family and see if they agree. This is an excellent group exercise and each family member (or friend, in particularly small businesses) should be able to have a very honest and open discussion around this topic, with the goal being to work to each individual's strength.

I have seen this completely transform numerous businesses over-night.

Never stop having fun, playing, and, most importantly, celebrating your victories

When you work with family, friends or lovers, the lines between home and work are often blurred and can roll into one. It's great when families have a lot of fun together and celebrate their successes within the business. But over time, as the pressure of business builds, the fun and celebration can end, both in the business and at home.

Fun and playfulness are vital for stress relief, and working with loved ones can certainly be stressful, especially in your own business. Sometimes we need to remind ourselves to lighten up, relax and not take things overly seriously. If you own the business, you are the business barometer, a point I have made earlier in this book. If you are stressed out and serious all the time, everyone else will be walking on eggshells and feeling equally as stressed. This is not an environment conducive to long-term business success.

We also need to make sure we celebrate our victories, both large and small, on a regular basis. Acknowledge where you have come from, the things you have accomplished and the fact that you achieved these things together.

I actually suggest that every year you make a point of picking a date, getting together with everyone involved in your business, in particular your family members, and listing everything you have achieved together in the past year. Acknowledge your successes and the roles that specific individuals have played, and laugh about your challenges and what they taught you. But most importantly of all, spend time appreciating each other, thanking each other, loving each other and laughing with each other.

If you leave the business, leave the business

If you decide that the time has come to leave the business and perhaps hand over the reins to your children or other family members, make sure you actually do so: it is a recipe for disaster to *tell* them you are handing over control but then continue to interfere.

Of course, your expertise and knowledge of the business is priceless, but just as we have to let our children figure out their own way in the world, the same applies to whomever we entrust to take on the business.

A lot of older business owners really do struggle with this. I have seen wonderful transitions where the founders of the business embrace the change and get excited about the new directions, initiatives and ideas that come with handing over to a new generation. But at the same time I have seen businesses literally tear themselves apart because a matriarch or patriarch can't let go.

If you make the decision to leave the business, then make sure you leave the business. If you can't let go, take a long holiday. Accept that the business will be different without you—not better or worse, just different.

22

In case of a business emergency, READ THIS

If you are going to operate a business, there is always the very real risk that at some time you will face an emergency of some sort. For most businesses, this will be a financial crisis.

In recent years many of us have experienced struggling with cash flow, trying to find credit or losing major customers who have gone broke or dramatically reduced the size of their operation. Running a business in the toughest of times, when the future has become uncertain, can be very scary for any business owner.

Generally these uncertain times are accompanied by lots of closed-door meetings, seriously stressed people, rumours of massive cuts, and general panic. You find yourself in a war battling for survival with no way of knowing whether or not you will succeed.

I have been in this situation myself and I have worked with many businesses and corporations in the same place. It is tough, it is emotional, hard decisions must be made, and it takes a very large toll on all who are caught up in it.

I have also watched many organisations slide into bankruptcy at times like this because they fell apart, lacked leadership or because the momentum of the disaster overtook the reality of the situation. In other words, these organisations could have survived if the right actions had been taken by the right people. The following information will point you in the right direction, regardless of the size of your business. The rest is up to you.

- Take action immediately
- Let those close to you know the seriousness of the situation
- Get advice, and then get a second opinion
- Cut costs without destroying your business
- Have someone close by to confide in
- Think outside the box
- Your suppliers don't want to see you go broke
- Don't over-promise and under-deliver on repayments
- Make the tough decisions and make them fast
- Keep one eye on where you are and one eye on where you're going

Take action immediately

John Hill is a long-time client and a very close friend of mine. He is a giant Canadian, with a dangerous moustache, who has owned many businesses over the years. We first came into contact when he purchased a restaurant called Mango Jam in Port Douglas in far north Queensland. From the day I met him I realised that not only was he intelligent and savvy but he was also the epitome of the smart businessman. What impressed me most was that he took action immediately whenever the situation warranted it.

Running a restaurant in a tourist town is about as tough as it gets. Over the last ten years there have been a number of major challenges (and opportunities) for this type of business. Whenever a major announcement of some sort was made in the media, be it good news or bad, John responded immediately. He started by asking smart questions that would lead him to a plan of attack. How will this affect our business? What changes do we need to make? Who do I need to talk to about this issue? What shall I tell the staff? How much will this cost?

An example of one challenge John faced was the introduction of budget airlines into Australia. He had observed what had happened in North America when low-cost airlines started operating there. He had learned that more people travelled more often and that these people were generally budget-driven. This increase in accessibility to tourist destinations meant that affluent travellers tended to look for places that were more exclusive in order to get away from the crowds.

So not only does a budget airline bring more budget-driven customers to established tourist regions, it also scares away the more affluent travellers. This means that a business in this region needs to completely rethink its approach, unless it is already catering for the budget market.

John called a meeting with his astute wife, Liz, who managed the finances, the restaurant manager, David, and me to determine what needed to be done for the restaurant to survive in this changing market. We brainstormed for several hours and came up with a number of ideas that would make the restaurant more appealing to budget-conscious travellers. We looked at improving the meals to show value for money and to encourage more people to come into the restaurant. We offered special deals for diners to come back a second time and we created giveaways for children. At the same time, we undertook a major renovation on the restaurant, at a time when everyone else had stopped spending. We knew that we had to look the part, offer great value and encourage people to come back time and time again.

Of course, the market did change dramatically. Many of the restaurants and businesses that were too slow to adapt died, but Mango Jam is still there and makes a good profit every year. It isn't a big, flash, fine-dining restaurant—it just serves good-value food in a fun way and tens of thousands of people keep coming back year after year.

In the face of the avian flu crisis, the 9/11 terrorist attack, the Sydney Olympic Games and any other event that would affect his business in either a positive or a negative way, John and his team reacted in exactly the same way. We talked it through, we made a plan and we took swift and decisive action.

Perhaps this example may seem irrelevant to someone who runs a large corporation, but the strategy in fact works for any organisation. A business that takes immediate action, develops a logical plan of attack and then actually follows through and implements the plan will be far more likely to survive than one that doesn't.

When faced with a crisis in your business it is very easy to freeze, to live in hope that something miraculous will happen that will change everything. You might be lucky and this miraculous thing might actually occur, but from my experience it usually doesn't. There were times in my own business when I went into denial, frozen with fear about what was happening around me. I lay in bed at night praying for a miracle. Nothing changed; the situation kept getting worse. It only improved when I leaped out of bed, looked at myself in the mirror, gave myself a stern talking to, stepped up to the plate, became the leader I needed to be and took swift, smart and decisive action.

A business will survive or not based on the actions taken by the people running it. If you don't feel you can make the hard decisions and act on them immediately, then perhaps you should skip this chapter and move on to Chapter 23, 'How to survive if your business doesn't'. I know this may sound harsh, but if your business is in a state of crisis, now is the time you need to step up and take responsibility and action.

Let those close to you know the seriousness of the situation

Often we are too fearful or paranoid about what will happen if anyone finds out just how bad the situation is. Will our customers dump us if they discover that we are doing it tough? Will the staff file out the door en masse if they hear a rumour that we are in trouble? Will my spouse or partner leave me if I tell them that my business is on the verge of going broke? What will people think? Well, none of these thoughts is going to help in any way, shape or form. Now is not the time to be ruled by fear, even if you are scared.

From my observations, there are two ways a crisis can be managed. The first is through a series of cloak and dagger late-night meetings. No one tells the staff what is going on until finally they are told that half of them will be losing their jobs. This is not a good way to manage a tough situation and it certainly doesn't encourage staff to rally around the company flagpole and do whatever it takes to work through the challenges at hand.

The second approach is one of engagement. This is where everyone, including your family, your staff, your advisers and any other relevant stakeholder, is told exactly what is going on. In my view, this approach works far more effectively than a secretive, fear-driven approach, with one condition: you must also tell everyone what you are planning to do to deal with the crisis. Of course people will panic if you say, 'Our business is in the poop and we have no idea what we are going to do about it.' You need to have a clear plan of attack with a range of options, and you have to let the people around you know what you need them to do to support you during this process. No one wants to see you go broke—well, maybe the competitor up the road, but even they will be realistic enough to know that if you go they may be next, or perhaps an even bigger and more aggressive competitor will come along to take your place.

You may be surprised by how people around you will respond when you open up and tell them about the severity of the situation. Your family might just throw their arms around you and offer love and support and a promise to help you in any way they can. You may find your staff are willing to do whatever it takes to get through the crisis, even if it means taking a pay cut, working longer hours, chasing business any way they can, or even just settling for dated equipment.

At a time like this, anyone in a position of control—whether it be the CEO of a company with 10,000 staff or the small business owner with a staff of two—needs support. But you have to let people in and tell them what is going on. I guarantee you will be surprised by the response you get.

Get advice, and then get a second opinion

I used to believe that for a business in trouble there was a very clear, defined path that had to be followed if bankruptcy was to be avoided. However, over the last few years, having dealt with some very complex situations in both my own and my clients' businesses, I have come to realise that it is not this simple. There are actually many options and alternatives, and some are certainly more likely to succeed than others. That is why you need to get good advice that is relevant to your particular situation, and I believe that you should also spend the money to get a second opinion.

I also used to be one of those people who believed everything that a solicitor, accountant or business adviser told me, usually because I didn't know any better. I am not one of those people now. I don't wish to offend anyone in these professions, but over the years I have been given some very bad advice and I have paid a lot for it, both emotionally and financially. To minimise the chance of this happening, you have to step up and take responsibility for your business. Taking advice blindly is dangerous.

So am I saying to get advice and then not to listen to it? Of course not. I am saying get the very best advice you can but don't just accept it as gospel. Question your advisers, analyse their advice and if you have to make a critical decision in a hurry, get a second opinion. I know this will slow things down and cost more, but it could stop you from making a huge mistake.

A while back I was about to sign a deed of arrangement with a former business partner that was going to cost me a fortune and which, in all likelihood, I would have struggled to pay—it could have led me into bankruptcy. My solicitor at the time was advising me to sign the deed. Luckily I had a call from a friend who, as a corporate restructuring expert, had handled many a big corporate crisis. He stepped in and took control, and we took the deal off the table. He made me realise that the deal was ridiculously generous towards my partner and that I would have been paying it off for years if I didn't go bust in the meantime. A long and drawn-out process ensued but it ended up working out much better for me, and in many ways for my former business partner as well. We could both have lost everything.

Today I have great advisers, but on any issues that are critical I always get a second opinion. There is always an alternative route to take, there are always options, even when you are being told there are none.

Cut costs without destroying your business

Cutting costs too dramatically puts you at risk of not having a viable business when the crisis is over. All too often businesses become obsessed with cutting costs at the expense of doing business.

A construction company I have worked with for many years got into difficulties and so a moratorium was placed on all spending. Now, this company makes its money by winning tenders in an industry that is highly competitive and cutthroat in every way. To me, the value of having the very best tender documents and proposals seems obvious, yet one of the areas where spending was to be cut was on the development of a more professional-looking cover and format for the submission documents. This would have resulted in an annual cost of around $2500. Given that the company sends out about 250 tenders per year, the cost per tender would have been about ten dollars. This business turns over well in excess of $100 million per year.

Surely you want any competitive advantage you can get in tough times. And while I don't doubt that a flash-looking document alone is not going to win a tender, it does say a lot about the professionalism of the business.

The reason this sort of thing can happen is that the person doing the cost cutting doesn't understand marketing or see value in the proposed spending. And this is the danger. Every cut in costs has ramifications and these need to be considered fully. All too often the tangible cuts, such as sacking staff, are clear, but the less tangible cuts, such as reducing meal sizes in a restaurant, are less apparent. However, the end results are the same—customers get disgruntled and head elsewhere.

There are many ways to cut costs when times demand it, but if cutting particular costs has the potential to impact on your ability to make an income, my belief is that these cuts must come last and only when you are truly in a state of desperation. The phrase 'cut costs however you can' can be a very dangerous directive. I saw an example of this when I was working for a subsidiary of a large shipping company. One day head office sent a fax to the CEO of our company, saying simply that all costs must be cut by 10 per cent.

We had a big powwow, looked at how we could make this happen and eventually worked out a plan of attack. During the next month we did actually cut our costs by the required 10 per cent. A couple of months later, our CEO got another fax from head office, again asking him to cut costs by a further 10 per cent. So again we set about figuring out how on earth we could do this. We made some very silly moves that ultimately cost the company a lot of money, but we achieved the 10 per cent cut and head office was advised.

We lost staff, we did less marketing, we stopped servicing equipment as often as we should have, we didn't replace uniforms, we cut back on cleaning services and we stopped doing many other things. Of course, this meant that our level of service dropped, the boats became grubby and less reliable, we lost business because we had cut back our marketing dramatically and staff morale went through the floor.

Several months later we got another fax, asking that yet another 10 per cent be cut from our operating budget. The CEO flew into a rage and sent a heated fax to head office about the ridiculous nature of the cost cutting and how we couldn't possibly cut costs any more and be left with a viable business. The response from head office was simple: they said, 'Okay.' An interesting little exercise. Head office just wanted to see how much we could reduce costs and we were driven by fear to do what they asked. The business never recovered from these cost cuts and it eventually faded into oblivion.

The moral of this story is that, yes, we have to cut costs, but we have to do it in a smart way, not in a panicked or illogical way. If you cut too deep, you may actually destroy your business.

Have someone close by to confide in

When we are in the midst of fighting for the survival of our business, there are so many issues to deal with, challenges to manage and emotions to keep under control that it can be somewhat overwhelming. Having someone close by who you can really open up to and confide in is invaluable.

This person needs to be someone you trust, someone you respect and, most importantly, someone who will tell you the truth, even if the truth is not what you want to hear. There is nothing to be gained from surrounding yourself with people who agree with you no matter what.

I feel that it is better if this person has a good general understanding of business, even if they don't necessarily understand your business in particular. They can be a sounding board, someone you can run your ideas by, especially if you are having trouble making a difficult decision. In among the madness, stress and pressure associated with turning a business around in a crisis, having such a person close by can be very reassuring.

Finding your own 'special adviser' may not be as hard as you think. Often they are around us already. They may be retired business leaders, they may be relatives, or they may be community leaders who are starting to wind down their careers. Once again it comes back to the key strategy of having a good network around you. Spend time building this network and you will find someone who fits the bill and who can give you specific advice from an impartial perspective that will prove invaluable. If you are going to have a confidant like this, you have to be open and honest with them. They can only give you their best advice if they have all of the information. Let them help you and they will.

Think outside the box

When we find ourselves between a rock and a hard place, where not surviving seems more likely than surviving, we need to be creative. If debts were mounting and the suppliers had started circling, I used to believe there was only one possible outcome—going broke. Now I know that nothing is further from the truth. At times like these we need to get creative and open our minds to potential opportunities.

I had a client who ran a web-hosting business and was struggling to make ends meet. He couldn't see any way to solve his biggest problem—repaying a $100,000 loan that his parents had provided for the business. He was getting depressed, working ridiculous hours and not getting anywhere. He came to me for help.

My suggestion was that he approach some of his biggest customers to talk about merging or even selling his business. The asking price was the amount he owed his parents. One of his customers expressed interest, as my client's business was a perfect fit for theirs. He ended up with a highly paid job running a division of the newly merged business, and with far less stress and angst than he'd had for years.

I recently heard of an architectural firm where all the staff agreed to cut back to working four days per week for 80 per cent of their salary. The business remains viable and everyone has kept their job. When things improve and demand picks up, they can all go back to full time.

There are many ways you can be creative. For example, you can look for ways to encourage your customers to buy more from you. My partner is a chiropractor who takes a holistic approach to health and offers colonic hydrotherapy in her clinic. She developed a special colonic package that encourages her clients to buy six treatments at once, which is better for their health and much better for her business. To find new customers, target specific businesses to which you may be able to offer a deal that will save them money or time or both. Everyone is interested in having more of these commodities.

Talk to your staff about ways to either save money or generate more work, or ideally both. Get them involved and active and they will surprise you with incredible ideas that you may not have even considered. Chat to your clients and customers. Ask them for ways that they think you could save money or generate more business. Again, I bet you will be surprised by what they come up with and by how many will have a genuine desire to help you.

Being creative doesn't work if you are exhausted, stressed out and fearful. If your business is in dire straits, as hard as it may be, try to get some rest and stay healthy so that your mind is open and receptive, so you can think outside the box and come up with ideas that may just save your business.

Your suppliers don't want to see you go broke

Suppliers can make or break you at a time like this. But why on earth would they want to see any of their customers go broke? In tough times, suppliers are not the enemy—they will want to work with you.

I always remember a very flamboyant client of mine who ran a big art gallery. He had a very busy high season and a painfully slow off season. He worked out an arrangement with his suppliers whereby he paid them within seven days in the high season and ninety days in the off season. It worked for him, it worked for his suppliers and everyone benefited.

In tough times some business owners start avoiding suppliers' calls, not responding to their letters and emails and generally shutting down all communication. This is the best way to get a supplier to stop supply or take legal action. The middle of an economic crisis is not the time to have no stock or to have the supply of essential items or services cut off. You need to work with your suppliers, to communicate with them often. You need to keep them abreast of your situation and tell them what you are doing about it.

Whenever I have been in a tight spot financially I have always managed to work through it with my suppliers. When I give a promise I do everything in my power to keep it. I ensure that either I talk to them often and keep them up to date or that my accounts team does the same. If anything changes our plans, if extra issues or problems arise, we work them out.

I have developed a reputation among my suppliers of always paying my accounts. They know I always will, even if there are times when I am a little slow. And it works both ways. If one of my suppliers gets into financial trouble, I pay my account upfront or at least much earlier than required. Sometimes I will pre-purchase stock, to be delivered in a few months. My motto is if they help me, I will help them.

Having strong relationships with your suppliers will get you through many tough spots. Pick up the phone, talk to them. Ask them to work with you and most of the time they will.

Don't over-promise and under-deliver on repayments

When the cash gets scarce it's almost impossible not to struggle to meet repayments. If you are already struggling you will know what it's like. Every phone call seems to be someone chasing money. Your bill folder is bulging and you can't figure out how on earth you are going to pay them all.

What you have to do is try to come to some arrangement with your creditors. Banks and finance companies may let you defer payments for several months; there will be charges, but it can help to get you past the current cash crunch. If you owe government departments like the taxation office, again they are likely to give you extensions and time to catch up. As discussed in the previous tip, suppliers will generally be more than happy to work with you to help you get past a crisis, depending of course on their own issues.

When making repayment deals, it is easy to feel intimidated. For example, if a debt collector calls to say you have to pay $10,000 in one week, you agree, even though you know that you can't possibly make that payment, because it buys you a week to think. This is a mistake— when you go into default, you can expect that much more serious action than a phone call is going to be taken.

When you make a payment plan it is imperative that you stick to it. So the key is to be realistic about what you can pay back and when you can pay it back. Many times I have made the mistake of over-committing to a repayment schedule and then under-delivering.

No matter how hard it is, don't get pressured into committing to a payment plan that you know in your heart you will not be able to meet.

Explain this to the person you are negotiating with. Odds are they will appreciate your honesty. They may not accept your proposal, but that is the risk you have to take when you are in this position.

Make the tough decisions and make them fast

In a difficult situation, you are going to have to make some hard decisions. My advice is to make them fast and carry them out faster. All too often a business goes broke while the owner is deciding what to do.

Without doubt there will be pain involved. You will probably have to sack some staff members, through no fault of their own. This is the hardest part of being the boss. You might have to downsize from your nice office to the shed at home and face the embarrassment that you think will come with that. You might have to ring a supplier whom you respect very much to tell them that you are struggling to pay their account.

All these things are really hard to do, but you have to do them. An old friend of mine who was as tough as nails used to say, 'If you've got a problem, front it!' No matter how hard the task may be, no matter how upset you may feel, take the bull by the horns and do it.

A problem of mine is that I have always been much too soft in business. Over the years I have had a number of wake-up calls telling me I needed to take action fast and I didn't because I didn't want to upset or hurt anyone. I kept staff on when I was going broke. For two years I remained with a business partner who did little but cost me money. I stayed in an expensive office because my staff liked it. Over the years this softness and failure to act cost me a lot of money.

I don't want to become a hard, miserable businessperson, but I do want to run a profitable business and not have to worry about making ends meet. To do that, I have to make hard decisions and now I can. I have learned that it is much more painful if you put off doing something out of fear of hurting people. In the long run there is always a price to pay.

No matter how hard the decisions that are needed to save your business, you have to make them, and you have to carry them out without delay.

Be sensitive but don't wait out of fear—take decisive action straightaway. Remember, if you have a problem, front it!

Keep one eye on where you are and one eye on where you're going

When you feel your world is about to collapse around you, it can be overwhelming and it is often hard to see beyond the day ahead. I remember times when I woke up at 3 a.m., filled with dread about what I had to face that day. I would lie in bed worrying about what would happen and wondering if my business would even survive. I felt my world was coming to an end and that there was no way through it.

In the middle of this madness, Terry Russell, a close friend of mine who also used to be my boss, took me aside and told me something very simple but very important—he told me not to get distracted by the trees that get in the way when you are trying to walk through the forest. Corny, glib, a cliché? Perhaps, but on that day these words made me sit up and take notice.

I realised that, right here, right now, all I could see were obstacles. But when I stopped focusing on the obstacles and looked beyond them, I could see where I was heading and everything became easier. I realised that what I was going through was only a temporary crisis. Whether my business survived or not, there was a life beyond the obstacles that had become the focus of every waking moment. This made me feel a lot better and took away a lot of my angst and fear.

I think there are many times in our lives where we forget to look over the obstacles to see where we are going. If your business is in crisis and you are not sure if it will be there tomorrow, please know that there is always life after this business. If you fail, so be it. But if you succeed—wow!

Think about how you will feel when you get to the other side of the forest and you have overcome obstacle after obstacle. Imagine what you will have learned and how much better you will be able to deal with challenges in the future.

Spend too much time living in the future and the present will fall apart. But spend too much time living in the present when it is heartbreaking, difficult or scary and it's almost impossible not to lose hope. Finding a place in between is the way to survive it.

23

How to survive if your business doesn't

We have all heard about the terrible failure rate of small businesses in virtually every Western country. In some reports, depending on where you get your figures from, as many as nine out of ten businesses fail to survive over a five-year period, with the majority going bust in the first two years. Often big businesses seem to struggle just as much, but they tend not to go broke. Instead they get taken over by another big business and a new entity is formed. Along the way, though, there is generally a trail of destruction.

Starting or buying a business means taking a risk and there is absolutely no guarantee that it will be successful. Yet every year, in every country around the world, thousands upon thousands of people take the plunge and start their own business. Economies change, competition increases, property prices fall, supply problems arise, people get sick, buying habits change and many other events occur which are to blame for this failure rate. And sadly, behind every closed business door, there is a tale of struggle and anguish.

For anyone who starts their own business, who puts their life savings on the line, who works ridiculous hours, who overcomes the many challenges along the way, and who sacrifices time with their family, losing this business is like losing a loved one and it takes a huge emotional toll. In fact, the suicide rate among business owners who go bankrupt is extremely high. They see no other escape from the embarrassment, the sense of failure and the financial loss.

I have certainly come close to the brink of financial ruin myself on a number of occasions. It is a scary place to be. You feel as though your life is out of control and that the world as you know it is coming to an end. I spent many nights sitting and staring into space wondering if the next day would be the day I went broke. I worried about the shame, the embarrassment, what I would live on and what my family and friends would think. I asked myself, on more occasions than I wish to remember, if it was worth going on. I was so close to becoming bankrupt that I could smell it, and this is what scared me into fighting my way out. I got through those turbulent times, mainly because I became desperate enough to do what I should have done in the first place. But not everyone gets away like I did.

As a public relations consultant, I have had to work closely with many clients during the financial demise of their business. I have been the spokesperson in situations like this for companies that turned over hundreds of millions of dollars right down to small 'mum and dad' businesses. There is always someone who has invested everything in their dream, and the ramifications of losing that manifests as fear in their eyes. It breaks my heart every time. I really think you have to spend years building your own business to understand just how hard it would be to lose it.

There are also many people who don't actually go bankrupt, but they do lose everything. I met a lady who bought a beauty salon in a remote regional town for $180,000. She then invested another $100,000 and ultimately ended up with a business worth nothing due to her lack of business experience. The house she owned with her husband had to be sold and they literally were left with nothing after twenty years of marriage.

There are plenty of books written to help business owners succeed but none that I have seen about what to do when your business goes broke.

The following advice and practical suggestions come from interviewing people who have been in that very situation. Some lost relatively small amounts of money, others hundreds of millions of dollars. From them I have learned that you *will* get over the loss of your business. Life will continue and you will certainly be wiser as a result of the experience.

I have met many small business owners who have gone bankrupt and this is the advice I have given to them over the years.

- Figure out what went wrong and learn from it
- Accept that businesses go broke
- Talk about your feelings and get help if you need it
- Stay healthy
- Other people will value your skills
- Use your time wisely
- People really do understand
- Let go and get excited about your future
- List the great things you got out of your business
- This may be the best thing to ever happen to you

Figure out what went wrong and learn from it

When it comes to figuring out where the business went wrong, we have to be honest with ourselves. It is really easy to blame everyone and everything around us for the demise—the economy, the nasty financiers, the fickle customers, global warming and, of course, the GFC. But if we want to get something of value out of what has happened, we need to be brave enough to admit our own mistakes.

There are many reasons why a business fails but from my experience the main cause tends to be bad decisions made by the business owner, simple as that. We can read a million books on how to run a business or perhaps do a course of some kind, but in reality we learn how to run a business by doing it. Unfortunately we have to learn on the job and this means mistakes get made, sometimes with dramatic ramifications.

Often businesses fall over because of seemingly simple mistakes like buying things when we shouldn't, taking our eye off customer service, failing to take action when we should, not marketing enough, poor money management, taking too much money out of the business, or perhaps we simply get too busy to do what we need to do. Then 'suddenly' we find that we have got into serious trouble. Often the simplest mistakes bring a business down. Many large corporations that have fallen over have come undone through the same simple mistakes.

While I don't advocate beating yourself up over where you went wrong, I do think it is very important to clearly understand what mistakes were made and how you would do things differently next time. I look at my business mistakes as my university degree. I figure that as long as I learn from them I will get something from the whole experience and that makes it a worthwhile investment. I weigh up what I have lost and in my mind I allocate it to the column headed 'training expenses'. But, most importantly, I learn to be grateful for the experience because next time I find myself in the same situation, my experience may end up saving me millions of dollars, not just a few thousand.

I advise people who go broke to spend some time clarifying what their main mistakes were and what they will do differently next time (there will be a next time if you want it). While this may be somewhat frustrating, I feel it is the first step in letting go of the business and coming to terms with what has happened. Smart people learn from their mistakes and move on. This is an opportunity for you to do the same.

Accept that businesses go broke

When a business goes broke, the owner generally struggles to see beyond the current calamity. It feels very personal and there is a real sense of loss and failure. But the hard truth is that millions of businesses have gone broke before us and that millions will go the same way long after we have gone. It is simply a fact of business life.

I had to put a company of mine into voluntary administration a few years back in the midst of a partnership dispute. It was really tough as

I basically had to hand a stranger the keys and chequebooks for the business. I felt as though I was the only person in the world in this situation. My receiver was a lovely man and he laughed when I told him how I felt. He took me to his file room and showed me the 400 other cases he was working on at that particular moment—and I felt much better.

We have to take the emotional aspect out of the situation and simply accept what has happened. Clearly this is easier said than done, but even if the business has gone broke because of our own mistakes, nothing can be gained by holding on to a sense of failure. I have met people who have gone bust and held on to their sense of failure for decades. It has stopped them doing so many things with their lives and they have grown old and bitter. Now that is a tragedy!

We can struggle to accept the reality of what has happened, we can lash out in anger, or we can go into denial. I have been in an office when the men in black arrived and started removing all of the computers and files and changing the locks while the owner of the business sat sobbing and refusing to let go of his desk until the police came and threw him off the property.

Yes, it is hard and yes, it seems unfair. If only we had an extra month, or a few extra thousand dollars—but really, would it have made any difference? I doubt it. Businesses don't go broke in a few days. It happens over time and there are plenty of warning signals. So the sooner you can accept that the business is finished, the sooner you can get on with life and start looking towards the future.

How many inspiring stories have we heard or seen on television about people who have gone broke a dozen times and finally made it? When you think about it, there is a certain logic to this. As you learn more in business you make fewer mistakes, and as a result you achieve the success you desire. If you make some big mistakes along the way, it is unlikely that you will repeat them. The people featured in these success stories simply learned where they went wrong and kept on trying. Many got it wrong time and time again, but eventually they got it right.

Where you come from doesn't matter, but where you are heading does. Right now, accept that businesses go bust and even though this has happened to you, it is not going to ruin the rest of your life. This is an opportunity for you to pick yourself up, dust yourself off and look to the future where there are endless opportunities. The best part is that you are going to chase those opportunities a little smarter and better equipped than before.

Talk about your feelings and get help if you need it

When faced with going broke or being made bankrupt, there is a lot to deal with. Bottling up your feelings isn't the smartest thing to do, no matter how embarrassed you may be.

At times like this you need to have people around you whom you can confide in openly and honestly, people you can cry in front of and not feel embarrassed, and people who love you for who you are not what you do.

The problem is that many of us measure our self-worth by what we achieve, not by who we are. If our business is worthless, then we feel worthless. Clearly this is crazy, but I spent many years believing this without even realising it. Today I understand how unhealthy this can be, but I didn't when I bought my first business at the age of eighteen and spent the next five years fighting off bankruptcy. I lost all confidence and considered myself a failure because I couldn't make my business work.

When you are in this zone, you start to hold it all in. If someone asks you how business is going, you automatically say it's great. You don't want anyone knowing that you are in trouble. And it takes a huge amount of energy to maintain the facade that everything is wonderful when you know that at any moment someone could come through the door and issue you with a bankruptcy notice.

I never used to talk to people about my financial issues. Instead I preferred the 'go insane slowly' principle, one that I was particularly good at. In the last ten years, however, whenever I have had financial problems, my staff have known as much about it as me. I shared the pain and the burden and they returned that trust by going the extra mile for me.

321

It is always good to talk to someone who has experience with what you are going through. Find someone who has gone bust and ask them how they coped. Believe me, you won't have to look far. Most people are happy to share their story and experiences. If you can't find someone like this and you feel that you are losing the plot, talk to a professional. Find a counsellor, psychologist or psychiatrist and open up. Just getting it all out of your system will help you feel much better.

I am not recommending a once-only five-minute conversation. You need to be able to talk to people often. When your business is in the death throes, you will experience a roller-coaster ride of emotions. You will have good days and bad days and it is really important that you have access to people with whom you can share your feelings, your fears and your pain.

For some people, losing a business is as difficult as a relationship breakdown, a serious health issue, or even the death of a loved one. We go through similar stages such as shock, disbelief, anger, grief and depression.

If you are reading this and someone you know is going bankrupt, try to get them to open up or at least let them know you are there whenever they need a friend's shoulder to cry on. In the midst of a crisis it is easy to feel very isolated and alone.

Stay healthy

As I mentioned earlier, businesses don't just go broke overnight. Normally they experience long periods of tight cash flow and the associated stress that comes with trying to juggle money and ward off debt collectors, all the while wondering if the business will survive. Sometimes this goes on for years until finally the business is either closed voluntarily or forced to close. The stress and fatigue associated with this can be incredible. I have heard business owners saying that it was actually a relief when the business finally came to an end.

If you find yourself in the unfortunate position of having to deal with a business that is going broke, it is very easy to slide into physical decline, self-abuse and depression. Sadly I have known quite a few people who literally drank themselves to death following the collapse of their business. Drugs and alcohol tend to become crutches at times like this. Often it starts with a drink or two to relieve stress, or a pill to help you forget the pain and sleep at night. The problem is that the stress and the pain will still be there the next day and the next, and will remain until the situation is resolved. This is a very dangerous time to turn to drugs and alcohol. In the end they will make the situation worse, especially as you may also be depressed. Nearly everyone who faces a business going bust has to deal with some sort of depression.

It is important to be aware of the risks and to take action immediately, no matter how hard it is to get yourself motivated. The very best things you can do are to exercise, eat well and get plenty of rest. If you can afford it, a long holiday away will work wonders. While a trip to the gym may be the last thing you feel like doing, there is a definite link between lack of activity and depression. The more you move, the better your state of mind will be. I love yoga. I find it the very best way to get rid of stress and recharge the batteries and it has certainly helped me to get through some very challenging times.

The quicker you take action and the better you look after yourself, the sooner you will feel better and the more able you will be to move on. Make this a time to reconnect with your body, to rid yourself of stress by working hard physically and eating well. You will sleep better, your health will improve, and you will lose that feeling of being powerless. When you build a strong, healthy, energetic body, you take control of your life.

Other people will value your skills

One of the biggest concerns for a person who has lost their business is how they will make a living. When working with clients in this situation I am often asked, 'Who would want to employ a failed business owner?'

Well, interestingly enough, lots of people. Generally people who start their own businesses are good at something. It may just be that the thing they are not good at is running a business. There are plenty of people out there who understand this. They will gladly employ a person who has the right skills. The fact that their business didn't survive is pretty much irrelevant.

In fact, many business owners who go broke end up being employed by their old suppliers or even their competitors. I see this a lot and to me it seems like a smart thing to do. The new employers know they are hiring people who have great skills in certain areas, and they may also pick up some of their customers in the process.

As well as the skills you have that led you to start your business, you will have learned a whole lot more while running it. You will have learned to be self-sufficient, a good people manager, and skilled in accounting, financial management, marketing, customer liaison, communication, negotiating, counselling, stock control, legal expertise and many other areas. How many jobs require you to possess or use such a diverse range of skills? Not very many.

So even though your business hasn't survived, please don't think you have no value in the workplace. In fact, once the dust settles you may be surprised by who approaches you to come and work for them.

What will work against you is wallowing in self-pity and feelings of uselessness. There is nothing to be gained from this. So take a few minutes and think about the list of skills you developed while running your own business. Think about the types of businesses that could use someone like you. Go one step further and write up your résumé. Clearly you have plenty to offer and it won't take long for you and others to realise this.

Use your time wisely

For the first time in possibly years you may suddenly have a lot of time on your hands. It is imperative that you use this time wisely and in a positive way.

Think about all the things you have wanted to do over the last few years but didn't, your excuse being that you didn't have the time. Sure, you might not have the money to do some of these things now, but I bet there are plenty on the list that don't cost much money. Things like spending time with family and friends, reading, camping, exercising, learning to cook, going to the movies, helping out a local charity or perhaps your kids' school, writing that book you have always wanted to write, calling people you love just to have a long chat, playing an instrument and so on. I am sure that your list will be much longer than this.

You will now have a lot more time to do the things you enjoy. Even if you go out and get a job tomorrow, it is unlikely that you will work as hard as you have over the last few years in your own business. This extra time is a gift, one that you can use wisely.

One of the best ways to feel better about yourself is to help those who are less fortunate. Volunteer at a local old people's home, or animal shelter, or kitchen for the homeless. Helping others in need helps us gain a better perspective on our own life, to become more balanced in our outlook. We learn that the things we worry about and fear are often not that important.

One morning while writing this book, I got up feeling under a lot of pressure. I had so much to do and so little time to do it: work to complete for clients, writing deadlines to meet, people who weren't paying their bills to chase. So I put on a CD by Dr Wayne Dyer, a popular American psychotherapist and self-help advocate. As I listened to Dr Dyer telling the story of Kaye O'Bara, a woman who had looked after her comatose daughter, Edwarda, for over 27 years, I couldn't believe what I was hearing.

Mrs O'Bara has to feed her daughter every two hours. Imagine never being able to sleep for more than two hours at a time, or never being able to go to the shops for more than a few minutes, or see a movie, or go on a holiday, or out for a meal. Kaye is alone. Her husband died of a heart attack not long after Edwarda went into the coma.

Kaye has no money. She has to find over $3000 per month just to look after Edwarda. She borrows from loan sharks, juggles credit cards and sells cakes to try to make ends meet, all the while going deeper into debt.

When asked how she survives this life, she answers humbly that she feels that it is an honour to be able to look after Edwarda, her beautiful daughter. What an amazing story of incredible devotion.

So why did I share this story? Because it shows two things. The first is that when you spend your time wisely, helping others, doing positive things, your life will be better because of it. The second is that no matter how bad you may think your life is, we all know that there are many people who are not just a little bit worse off, but incredibly worse off.

Use your time wisely. Invest it in getting back to being the person you truly want to be. Learn, serve, give—three keywords to help give you direction when it comes time to work out what to do with your time.

People really do understand

One of the biggest challenges any business owner faces when their business goes bust is the sense that everyone is looking at them as a failure. The reality is while some people will think this way, many others will not.

Every single business owner in the world knows that one day they could be the one going broke. It may be due to circumstances out of their control, or it may be 100 per cent due to mistakes they have made. But it is without doubt a risk that we all face when embarking on a career as an entrepreneur.

I have sat in on many creditors' meetings, where a business has gone into liquidation and the administrator is working to finalise the details. Normally representatives from businesses who are owed money by the failed business attend. They are not very cheery get-togethers, as most people there know that they are going to get paid very little of the money they are owed.

When I sit in on these meetings I have a different view. I know that the person who has gone broke has normally lost more than everyone else sitting around the table combined. They have to deal with the enormous angst, pain and embarrassment of going bankrupt and it is tough. No one wins when a business goes broke. People who have been in business for a while know that and they understand this point.

Going broke can be humiliating, but there are plenty of people who really do understand. For someone in this situation, you can take solace from this fact. The rest of the world is not looking at you as a failure, so don't shut yourself away from the world and hide for the next few years, even if that is what you feel like doing. Businesses open and businesses close. This is all a part of a very normal cycle. Get on with your life and hold your head high, knowing that at least you gave it a go.

Let go and get excited about your future

More than twenty years ago, I had a terrible experience. At the time I owned a scuba-diving retail shop and school on the outskirts of Sydney. I had owned the business for about four years and had just sold a share to a man who worked for me. Part of the deal was that I would take a holiday as soon as he bought into the business, as I was badly in need of a break.

I headed out into the open ocean on a sailing trip for a few weeks. While I was out at sea, my creative business partner held a huge sale in our shop. In fact he sold everything, including the kitchen sink, and then he disappeared. I got back to Sydney and found my dive shop looking like the Arizona Desert—nothing but tumbleweed rolling across the floor.

I was left broke, in debt and really angry. I didn't know what to do, so I grabbed a paper and applied for the first job I could find, which happened to be selling encyclopaedias door-to-door in Tasmania. I was determined that I was going to save up enough money to get my former business partner 'dealt with' by some people I knew. This became an obsession and after two years I finally had enough money in the bank. By then I was working in the middle of the Western Australian desert for a gold exploration company. I still remember the day when my pay slip arrived and I knew I had enough money to sort out my old business partner once and for all.

But now that I had the money, something made me sit down and think about the last few years. I was always run-down and sick, I had nasty boils all over my back, I was angry and unhappy, and I had no real plans or goals other than my burning desire for revenge. I began to question what I would gain from a violent reprisal and I also realised what this grudge was costing me physically and emotionally. When I made the decision to 'let it go', right then and there, something unexpected happened. My body started to heal itself, the boils disappeared within a day or two, I stood taller, I smiled all the time, like I used to, and I got on with my life.

I had learned one of the greatest lessons in life: we all need to let go of situations that no longer serve us or have any bearing on our life. Hanging on to the anger, bitterness, resentment and hurt that comes from losing a business only brings more of the same. If your business has gone bust, you have to let it go. Far too many people hang on to the emotions that surround the loss, just like I did, and it sets the stage for the rest of their lives. Nothing good comes from hanging on to negativity.

When you do actually let go of the past, you can start to look forward to the future. You can get excited, you can make plans and you can get your life back. Where we have come from doesn't matter, but where we are heading does. Just because you have gone broke doesn't mean that you have to pay for it for the rest of your life.

List the great things you got out of your business

In life, whenever we face challenges we tend to focus on the bad things. When a relationship ends we talk about the awful stuff our ex-partner did that drove us crazy. In a lousy job, we focus on everything bad about it, or the rotten organisation we work for. The same happens when a business goes broke. We spend a lot of time thinking and talking about all of the terrible things that happened to us over the years as a result of the business failing, but we rarely sit back and consider the wonderful things that our business gave us.

If you go into business purely for the financial rewards, I think you are destined to feel unsatisfied, particularly at a time when you are facing business failure. Sure, losing a pile of money stinks, but there are many other rewards to be gained from running a business: being able to contribute to society or make other people's lives better, being able to do what you are great at and getting a sense of satisfaction from your work, and hopefully learning and growing as a human being along the way. There are many really good things that we get to experience and be proud of when we have our own business.

One of the keys to getting past the loss of a business is to look for these positives. I suggest that you take a few minutes to write a list of everything your business gave you. Make it as comprehensive as you can, and include:

- material possessions
- skills you have now that you didn't have before
- lessons you have learned
- places you have visited
- friends you have made
- charities you have supported
- people on whose lives you have had a positive impact.

Focus on the good things not the bad and everything changes. I have yet to meet a person who could not make a list of at least twenty wonderful things that occurred because of their business.

Once you make your list, stick it on the wall, keep it in your diary, or put it on the bathroom mirror. Read it every day and be grateful for these wonderful gifts that your business gave you. On those days when you find the going tough, read your list more often and close your eyes and visualise the good things. I know that some people may struggle with this concept, especially when the pain of going bust is fresh, but it really does work.

Business owners who have to deal with the reality of bankruptcy can be divided into two types. One type accept what has happened, understand where they went wrong and, most importantly, work out what they would do next time. They take the time to regroup, and to focus on their mental and physical health and wellbeing. The other kind become overwhelmed by a sense of failure, they abuse their body, get depressed, lose direction and hope and they never really recover from their loss. The difference between the two groups is their state of mind.

Learning to be grateful is one of the best ways to develop the right state of mind and even if right now it is hard to find anything to be grateful for, you will in time.

This may be the best thing to ever happen to you

I spent a lot of time looking for the right words to start this tip. I found them in Napoleon Hill's motivational book *Think and Grow Rich*: 'Most people have attained their greatest success just one step beyond their greatest failure. This may be the case for you. Your greatest success may now be one step closer.'

I have a very dear friend who ran a big transport company. He built it from the ground up, investing incredible amounts of time, energy and money. Through a series of unfortunate events, he had to place the business into administration and ultimately he was made bankrupt. In the years leading up to this my friend worked himself nearly to death and he abused his body big-time, mainly with cigarettes and alcohol. I have no doubt that he would have been dead at fifty if something hadn't changed.

When he lost his business, he turned over a whole new leaf. He stopped smoking, virtually stopped drinking and he took up yoga. Today he lives almost like a Zen monk; he is happy and content with a simple life, in a loving relationship and able to enjoy the things that are most important to him. In a strange way, going broke was the best thing that ever happened to him, because he got his life back.

Anyone who has ever had their own business knows that you don't own it, it owns you. A business is the most demanding relationship we can have. It creates great highs, terrible lows and generally you can expect a roller-coaster ride every step of the way. Having said that, it can also be one of the greatest experiences in life and one where you learn a lot about yourself and what you are capable of.

If you are feeling like a failure because your business didn't survive, remember it is only one chapter in the book of your life. You had many before it and you have many more to come. What you have learned from this experience will change you forever and it will change you for the better. Often we simply need to let the story play out. Who knows where we will be in twenty years? But wherever we are, this experience will have led us there.

A final word

Well, if you made it this far you deserve a pat on the back. You now have hundreds of practical tips and ideas that I absolutely know will help you to build the business of your dreams.

One of the biggest challenges facing most business owners is balancing their business and their life. It takes a huge amount of energy, passion and commitment to build a business and that tends to lead to the 'entrepreneurial crash-and-burn cycle'. Master this challenge and you will have a very long and successful entrepreneurial life ahead of you.

Reach out and help others wherever you can. Share your own expertise and never underestimate just how much you have learned in your own journey as a business owner or how much of a difference you can make to others.

But perhaps most importantly of all, keep that passion alive. Passion equals profit; I see it every day. Smart business owners never stop learning, they invest in themselves, they reward themselves and others, they treat their staff and their customers with enormous respect and they are proud of their business—and it shows.

I wish you every success and I would love to get your feedback on *The Big Book of Small Business*.

Andrew Griffiths
Email: info@andrewgriffiths.com.au

IF YOU'RE LOOKING FOR A PASSIONATE, FIRED UP, STREET SMART ENTREPRENEUR TO INSPIRE YOUR AUDIENCE, LOOK NO FURTHER.

The "Andrew Griffiths" name has become synonymous with smart, practical advice, mainly delivered through his series of bestselling books. As a result of his successful writing career, Andrew has gained a reputation as a sought after speaker, presenter, trainer and motivator. He is now widely acclaimed as one of Australia's most energetic, humorous and charismatic speakers.

Andrew has successfully conducted a broad and diverse range of presentations and training programmes for iconic companies including Telstra, Hertz, Jetset Travelworld Group, ING, One Path, Suncorp, Ray White Real Estate, Dymocks, L'Oreal, Bendigo Bank and many more.

For a complete list of topics that Andrew presents on or to find out about his fully customised presentations and training programmes please visit:

www.andrewgriffiths.com.au

ANDREW★GRIFFITHS ENTERPRISES

ARE YOU REALLY SERIOUS ABOUT TAKING YOUR SMALL BUSINESS TO A WHOLE NEW LEVEL?

This is a big question, but it is an important question. Do you want to just coast along and skirt around a zero bank balance or are you really ready to get serious and build the Small Business you want and deserve? I firmly believe that business success or failure is hugely dependent on your attitude, the new skills you learn along the way and some simple but vital customer related strategies.

If you have made the decision to build a really successful business I strongly encourage you to join my Small Business Academy of Success. This is a membership based academy where I will share some of the greatest Small Business building tips with a limited number of people. Like this book, the information I share is based on my own Small Business trials and tribulations as well as those of the countless businesses I have worked with over many years.

If you think your business could benefit from this expertise, for a low monthly fee, then check out the Small Business Academy of Success website. I guarantee it will change your Small Business life forever.

www.smallbusinessacademyofsuccess.com

SMALL BUSINESS ACADEMY OF SUCCESS.com

THE WORLD'S GREATEST ENTREPRENEURS SHARE COMMON CHARACTERISTICS. SO WHAT ARE THEY?

I have spent a lifetime working with and learning from some of the leading entrepreneurs on the planet. I certainly attribute much of my success to having great mentors.

After all this time, I realised that these amazing entrepreneurs share many common characteristics. We all know that success mirrors success, so logically if you want to be a truly successful entrepreneur the best thing you can do is to do what they do.

But of course that is easier said than done. Who has the time to do all of the research, to read all of the books, to watch all of the DVDs or go to all of the events?

Well now you don't have to. I have developed a programme built around the 30 most common beliefs, habits and actions shared by the worlds top entrepreneurs. I call this the Entrepreneurs Academy of Success and it will blow your socks off.

For a low monthly fee you will take your entrepreneurial skills to a whole new level. I have packaged the information up so that it is easy to take in and even easier to apply to your own entrepreneurial world. It is real, it is raw and it is relevant and it will be one of the best investments you will ever make. To find out more, check out:

www.entrepreneursacademyofsuccess.com

ENTREPRENEURS ACADEMY$OF SUCCESS.com

ALSO BY ANDREW GRIFFITHS

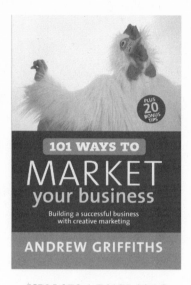

ISBN 978 1 74175 005 8

ISBN 978 1 74175 007 2

ISBN 978 1 74175 006 5

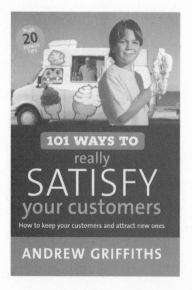

ISBN 978 1 74175 008 9

ALSO BY ANDREW GRIFFITHS

ISBN 978 1 74114 787 2

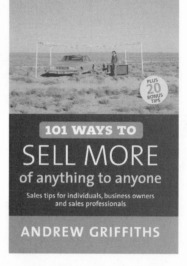

ISBN 978 1 74114 788 9

ISBN 978 1 74175 989 1

ISBN 978 1 74114 959 3